Reflections on the Cold War

Diplomacy in the Cold War

Edited by
Lynn H. Miller and Ronald W. Pruessen

Reflections on the Cold War

A Quarter Century of
American Foreign Policy

Temple University Press
Philadelphia

Temple University Press, Philadelphia 19122
© 1974 by Temple University. All rights reserved
Published 1974
Printed in the United States of America

International Standard Book Number: 0-87722-028-X
Library of Congress Catalog Card Number: 73-88279

Contents

Preface

The essays in this volume grew out of a lecture series at Temple University during the 1970–71 academic year. The series, which was sponsored jointly by the departments of History and Political Science, included as participants some of the country's leading historians and political scientists, as well as a distinguished journalist and diplomat—both with wide experience in observing and writing about major developments in the Cold War.

The lecture series was intended to provide a reassessment in historical perspective—short though that perspective may be—of American policy during the Cold War, an era which, if it has not come to a close, at least has been transformed fundamentally in recent years. In our view, such a reassessment is an important undertaking today, largely for two reasons. First, and of obvious importance to the scholar, is the growing availability of information in the form of memoirs and formerly private papers bearing on crucial decisions made by American policy makers in the 1940s, 1950s, and early 1960s. Second, and perhaps even more important, because the Cold War has been transformed or even superseded in recent years, our perceptions of the earlier period are inevitably influenced thereby, and interpretations of events that once seemed plausible are often less persuasive today. As a result, the generally accepted folklore about the Cold War is being questioned today as never before.

Moreover, as the lectures in this series demonstrate clearly, the participants showed a keen awareness of the pertinency of the past to contemporary problems. In surveying thirty years, and in some cases more, of American foreign policy, virtually all began or concluded with a discussion of issues of current importance. In a number of cases, the war in Indochina served as a springboard for analysis of earlier years, its horrors providing a stimulus for looking back into the past, the desire to understand its course yielding efforts to chart our movements before. Not surprisingly, many of the participants came to argue that American foreign policy now is much the direct product of its course through the recent past. Patterns were established in earlier years which still cast shadows, which still determine the course of policy makers, and which have proved difficult or impossible to break.

This is not to say that all participants hold uniformly "revisionist" views of American policy in the Cold War. Some of the contributors to this volume are in the forefront of this approach, while others hew much more closely to traditional Western interpretations of the period. Yet virtually all the essays are critical of at least certain aspects of the conventional wisdom about the United States' role in the Cold War. In a time when the basic ends and means of America's involvement in world affairs are being questioned, it seems particularly appropriate to make available to a wider audience these constructive reassessments of American foreign policy in the recent past.

Reflections on the Cold War

Stanley Hoffmann

1
Revisionism Revisited

EDITORS' NOTE. From the very outset of the Cold War, there have
been numerous critics of the policies pursued by the United States
in its role as the principal antagonist of the Soviet Union and
leader of the "free world." Not until the middle 1960s, however,
did a group of these critics begin to emerge in America as a coherent school of historical criticism—now widely known as the
"revisionists." In general, and in varying degrees, the revisionists
have denied the common wisdom of the orthodox view of the Cold
War, in which the United States is viewed as the reluctant leader
of a defensive coalition to halt or "contain" Soviet expansionism
and aggression. Revisionists charge America with having taken
most of the initiatives, through the use of economic, political, and
military power, that have produced more than twenty years of
Cold War tensions.

Although the orthodox/revisionist debate began largely within
the academic community, it has vastly more than purely academic
interest and importance. The potential impact of the debate has
been heightened by the fact that large sectors of the American
public have within the past few years raised new and fundamental
questions about the principles and perceptions upon which recent
United States foreign policy has been based. Responding propor-
tionately, it seems, to the escalation of American involvement in
Indochina, curiosity and cynicism have by now reached far back
into the past. As a result, major attention has been focused on
the nature of United States actions during the entire span of the
Cold War.

This is by no means the first great debate between opposing
interpretations of a period in American history, nor will it be the
last. In fact, since men must always interpret the past in the light
of their own experiences, they must constantly sweep away the

3

dogmas of the past as these dogmas lose their strength—that is, their sense of truth or explanatory power—in the face of changed conditions. In this connection, it is important to remember that what is currently identified as the orthodox view of the role of the United States in post–World War II foreign policy was by no means orthodox when it was first espoused: originally, it constituted the doctrine justification of a massive, and successful, effort to change radically the role of the United States in world affairs. Should revisionism succeed in becoming the "new orthodoxy" about United States foreign policy, as Professor Stanley Hoffmann suggests is happening in the chapter that follows, it is certain that it too will be challenged by a future generation of historians grown up in a world that is considerably different from the present.

Despite its lack of uniqueness, the type of revisionist versus orthodox debate that is currently raging over recent American foreign policy is most valuable. Questions have been raised, sources scoured, and answers essayed that might never have seen print if a challenge to an accepted interpretation had not been made. It is certain that the very process of debate and disagreement will make possible a far fuller picture of what has actually happened than would otherwise have been possible. "Revisionism Revisited," for example, provides ample evidence of what one scholar believes has already been accomplished. In focusing primarily on what is usually termed the "origins" of the Cold War—that is, the events and policies of the mid and late 1940s—Professor Hoffmann takes what might be called a balanced look at the two sides of the debate. He concludes that both orthodox and revisionist spokesmen have been right in certain aspects of their interpretations. He does believe that both schools have tended to be too dogmatic in failing to acknowledge the significant gaps which usually exist between men's intentions and their actual accomplishments. In his words, "the key problem is not to look for a master explanation but . . . to try to understand the contrasts—the permanent, ironical contrasts—between what people think they are doing and what they are actually achieving."

Professor Hoffmann's review of the principal arguments and issues dividing the orthodox and revisionist approaches provides a useful initial framework for the more specific discussions of events and policies that follow.

We are intensely aware today, particularly in the United States, of the growing challenge to the orthodox view of the origins of the Cold War. I would like to begin by discussing these competing interpretations and, in particular, the revisionist view. After a brief critique of these two contrasting conceptions, I shall present some views of my own about the process which led us into twenty-five years of Cold War. It is a complicated and interesting process.

It is not surprising that we should now be faced with two conflicting interpretations—one which is a kind of official justificatory conception, and one which is iconoclastically revisionist. The growth of this challenge to the "official" view of history has happened in America after practically every war. That it has developed now with regard to the Cold War is interesting in itself because the Cold War is, after all, still with us. The debate between the two explanations is interesting also because it is important to know how we got into it—and not only to understand why we ended with the Vietnam war. Moreover, this debate tells us something about how history is written, and perhaps something about how history should not be written. Finally, an examination of these competing views also tells us something about how United States foreign policy is made.

The official view of the origins of the Cold War—which was most recently presented, implicitly at least, in Dean Acheson's modestly titled book *Present at the Creation*—is that, on the whole, the Cold War began because of bad Soviet behavior. This particular view generally starts with the wartime alliance. It emphasizes how the United States trusted and helped the Soviet Union during the war, and it assumes that the Soviets themselves were, in fact, largely responsible for the war itself, which might not have started if Stalin had not made his deal with Hitler in 1939. Throughout the period of the wartime alliance, the United States expected that the Soviet Union would join us after the war in the creation of a new world order which would be based upon the cooperation of the great powers, in which democratic regimes would prevail and be safe from outside intervention, and in which spheres of influence—even disguised as "regionalism"—would be scrapped.

STANLEY HOFFMANN is Professor of Government at Harvard University. A student of American foreign policy, French politics, and international relations, Professor Hoffmann is currently preparing a work entitled *The Burden and the Balance*.

Such a view was reflected in the United Nations charter. Parenthetically, it is interesting to note that in working out schemes for this postwar world order in the years 1943 through 1945, the most serious conflicts were not between the United States and the Soviet Union but between the United States and Great Britain. These conflicts centered on such matters as the international monetary and trade systems, the emancipation of colonial territories, and so on.[1] Finally, the orthodox thesis states that the United States had no intention of becoming a world policeman after the war—certainly not *the* world policeman. In fact, it shows that throughout the war the United States overestimated the power which Great Britain would still have afterward, and expected a large measure of American disengagement.

All this, according to the official thesis, was destroyed by the aggressive behavior of the Soviet Union, which gradually increased its domination over Eastern Europe. As early as 1942 and 1943, the Soviet Union tightened its control of numerous Communist parties in the Balkans and in Western Europe, even beyond the line which the Red Army would reach at the end of the war. As examples of Soviet maneuvers which made cooperation difficult, this thesis points to: the Soviets' manipulation of Polish Communists in order to eliminate non-Communist forces from Poland; the establishment of bilateral links between Moscow and its neighbors, and Moscow's opposition to any linkages between these states which it might not control; Moscow's violation of the Yalta understanding on free elections in Poland; the Soviets' behavior in occupied Germany, in various interallied commissions, and in peace treaty conferences.

According to this view, the United States was then obliged, as the result of Soviet behavior, to face a choice it had not wanted. It was a choice between: on the one hand, tolerating a vacuum which could have been filled only by the Soviet Union, given the decline of England, the collapse of Western Europe, the decrepitude of China, and the fall of Japan; and on the other, taking leadership in a world in which there were now no major powers other than the Soviet Union and the United States. In other words, according to this first view, the United States had no imperial designs, but found itself forced to assume the leadership of a coalition. Nor was it the United States' fault that this was a coalition of unequals. The coalition it found itself leading was defensive, not offensive; leadership of that coalition was imposed, not planned.

This is the official line. If one looks at the facts—which is sometimes useful—one finds that this line goes much too far. Although it is certain that the Soviet Union deliberately extended its influence, these were limited moves and, certainly in the case of Germany, moves that seemed to be more preventive than anything else. On the whole, the Soviet Union did stick to and respect the divisions into national spheres of influence that it had arrived at with Churchill (it had been difficult to get the United States to agree). If one looks at the situations in Greece and in China, one finds that the behavior of the Communist parties in these two important countries was not at all dictated from Moscow. As for Germany, where the Soviets used their occupation zone as a major bargaining tool, the Soviets obviously had security fears and enormous economic needs which they wanted to satisfy, given the destruction they had suffered.

To be more specific, there was a fundamental ambiguity in Soviety policy in Germany, where they did not have one basic approach. But if any consistent thread did appear in Soviet policy there immediately after the end of the war, it was the need to take certain strong positions which could be exploited later for bargaining purposes and as leverage (for instance, in order to weaken any United States resolve to remain in Europe) rather than anything more precise. Most important, if one looks at the behavior of Communist parties in Western Europe in the period 1945 through 1947, one finds that they were far from being huge, disruptive, subversive organisms. In fact, they were still in their patriotic nationalist phase, willing to participate in coalition governments and to play the game of electoral democracy, telling their supporters, particularly the workers, to work and produce and rebuild these countries.

Clearly, then, the standard thesis goes beyond the facts. It does so, in part, because of something which the revisionists point out and to which I will return—the old tradition of anti-Communism and anti-Soviet suspiciousness in this country.[2] It may also have gone too far because of excessive Western—and especially American—expectations during World War II: the dream of harmony and cooperation after the war was bound to be disappointed, and disappointed Americans tend to overreact.

There was also a large amount of confusion in American thinking. It was not always clear whether what was lamented about Soviet behavior after 1945 was the division of Europe into spheres of influence—that is, the Soviet domination of one sphere—or the tendency which we thought the Communists had of going *beyond* their sphere of influence. The best example of this confusion we find in Kennan's own writings, in his memoirs. On the one hand, he indicated, in his own messages from that period, his conviction that Soviet control in Eastern Europe was shaky. He wrote that the Soviet threat was not military, that Soviet behavior was not adventurous, that the Soviets were interested primarily in a security zone. Yet there are other passages in his memoirs in which he talks about his fear of communization of the whole of Europe, and his description of the means of Soviet diplomacy suggests, at least implicitly, that he felt they had universal ends. So there was a confusion, based on uncertainty and fear, in America's image of Soviet behavior.

Eventually the revisionists entered the field and offered their own images. First, all of them go back for their interpretations much farther in time than the end, or even the beginning, of the wartime alliance. They generally start with 1917, not with the 1939 Hitler-Stalin pact or with 1941. One of the most representative spokesmen for the revisionists, Arno Mayer, presents the theory of an international civil war that has been going on at least since the Russian Revolution of 1917.[3] He describes the constant Western hostility to, and horrified fascination with, Communism, which resulted in recurrent attempts to intervene against Russia after 1917, as well as occasional strong sympathies for, or at least nonantipathy toward, Fascism in its anti-Communist implications. Revisionists also often concentrate on the immediate prewar years—in particular, on the impact Munich had on the Soviet Union, which felt itself rejected by the powers of Western Europe despite its offers to join in anti-Nazi collective security.

Insofar as they examine the wartime behavior of the Soviet Union, revisionists view it as essentially defensive and nationalist. They insist that the main objective of the Soviet Union was security in areas which had been traditional zones of Russian interest: in Eastern Europe and in the Balkans, in Turkey and all along the borders of the Soviet Union. They stress that the Soviets avoided major provocations and behaved with great prudence in

Western Europe, precisely by encouraging the Communist parties to work in national coalitions—even at the cost of sacrificing chances of social revolution. They show that Stalin was eager to avoid provoking the British there and in the eastern Mediterranean, and that the whole emphasis within the Communist parties was on nationalism, not on Communism. They show that Stalin expected agreements with the Western powers along sphere-of-influence lines and accepted Russia's exclusion from any significant role in Italy or Japan.

So what went wrong, according to the revisionists, is largely the result of American imperialism, whose existence they attempt to prove as follows: first of all, there was the rejection, in at least three forms, of economic aid to the Soviet Union as soon as Roosevelt was dead. The United States immediately ended Lend-Lease, refused a loan to the Soviet Union, and decided to put an end to reparations from West Germany to the Soviet Union. These were moves against which Henry Wallace protested when he was still vice-president.

The second fact was what the revisionists call the American attempt to intimidate the Soviet Union in areas of legitimate Soviet concern, such as Eastern Europe, with an American demonstration of strength through the use of the atomic bomb. Alperovitz, in his well-known book,[4] presents the American decision to use the bomb on Japanese cities as being intended largely to impress the Soviet Union with America's monopoly. Similarly, as Kolko shows throughout his enormous volume on the American politics of war, the United States' constant wartime support to the London Poles—the most anti-Communist Poles—must have appeared to the Soviets as an attempt at intimidating them and at insuring the future of an anti-Russian regime in Warsaw.

Finally, according to the revisionists, came the postwar attempt to universalize the Open Door, as symbolized by the Baruch Plan; it would have provided an international monopoly for the production of nuclear energy which would have been able to function without any veto by the Soviet Union. It was, in other words, a scheme that would have resulted in the sending of inspection teams into the Soviet Union, and it was based upon the notion that the United States would keep its nuclear weapons and not destroy them until and unless this Open Door international organization had been established. Incidentally, while the United States proposed this scheme, it excluded the Soviet Union from any part in the control of Italy, Japan, and West Germany. Concern for the Open Door—that is, preserving polities and markets for American influence and business—also manifested itself in Greece and Iran, as well as in America's opposition to British schemes for world trade and monetary arrangements (with the United States using now, against Britain, the ideology of free competition which the British had used against the Continent a century earlier).

These are the facts—accurate in themselves—which the revisionists mention. What about the value of the theory?[5] I think that the revisionists are far more nearly right than the official thesis in their treatment of the Soviet Union, in pointing out that the Soviet Union had limited territorial ambitions and that these ambitions were of a traditional nature. They are right too in pointing out that the leaders of the Soviet Union acted not as the brains behind a worldwide, Communist, ideological Frankenstein monster but as if they had read Hans Morgenthau's theory of power politics—which, incidentally, had not yet been propounded. The Kremlin leaders were much more concerned with the Russian national interest than with worldwide Communism. And the revisionists are right also in pointing out the complex nature of the Soviet Union's relations with outside Communist parties. This is a fact rightly stressed by Kolko—that the Soviets had little or no control over the Yugoslav, Greek, or Chinese Communist parties. The revisionists are right in pointing out that there were no instructions from Moscow to the Western European Communist parties to seize power or even to keep the arms they had accumulated during the resistance. They are right in pointing out the ambivalence of the Soviet Union toward Germany and the constant oscillation of Soviet policy between two possible lines: joint control of the whole of Germany with the Western powers, if at all possible, and—only if this was not to be possible—partition. Neither line entailed exclusive Soviet domination of all Germany. The revisionists are right in stating that the Soviets were concerned essentially with preventing Germany from becoming a Western, and potentially anti-Russian, preserve, and did not set up the East German regime until after the United States and Britain had begun to organize a West Germany entity. Thus the tragedy of partition grew out of Anglo-American hostility to the idea of a neutralized Germany under four-power control. (Whether this idea would have been workable at all is another story; my own opinion is profoundly skeptical.)

I think the revisionists are right also in showing that the notion of a worldwide Communist conspiracy was essentially a projection of America's own universalism. They are right in emphasizing that the United States in 1945 looked at the Soviet Union from a long tradition of distrust, which made us expect the worst. Americans felt a kind of disbelief about the Soviet Union, which was suspended only when it had to be—during the days of the Grand Alliance; this disbelief started all over again as soon as the Soviets proved to be difficult partners. And the revisionists are right in stressing that the United States faced world affairs with its own set of principles. As de Gaulle would say in one of his memoirs, "The United States looks at the world with complicated methods and simple ideas." In other words, American leaders did have some notion of designing a world which would look very much like the United States.

So the revisionists point to a paradox that, I think, has some validity. Whereas it was the Soviet Union that behaved according to a classical theory of power politics, it was the United States that behaved not at all like a classical great power playing a balance of power game but like an ideological power with a global vision. The United States behaved, then, in the way we thought the Soviets were behaving. In this respect, incidentally, the real father of revisionism, the one who first criticized this tendency of the United States to face the world with a set of principles of its own, was Walter Lippmann, in his writings about the Cold War in 1946 and 1947.

However, having said where the revisionists are right, I should also add that they are in danger of developing a new mythology of their own. Here I would like to stress where their realism goes off into a fantasy world.

It does so, I think, because the revisionists all look at American foreign policy with an a priori ideological conception; they announce what United States policy is, which often makes it unnecessary for them to look at the data or at least to interpret them correctly. This isn't true of all the revisionists. Some of them make a valiant effort to look at the data—certainly this is true of Alperovitz. As for Kolko's large book, I suggest that none of the chapters is better than the bibliographies he lists for each of them; and in the bibliographies, some of the listed books are of questionable value. There is in his book a kind of grand overview to which all details are subordinated. At its most extreme, the revisionist approach gives a kind of systematic, quasi-conspiratorial view of American foreign policy as an East Coast establishment plot. At the core of that plot is the economic interpretation, which assumes the need for ever-expanding markets. (Some emphasize the business drive; others stress agricultural expansionism.) This is an adaptation of the traditional socialist theory of imperialism; it sees United States foreign policy being led by men who, as Kolko puts it in his second and shorter book,[6] are all under the direct or indirect influence of the business interests. They are corporation lawyers, business executives, and the like. Everything is fitted into this design, and many quotations are strewn about to buttress the economic interpretation and present the search for new markets as the master key. Each time somebody talks about markets, you can be sure that even if the speech is made for purely Rotarian purposes, it is going to be picked out as damning and decisive by the revisionists.

Now this raises the essential problem of how one builds up an interpretation of a foreign policy. There is a serious danger in any a priori or ex ante method, be it Marxist or other. First of all, any approach in which you know the answer before you have asked the question effectively eliminates contradictions. The difficulty is that contradictions exist in every aspect of life. Second, it blows up small parts, or partial aspects, of the whole picture. And finally, it raises an interesting psychological problem: how is one to interpret the dynamics of foreign policy? If, in case after case, you find that what people thought they were doing is different from what the theory says that they were actually, really, "objectively" doing, then you have a problem. You must assume that people are in fact either mere puppets manipulated without their awareness—puppets who are now being told there was, for their motivations and actions, a purpose of which they were not aware—or else purposeful puppets conniving for, but carefully disguising, their real goals. But are policy makers either programmed automatons or cunning conspirators?

It isn't that what the revisionists say is necessarily false, but that they do iron out the kinks in history. It is a fact that through most of its history the United States was more concerned with raising the barrier at its gate—protectionism—than with enforcing open doors elsewhere—free trade. It is a fact that throughout this period the United States, at the same time that it was getting into trouble with the Soviet Union, did make effort after effort at accommodation. Truman might have been highly annoyed at the Russians—telling Molotov, quite literally, to go to hell—but he also sent messages to Stalin trying to patch things up. It is a fact that there were disagreements between the architects of United States policy—between Roosevelt and Hull, Hull and Welles, Truman and Byrnes, Acheson and Kennan. It is a fact that policy in the Third World was neither high-priority nor consistent (cf. Indonesia versus Indochina).

A different kind of contradiction, as I see it, is provided by the experience with the Marshall Plan. If the Soviets had accepted the Marshall Plan, which was offered to all of Europe, including the Soviet Union, they would have submitted themselves to receiving American aid and opened themselves to American industry, so that the outcome of the Marshall Plan would be evidence of American imperialism.[7] Yet the revisionists are also inclined to say that if Marshall aid had not been offered, this would have been a worse sign of American imperialism, because it would have proved that the United States wanted to cut the Soviet Union out. In other words, whatever the devil does is devilish. There is another of these contradictions in the fact that American economic investment was particularly high in areas that were not contested by the Soviet Union; areas in which the United States was supposedly in contest with the Soviet Union, such as Eastern Europe, were of practically no importance for American economic interests.

Now we come to the matter of blowing up parts of the picture. Alperovitz, in his book *Atomic Diplomacy,* discards or minimizes literally all the evidence that one could use to show that the Soviet Union was perhaps not the main target of the bomb dropped on Japan. Isn't it possible that the main target was Japan? Truman said that the atomic bomb was a weapon, that weapons were meant to be used, and that the decision to use it never cost him five minutes' sleep. Sometimes simplicity is its own answer. Perhaps things were not as complicated and men not as cunning as the revisionists believe. At least this alternative explanation should have been fully considered. Similarly, on the cancellation of Lend-Lease, the revisionists have made too much of the matter. Cancellation was largely a routine act by a new president who was inclined to the belief that when the war stops aid does too. Incidentally, this decision hit England at least as hard as it hit the Soviet Union.

Finally, on the problem of interpretation of the dynamics of foreign policy, one must ask oneself why, if the moving force was economic expansiveness (or expansionism), it is so hard to find evidence of its impact on actual decisions (by contrast with its presence in speeches). One must ask oneself whether American officialdom really intended ever to go back on the concessions made at Yalta and to force the Soviet Union out of Eastern Europe or East Germany, as Christopher Lasch has charged, or whether it was merely expressing indignation at what we thought they were doing beyond what we thought had been agreed at Yalta. Had we intended to "roll back" the Russians, we would have behaved as the world's most clumsy imperialists, since we began by letting the Soviets take Berlin, Prague, and Vienna when we could have prevented them from at least seizing all three, and continued with a colossal demobilization—a point neglected by the revisionists. How did American officials actually see their objectives? If they did not see them the way the revisionists said they saw them, this does not mean that American objectives could not have appeared to the Soviets the way they now look to the revisionists, or that the results of American policy do not look the way the revisionists see them; but it does mean that there may perhaps be a gap between American intentions, as Americans understood them, and the eventual outcome. So the key problem is not to look for a master explanation but, as Max Weber and Raymond Aron have pointed out, to try to understand the contrasts—the permanent, ironical contrasts—between what people think they are doing and what they are actually achieving. In other words, the key is to be found in the realm of perceptions.

When we're dealing with theoretical work on international systems, we may not have to go into the problem of perceptions. At that level of abstraction, people don't even matter; only systems—that is, patterns of relationships—matter (although I've never met a system in the street). But if one is going to explain foreign policy, he must take perceptions into account. At the heart of this debate is the question: what shall social science look for? Should it, à la Marx, look for a grand philosophy of history and a grand explanation which provides the key to everything, in which case one can relax—and act—or should it follow Thucydides, and focus on people's perceptions and intentions, and on the frustrations and contradictions people get into when what they achieve is different from what they intended? I lean toward Thucydides, in this respect at least. And this leads me to conclude that while the revisionists are more nearly right when they deal with Soviet behavior than in their account of United States motivations, the official thesis, which distorts Soviet conduct, correctly reflects American perceptions (or misperceptions) and the self-image of American leaders. If American actions formed patterns that invite the revisionists' wrath, the explanation must be sought in the nature of America's style and institutions rather than in the realm of counterrevolutionary motives and economic drives.[8]

Let me now present my own view of what the Cold War really was about and what the process became. I think, first of all, that one has to look at objective realities. The existence of a huge power vacuum in Europe and of another one in Asia, following the collapse of the Axis power, is such a reality. Next, one must look at intentions. Here, the revisionists' view of Soviet intentions is closer to the truth than their analysis of American intentions. When one looks at the latter, one should avoid projecting the 1960s backward. One has to keep in mind that much of American foreign policy at the time was extraordinarily improvised. Franklin Roosevelt's foreign office was still small, and his foreign policy machinery was extraordinarily primitive. He was a president who didn't listen to his secretary of state, but who had his own sources of information and advice. By 1945, American foreign policy machinery was not far from what it had been in 1940–41, when it was practically nonexistent. The American conceptions of the world, largely abstract and disembodied, both reflected and reacted against the absence of America from world affairs before that period. Quite naturally they expressed a certain American style, which Wilsonianism had already displayed, and which could be described as representing the hubris of worldwide do-goodism.

Then, after intentions, we have to look at perceptions, and here what is most important is how each side saw the other one. For how each side saw the other determined how each side acted. This is where the stuff of tragedy, I think, can be found. The Soviet Union saw the United States as being far more deliberate and far more vigilant than the United States actually was. And the United States saw the Soviet Union as being far more ambitious and more in control of everything than the Soviet Union actually was. This can be confirmed by anybody who works in the field of perceptions:[9] each side always tends to see his antagonist as being infinitely more cunning, centralized, controlling, and competent than he is or than he himself is. Now the origins of this battle of misperceptions have only little to do with objective reality, for each side was doubtlessly inclined to perceive the present in terms of extreme past experiences, domestic or external. The United States had a kind of fixation about—this time—not allowing another Hitler and not succumbing to another Munich; after all, United States officialdom felt slightly guilty for not having been vigilant in the 1930s, for not having paid much attention to the European scene, for having practiced until 1940 the policy of the ostrich. They didn't want this to happen again and had a strong tendency to interpret what was happening now in the light of what had happened then. The Soviet Union, for its part, had its own theories about Western capitalist behavior, based on its own experiences of the early 1920s and the 1930s.

The final element we should examine is the opportunities for action. Here, we need to move from generalities to something more precise. First of all, there were asymmetries in the two Policies.[10] The Soviet Union was probably uncertain as to whether the wartime collaboration would continue or not. Stalin showed some willingness at Yalta and at Potsdam to make at least some concessions in order to assure the permanency of the collaboration, perhaps in the hope of economic rewards, and it was largely because of those concessions that the UN was finally established. There is no doubt that the Soviet Union was determined to pursue a sphere-of-influence policy in Eastern Europe and to have a decisive say in the settlement of the German problem. While this may have been a strictly defensive conception, it does raise some traditional questions about great-power defensive conceptions. What specific policies were implied? Would it be defensive in cooperation with others or in conflict with them? Nor was it clear as to what was their ultimate vision of world affairs to be served by this conception. Was it a conservative or a revolutionary vision? This is a question, incidentally, which Kolko never reaches. Now, the shape and features of a Policy depend on the long-range vision and on the tactical policies.

As for American Policy, it was clearer about economic schemes than about political issues. There was obviously a great desire on the part of Roosevelt for peaceful collaboration with the Soviet Union. The president had an understanding of Soviet security concerns, which often made him extremely annoyed with Churchill throughout the war. But we also hesitated to pay for such collaboration the price the Soviets requested—to endorse their political control over their neighbors, especially Poland. Moreover, the American long-term vision of world affairs was essentially neither conservative nor revolutionary. It might better be called a reformist vision, a kind of Wilsonian view, accompanied and sharpened by FDR's sense of the need for great powers to play a leading role. The United States, by way of contrast with Marxism or Communism, did not think of a world revolution. Yet its long-range vision was not conservative, because United States leaders distrusted such conservative techniques of conflict management as the balance of power; the United States preferred a kind of Wilsonian concerted cooperation on the part of the great powers. Whereas this was not incompatible with some sphere of influence policy—after all, the United States itself insisted on its sphere of influence in Latin America, and enshrined it in the charter of the United Nations—it was not compatible with two different factors. It was incompatible with what appeared to us to be the revolutionary vision of the other side. What was required by the American vision was at least a harmony of ends on the part of the great powers. Second, it was not compatible with any tendency of the other side to confuse a sphere of preponderant influence with a sphere of exclusive property. The distinction—between hegemony for security or economic reasons and controlling domination—was clearly made in Washington.

There is yet another paradox, which explains the momentum of the Cold War. The Soviet Union's policy was to a large extent defensive and cautious, but was pursued so vigorously that to many Americans and West Europeans, it looked like the policy of Genghis Khan reincarnate. On the other side, the United States had a policy which it viewed as defensive, but in some ways its own vision of the future was highly universal and implicitly imperalistic, in the sense that it wanted to see a world which would look much like the United States. And of course the United States, undevastated and indeed strengthened by the war, had the biggest weapons available to any nation in history.

Let us look at these ambiguities a bit more closely. What the Soviet Union started by doing was in itself ambiguous. Thus, (leaving aside Czechoslovakia, where the coup de Prague did not come until early 1948) the communization of Eastern Europe could be seen—as Louis Halle puts it in his book on the Cold War[11]—as a situational necessity for the leaders of the Kremlin. The Soviet Union found itself in countries essential for Soviet security—traditional invasion routes—yet where all the non-Communist forces were anti-Communist and anti-Soviet, and so what could they do? Obviously, the concern for external security led to measures of internal safety: they moved to eliminate the anti-Communist forces. But Soviet policy there could also be seen as a step toward ultimate world revolution. This ambiguity was present from the very start.

What was it that the United States perceived? What it saw was a shock to its own expectations. First, the United States, as a good, "liberal" power, was inclined to draw a clear boundary—its own Iron Curtain—between international politics and domestic affairs. The Soviets were viewed in Washington as entitled to a predominant foreign policy influence in Poland or Bulgaria or Hungary, just as they had in Finland, but they should not control the domestic affairs of those countries. Washington always made this perfectly artificial distinction without realizing that for the Soviets, at least in Eastern Europe, it was a hard one to apply, not only because in Marxist doctrine the distinction itself is absurd but also because of the political situation of those countries, where there was little middle ground between Communism and anti-Communism. Second, the United States, as a good, "liberal" power, saw international relations as a domain of give and take, and found itself facing Mr. Molotov's "nyet, nyet, nyet" intransigence instead. It therefore saw itself on the defensive. This is what the United States perceived by the end of 1945.

How the United States reacted to its own perceptions was in itself ambiguous. On the one hand, the United States discovered power; in fact, it did so with some glee, as manifested in Kennan's writings. The United States thus discovered what in a country like England had been known for many centuries: that in the absence of any world community, power means hard bargaining, not gestures; power means applying one's might locally to master local circumstances; power means having to discriminate between essential areas and the others. So, in 1945, the United States discovered what Morgenthau was to codify in 1948. But on the other hand, the United States also projected its own universalism, which was incompatible with traditional power politics, and in doing so, the United States reacted by supposing that if the Sovet Union misbehaved, it must be because of Soviet universalism. Therefore we translated from their acts—which, as we saw, were ambiguous—to their intentions; and the American response, based on this interpretation, was dictated by the American style. It was a response in universalist fashion, according to American values and practices. When something goes wrong outside, we offer economic aid and military assistance, because that is what we know how to do. Typical of American principles is the Truman Doctrine, which wasn't just an offer of aid to Turkey and Greece; it was a proclamation of the duty to protect free peoples everywhere against Communism. Then there was the "open society" element enshrined in the Baruch Plan, also typical of how this country reacts. Important changes in American foreign policy personnel—the departure of many of the Rooseveltian in-and-outers who had made the wartime alliance work, and their replacement by foreign service officers and military and civilian leaders deeply suspicious of the USSR—contributed to this response.[12]

How did the Soviets interpret an American reaction which was itself ambiguous? The Soviets obviously interpreted it as a challenge. The American scheme for an open international society, with majority rule and no veto, was seen as a grand design to suppress revolution and to subvert the Soviet Union. The Soviets naturally saw it as a challenge to their interests. What the Baruch Plan meant to them was that the United States would keep its bomb until such time as the Soviet Union knuckled under a majority scheme obviously controlled by the West. This was also the time when the Americans began to consolidate the western parts of Germany, when Communists were ousted from the governments of France and Italy. How did the Soviets react, following their interpretation of our ambiguous reaction to the ambiguous acts of the Soviet Union? The Soviets reacted with a considerable tightening of the screws. They mobilized the Communist parties in Western Europe in 1947–48 to go on strikes; they provoked a huge antibomb "peace" agitation in 1948; they established the Cominform. Inside the Soviet Union, they performed a similar tightening of screws, symbolized by the fall of Zhdanov; they staged—or helped—the coup in Prague, in February, 1948; and they established the Berlin blockade, which was essentially a reaction to American moves in Western Europe.

Now, whatever the implications of all these Soviet moves, they were probably not meant to be offensive. They were probably more, as Adam Ulam says in his book on Soviet foreign policy, an attempt to make the United States lose patience and heart, to drive a frustrated and exasperated United States back into isolationism.[13] We had practically promised Stalin that after the war was over we would go home. The United States, after all, had already demobilized, from about eight million persons under arms during World War II to less than half a million. Rather than moves toward promoting the Communist world revolution, Stalin's moves were attempts to show the Americans that staying in world affairs was going to be painful. Ironically, only now, after Vietnam and the beginning of a detente, has the long-expected and much-delayed isolationist swing in the United States reemerged.

How did the United States interpret these Soviet moves? Naturally, they were thought to be the justification of America's own vision and of America's old misgivings about Soviet universalism. The United States inferred from Soviet acts and capabilities to Soviet intentions, and reacted with an increase of pressure on the Soviets. Through a combination of power and universalism, the United States moved rapidly from Kennan's limited notion of containment, which was based on an assessment of the limits of Soviet power, and which would have been pluralistic, essentially nonmilitary, and transitional, to a wholly different policy—one symbolized, for example, by the Japanese peace treaty. United States policy was not pluralistic but hegemonic, in the sense that everything was to be under United States predominance; it put primary reliance on military pacts, presence, and support; and it became self-perpetuating, largely because the United States stuck to its universal vision—later christened "pragmatic" by Walt Rostow.

And yet, even when the United States reacted in this way, it kept trying to avoid a total militarization and division of the world. In the one place in which the United States did not react in military fashion—in fact, took its troops out—in South Korea, it thus provoked a power vacuum into which the North Koreans moved. The United States response to that action is well known. So even where the United States had not been consistent with its fears, there was a forced confirmation of its vision.

So much for the momentum. What lessons can one derive from this? Halle, in his book, talks about the interaction between the scorpion and the tarantula. The scorpion shows its aggressiveness toward the tarantula, but it merely reflects its defensiveness—its conviction that the tarantula secretly wants to kill the scorpion. And the tartantula naturally reacts by trying to kill the scorpion, thus confirming the scorpion's conviction that the tarantula is out to kill it. The story is instructive with regard to both the origins and the development of the Cold War. I think that it was a mistake then to attribute to the Soviet Union an aggressive, worldwide universalism, for one good reason—they didn't have the means for it. Whatever their dreams may have been, they had to adjust their ends to their means. Similarly, it is a mistake now on the part of the revisionists to attribute to the United States of 1945 an aggressive economic and military universalism. To be sure, the United States had the means for it, but many of these means were not converted into power. The nuclear monopoly was not converted into political power, and never were the Soviets more active abroad than in the period when the United States had a nuclear monopoly. Nor did American actions really correspond to those alleged imperalistic intentions. The Baruch Plan, for instance, was not intent on depriving the Soviet Union of its enormous superiority in conventional weapons. It didn't even deal with this. The Marshall Plan, for all its self-interest aspects, was not an imperialistic design either, for it obviously aimed at the restoration of potential challengers or rivals.

Why, then, did each side so badly misperceive the other's intentions, and act on the basis of those misperceptions? The answer is to be found in a mix of specific features and general factors. Who were the two opponents? They were not just any two powers. The Peloponnesian War did not involve just any two powers; it involved Athens and Sparta. Similarly here, there was a revolutionary, if cautious, power pitted against a reformist, although confused, one. On one side was the Soviet Union, which had a long history of invasion, of disappointments and suspicions in the thirties, and which was fearful about its security. On the other was the United States, with a long history of oscillation between total noninvolvement in world affairs and involvement in order to save the world. Then, next to those specific features was the dialectic characteristic of any bipolar confrontation in history. It always seems to oppose two self-fulfilling prophecies. Here we find, as usual, the paradox of two largely defensive universalisms, with its three features. First, in this kind of dialectic, what is essential to each appears threatening to the other. Soviet security, interpreted in Communist fashion as entailing Communist regimes in Eastern Europe, seemed threatening to us. And the American vision of an open world, without vetoes or Iron Curtains, seemed threatening to the Soviets. Second, what each one may have regarded as admirably restrained on its part appeared ominous to the other. Soviet behavior in Greece and Western Europe appeared ominous to us; the Baruch Plan, which foresaw that the United States would ultimately give up its nuclear arsenal, appeared menacing to the Russians, because it was only ultimately that our weapons would be destroyed. Finally, in this kind of a confrontation, each one interprets the other's defensive moves as offensive. This is true partly because each expects them to be offensive (this points to the enormous importance of the images each had of the other). The Soviets saw the United States as a capitalist power, and therefore necessarily offensive toward a revolutionary power such as the USSR. We saw the Soviet Union not as a "normal" state but as the seat of a revolutionary movement whose purpose was to undermine the international system. Partly, each viewed the other's moves as offensive, because sometimes they were—sometimes, when fears are acute, defensive acts have definite offensive overtones, which only confirm the opponent's expectation. Thus, out of fear for Iran's independence, we pushed the Soviets out; and out of fear for their interests in West Germany, the Russians staged the blockade of Berlin.

There remains one last question—the question one always likes to ask. Was the Cold War inevitable? To a large extent, it appears to have been so. By now, some twenty years later, all kinds of people tell us that it could have been avoided, if we had only had a somewhat more realistic diplomacy, if we had followed canons of moderation, such as not allowing power vacuums in important areas, and had not allowed ideological generalizations and escalations. Kennan, for instance, has generally taken this line, and criticizes the slant of the Truman Doctrine. This approach is, however, unworkable, partly because the givens had been provided by recent history and could not be undone—the power vacuums, for instance, and the presence of the Red Army in central Europe, or the economic preponderance and nuclear advance of the United States—and partly because the precepts of Kennan are those of a moderate, multipolar system, in other words, a system in which powers are not ideologically in conflict and do speak the same language.

Given what the world was like, it seems to me, first of all, that intensification of the conflict was inevitable, if only because of the actual and potential might of the antagonists. De Gaulle's diplomatic techniques were often as brutal as the Soviets', but they created no comparable fears in Washington, precisely because his might was negligible.[14] Might creates opportunities—as we well know from Vietnam—even when intentions are limited. The presence of large Communist minorities in Western Europe was an opportunity for the Soviet Union. The power vacuum in South Korea was an opportunity. The facts that the United States alone defeated Japan and that the Western powers alone occupied Italy and half of Germany also provided opportunities for the West to exclude the Soviets. Even if one defines interests so narrowly that they are necessarily in conflict, power creates interests in a broad sense. For a great power, security is a universal problem, which creates the temptation of camp building; and every great power has always believed that it had to increase its power to save the world. When one is strong, one's rival will always tend to jump from one's acts to one's capacities and to derive one's intentions from these.

Second, intensification also tends to increase without limit, because of ideology. Ideology is always partly a rationalization of great might. In modern history, many statesmen are elected—although sometimes it is the statesmen who elect the people—and normally these men are not cynical, but want to define their might in ideological terms. There is a human need to justify in one's own eyes, and in the eyes of others, what one does in terms of ultimate values beyond might. Moreover, each of these particular antagonists felt a need to offer its way of life to others, apart from any rationalization of its might. Hence, a dialectic developed, which was a combination of accurate perceptions—each party was aware of the hostility and of the long-range preferences of the other—and misperceptions as to what each side was up to in the short range.

The final contributing factor which made the whole process inevitable was the domestic styles of the two protagonists. Moderation was ruled out, not only by ideology and might but also by that style. The Soviet Union was led by a man who can be said to have had an absolute, cosmic distrust of everything that was not himself. We all know now, on the basis of more information than we care to have, what life under Stalin was like. Stalin needed the total subservience of everybody else around him, as was shown as much in domestic trials as in foreign purges. When he disappeared, his successors had the problem of their own security. They did make some limited gestures of moderation, such as the Austrian peace treaty in 1955, but there were built-in limits to those gestures, because these men too had to succeed, if only to consolidate their weak domestic position. Success at home is never enough for a great power. In the United States, there was always an incompatibility between people like Kennan, who advocated moderate and non-public diplomacy, and the political process, institutions, and culture of the United States. What characterizes Kennan is his intense dislike of the whole American political system, essentially because he well understands that it does not make for the kind of cool cabinet diplomacy of which he is so fond. Moreover, the United States had to deal also with insecurity, for this nation, which found itself a world leader for the first time, did not know what kind of world it would be. This insecurity expressed itself in extreme fashion, for instance, in the appearance of Joe McCarthy and in what his exploitation of collective paranoia did to various circles in American life, at home and abroad.

These are the reasons why it seems to me futile to look for one villain. If you like villains—and what American doesn't?—there are two to contend with. If you think, as Camus did, that in this world nobody is either entirely innocent or completely guilty, then the best explanation is that the Cold War developed between two nations which were partly villains and partly victims.

In the final analysis, perhaps the most significant shortcoming of the revisionists' new othodoxy is that it is so much the mirror image of the other orthodoxy. It merely reverses the black and the white, making the Americans the villains and the Soviets the moderates. The revisionists, like those holding the official view, look for grand explanations of a conspiratorial nature, although this time it is American economic imperialism rather than a world-wide Communist conspiracy that is the key. The revisionists, like their predecessors, oversimplify the history of others. (For example, the moment in Gabriel Kolko's book where I really had a sense of landing in a dreamland came when, at the end of the chapter on France, he explained that by October, 1944, the United States, which had long resisted the leadership of General de Gaulle, finally threw its support to him in order to suppress the French left. The French left, incidentally, got 67 percent of the vote in the election a year later, and so it had not been badly suppressed.) Finally, like the orthodox view, the revisionists' vision is somewhat abstract, vague, and too grandiose—it fails because it is too nearly perfect, because it refuses to take sufficiently into account all the little points about perceptions, intentions, misunderstandings, and just plain errors that I have tried to mention here. There has long existed this pattern of oscillation in American historiography; it has developed about World War I as well as about the Cold War. It is not up to me to decide whether this constant shift from one devil's view to another, without ever stopping in the middle, is the best way to political and scientific maturity.

NOTES

1. See, on these points, Gabriel Kolko, *The Politics of War* (New York: Random House, 1968).

2. See Arno J. Mayer, *Politics and Diplomacy of Peacemaking* (New York: Knopf, 1967); and D. F. Fleming, *The Cold War and Its Origins,* 2 vols. (New York: Doubleday, 1961).

3. See also his essay, *Dynamics of Counterrevolution in Europe, 1890–1956* (New York: Harper Torchbook, 1971).

4. *Atomic Diplomacy: Hiroshima and Potsdam* (New York: Simon and Schuster, 1965).

5. Two excellent critiques of revisionism are: Charles S. Maier, "Revisionism and the Interpretation of Cold War Origins," in *Perspectives in*

American History 4 (1970); and Robert W. Tucker, *The Radical Left and American Foreign Policy* (Baltimore: Johns Hopkins University Press, 1971).

6. *The Roots of American Foreign Policy* (Boston: Beacon Press, 1969).

7. See William Appleman Williams, *The Tragedy of American Diplomacy* (New York: Delta Book, 1962).

8. I have tried to describe the impact of America's style and institutions on foreign policy in *Gulliver's Troubles* (New York: McGraw-Hill, 1968).

9. See the work in this area of my colleague Robert Jervis.

10. By Policy, I mean the sum total of vision, objectives, and policies (or tactics).

11. *The Cold War as History* (New York: Harper and Row, 1967).

12. See a forthcoming Harvard University Ph.D. dissertation by Martin Wishnatsky.

13. *Expansion and Coexistence* (New York: Praeger, 1968).

14. Incidentally, even de Gaulle—normally more lucid about long-range trends—expected World War III to break out soon after the end of World War II.

Ronald W. Pruessen

2

The Objectives of American Foreign Policy and the Nature of the Cold War

EDITORS' NOTE. "Cold War" is a term that came into use as a result of growing United States–Soviet conflicts at the close of World War II. In the standard Western interpretations, the Russians' maintenance of a strong military presence in Eastern Europe after the close of the war, their communization of the governments of those states, accompanied by their intransigence against their wartime allies in conferences intended to produce peace in Europe—all were essential ingredients in the making of the Cold War. By March, 1946, Winston Churchill had coined the phrase "Iron Curtain" to describe the awesomeness of the barrier that the Soviets had presumably erected about the European territories they controlled. A year later, Walter Lippmann had written a book specifically entitled *The Cold War.* Europe was the theater, and Soviet hostility has been taken as the driving force for the opening of the Cold War era there.

As a result of these developments, according to the views that have long dominated American thinking on the subject, the United States took the great defensive steps in response to Russian expansionism that were to halt further Soviet moves in Europe and elsewhere and to define the boundaries between the "free" and the "Communist" worlds. The most notable of these early steps—the Marshall Plan and the Truman Doctrine—both related to the perceived Communist threat to Europe.

In the following essay, Professor Ronald Pruessen argues that the orthodox interpretations of these American initiatives in Europe have always been incomplete and, indeed, misleading explanations of American motives. In his view, the Soviet presence only made more ominous a situation that United States policy makers would have regarded as a serious threat to American interests in any case—the danger of Europe's complete economic col-

27

lapse. America's own economic health greatly depended on
Europe's economic recovery, and self-interest dictated that the
United States take action to encourage that recovery in such a
way that European markets would not be lost to America. Hence,
the American initiatives toward Europe in the postwar period
should be viewed largely as attempts to restore and expand those
markets. Professor Pruessen even goes so far as to suggest that
"the objectives of American policy makers would have been almost exactly the same if the Soviet Union had not even existed
in 1947."

That is a conclusion with which not everyone will agree, but,
as the following essay clearly reveals, United States policy makers
at the time were far from oblivious to the dangerous implications
for the United States of economic chaos in Europe. To some of
these policy makers, it seemed necessary to phrase the American
initiatives in terms of a response to Soviet hostility in order to
secure their acceptance by Congress and the public. To others,
most notably George Kennan, the use of ideological rhetoric—particularly in the Truman Doctrine—diverted attention from the
principal issue and raised to a dangerous level the emotional con-
tent of the international issues facing the nation. That there was
prescience in this latter view can hardly be denied in retrospect,
for the economic challenge to the United States in 1946–47 has
nearly been lost sight of during twenty-five years of Cold War confrontations in which the Soviet Union has been seen as the
archvillain.

More than twenty-five years have passed since the beginning of that era in international relations we have come to call the Cold War. The passage of that length of time should allow a step back from the fray and an assessment of some of its major characteristics as a historical phenomenon. In attempting to do this, it would be particularly interesting to observe the behavior of the United States in the early days of the Cold War. By far the most powerful nation on the globe, even before the end of World War II, the United States contributed most extensively in the mid 1940s to the forging of patterns in international affairs from which the world has yet to break free. American actions then and the way in which power was exercised still cast dark shadows across the decades.

An understanding of the behavior of the United States on the world scene during the early Cold War era requires the answering of certain basic questions. What were the objectives of American diplomacy in those years? Beneath all the events and actions and policy initiatives, what motivations were at work? Why did American policy makers see the problems they did? And what did they hope to accomplish by means of the policies they devised? These are by no means easy questions to answer, but they are of fundamental importance in understanding the nature of our times.

A meaningful initial observation to be made about American motivations during the first phases of the Cold War concerns the location of the actual arena in which international struggles were to be waged. If on a map of the world small markers were pinned on those areas which were the scenes of crises in world affairs during the early years of the Cold War, there would be a visibly impressive concentration in one particular geographical region: Europe and the other areas surrounding the Mediterranean Sea. It would be easy to observe that from at least 1943 to at least 1949, the physical center of that portentous struggle between the United States and the Soviet Union, between the "free world" and "communism," was to be found there. The briefest rundown of the sequence of initial Cold War crises demonstrates this amply through place names alone. Allied disagreements over the Italian

RONALD W. PRUESSEN is an Assistant Professor of History at Temple University, where he specializes in American diplomatic history. He is at work on a book-length biography of John Foster Dulles.

surrender, the future of France, and the structure of Poland before 1945; British and French economic problems, and American loans to these governments in 1945–46; the destinies of Bulgaria, Rumania, Hungary, Czechoslovakia, Yugoslavia; the negotiation of a peace settlement with Germany; Soviet relations with Turkey and Iran in 1946; civil war in Greece in 1947; the 1946–47 economic debilitation of Western Europe; the 1948 "coup" in Czechoslovakia; the 1948–49 Berlin blockade and airlift; and so on—virtually all the major international crises of these years obviously revolved around a particular geographic hub. In addition, most of the milestones in the evolution of specifically American foreign policy were unmistakably laid out on the same terrain: the American occupation of a zone in conquered Germany; the negotiation of the British Loan; the assignment of a United States fleet to the eastern Mediterranean; the Truman Doctrine; the Marshall Plan; and the North Atlantic Treaty Organization—all are cases in point.[1]

Such a European and Mediterranean focus in early Cold War crises is an interesting and significant aspect of the international relations of that period. The interest can be found in the simple phenomenon of geographical homogeneity; the significance lies beneath the phenomenon. In particular, consideration of American actions in these closely related early post–World War II crises yields revealing insights into the basic substance of United States foreign policy. What troubled American policy makers so greatly as they looked at Europe and the Mediterranean? What led these men and the nation to abandon what was supposed to have been a traditional aloofness from international affairs in order to become the crusading leader of a free world coalition? If policy makers in Washington, as conventional wisdom would have it, were responding in a determined fashion to an unfolding Soviet-directed Communist menace, just what was it that was being menaced— and why did these policy makers see it as dangerous enough to justify such bold responses? To a significant degree, in other words, it is possible to arrive precisely at the motivations behind American diplomacy by looking at European and Mediterranean policies in the early years of the Cold War.

A consideration of the geographically circumscribed crises of the mid and late 1940s and of the reasons beneath United States policies toward these is a significant undertaking in itself. And yet, in addition, some sense of American motivations will also make it possible to grasp something of the real essence of the Cold War as a historical phenomenon. American policies in Europe and the Mediterranean demonstrate how greatly historians and political scientists have become prisoners of Cold War rhetoric and mythology, how much they have come to depend on a simplistic, all-pervasive story line revolving around United States–Soviet relations, and how little they have appreciated the enormous complexities of international relations. It is not at all too much to suggest that the United States responded to this geographical area in this period on the basis of concerns that long predated the Cold War and in a way which, for many key policy makers, had relatively little to do with the behavior of the archvillains in Moscow. As other historians have now effectively argued, the usual harsh impression of the Cold War era has emerged in significant part from the tense rhetoric of policy makers seeking much-needed support from the public and Congress for programs serving traditional political-economic ends. The ideological uproar of the free world versus Communism syndrome was frequently a useful political camouflage.

An accurate appraisal of American objectives in the early years of the Cold War would have to grow out of a careful study of all the policy decisions in this period, and this is obviously beyond the scope of this essay. The examination of one particular case in some depth will, however, allow some tentative conclusions concerning these years as a whole. Such historical license is especially justified in this instance, since American policies in the mid and late 1940s have been seen by many historians as basically consistent, whatever their specific varying conclusions might be. Of all the possibilities for this procedure, no situation may be as revealing as those particularly crucial crises of early 1947. In what one participant has dramatically described as "The Fifteen Weeks" (February 21–June 5), both the Truman Doctrine and the Marshall Plan had their births, a fact which may justify a certain dramatic emphasis.[3] What considerations lay behind those emphatic foreign policy initiatives? What did American policy makers see as they looked at Europe and the Mediterranean, and why did it worry them so greatly?

As the men in Washington looked across the Atlantic in early 1947, they all saw a series of economic and political crises that filled them with foreboding. Before the year had run its course, many would give voice to fears for the very continuance of Western civilization, and few refrained from the frequent use of melodramatic terminology and expletives. It might be said that none of the serious problems plaguing that geographical region were new in 1947, or that Americans had hardly just come to see threats to their own national interests. But for all this lack of suddenness, the problems at the time seemed ever worsening, and the atmosphere in government offices became tense and electric.

First in 1947's unfolding drama were the critical situations developing in Greece and Turkey. Both countries faced similar problems. Each was experiencing grave economic weakness, and appeared to Americans to be under additional and compounding political-military pressures. Turkey was spending a major portion of its budget on armaments, worried that more momentum might be added to Soviet interference in Eastern Europe and the Balkans. Greece was facing a more overt and immediate crisis. A bitter internal conflict, between the traditional rulers of the land and the leftist and Communist resistance groups that had begun after the wartime departure of German forces, was still raging, and there were numerous signs that its reverberations were being felt in neighboring countries. Already in the previous year, American policy makers had seen their interests in Greece and Turkey as substantial enough to justify strong diplomatic support to the established governments and the initiation of military aid programs. Secretary of State James Byrnes had talked about both these matters at length with British Prime Minister Ernest Bevin during the July, 1946, Paris session of the Council of Foreign Ministers. The British, who had long cast a paternalistic cloak around this section of the Mediterranean, were facing such economic troubles of their own that their role was likely to be diminished for financial reasons. Byrnes assured Bevin of American interest in supporting the area in dealing with its political and economic problems.[4] By early 1947, in fact, a special United States economic mission was conducting an investigation of conditions in Greece which was to play a role in a consideration of the expansion of military aid. The problems reached a critical stage in February, 1947, when the British government notified the American State Department that as of April 1 it would no longer be able to provide military and financial aid.[5] While discussions and decisions in 1946 indicate that this could hardly have been a bombshell, the British notification did require quick decisions and actions by the United States. In that respect, it proved an immediate catalyst for policy makers.

The British note was delivered on February 21, 1947, and on March 12, President Truman addressed Congress and requested authorization for $400,000,000 in assistance to Greece and Turkey. In the three weeks between these dates, the arguments developed to justify this "Truman Doctrine" well revealed the substantive motivations behind it.

Explanations provide an early example of a line of reasoning which was to become endemic to American foreign policy during the Cold War—that is, what policy makers saw of greatest relevance to the United States in the critical situations developing in the eastern Mediterranean was not so much the problems of that immediate area as it was the potential impact of those problems on contiguous regions. Although the term "domino" was never used, visions of an all too neat progression of falling units were pervasive among policy makers in Washington.

One of the most famous policy sessions leading to the enunciation of the Truman Doctrine, for example, was the meeting held at the White House on February 27 at which President Truman and Secretary of State Marshall attempted to provide advance warning to Congressional leaders concerning the developing crisis. From all accounts, the key presentation of the day was an off-the-cuff elaboration by Undersecretary of State Dean Acheson which explained the great significance of what was happening in Greece and Turkey. It was serious enough in its own right, Acheson argued, that two such countries stood in danger of succumbing to Communist expansionism—but that was really only the beginning of the problem. Listing one country and then one continent after another, Acheson described the way in which the loss of Greece and Turkey would have horrible reverberations. Iran and the entire Middle East; Italy, Austria, Hungary; France and Germany; Africa—the dominoes would start to fall, and would not stop until all had been toppled. Acheson's audience was apparently awed by the progression of catastrophes whirling before them.[6]

Less than a week later, Undersecretary of State Will Clayton wrote a formal memorandum for the president on the developing situation which took precisely the same line Acheson had developed. "I am deeply disturbed by the present world picture," Clayton began. "The United States must take world leadership, and quickly, to avert world disaster."

> If Greece and Turkey succumb the whole Middle East will be lost.
> France may then capitulate to the Communists.
> As France goes, all Western Europe and North Africa will go.
> These things must not happen.
> These things need not happen.[7]

And in President Truman's own major statement to Congress on March 12, no new explanation of motives emerges:

> It is necessary only to glance at a map to realize that the survival and integrity of the Greek nation are of grave importance to a much wider situation. If Greece should fall under the control of an armed minority, the effect upon its neighbor Turkey, would be immediate and serious. Confusion and disorder might well spread throughout the entire Middle East.
> Moreover, the disappearance of Greece as an independent state would have a profound effect upon those countries in Europe whose peoples are struggling against great difficulties. . . . Should we fail to aid Greece and Turkey in this fateful hour, the effect will be far reaching to the West as well as to the East.[8]

In fact, the truly crucial aspect of the Truman Doctrine is in actuality not so much what it itself involved but what it began. The $400,000,000 eventually authorized by Congress, for example, was to become a relatively small sum in the context of evolving programs over succeeding months. "This is a serious course upon which we embark," Truman told Congress on March 12, and he fully recognized what he himself called the "broad implications" of the actions then being considered. Subsequent events well demonstrated the recognition of a beginning in those words.

The Truman Doctrine, even before its official presidential enunciation, was clearly only a first move designed to deal with critical situations that had spread far beyond the eastern Mediterranean. As one State Department figure described it, "the specific project of aid to Greece and Turkey had sandbagged only a tributary to the main stream, which was now out of banks."[9] On February 26, for example, in one of the first high-level meetings on pressing

Greek-Turkish matters, Dean Acheson met with Secretary of the Navy James Forrestal and Secretary of War Robert Patterson to discuss the problem of formulating an overall response to the British note on Greek and Turkish aid that had arrived a few days earlier. Forrestal and Patterson conveyed their own sentiments and those of Chief of Staff of the Army Dwight Eisenhower that large-scale aid to countries *other* than Greece and Turkey had to be considered immediately. Acheson agreed that wide-ranging studies should be undertaken, but convinced his colleagues that "the suggested study would take a very long time to prepare, that getting a general aid bill approved by Congress would be extremely difficult and in any event would take a very long time, and that the Greek crisis required the fastest possible action."[10] Acheson had earlier proved that he felt the "broad implications" which Harry Truman had mentioned. His own description of the falling dominoes to congressional leaders was now to be followed by an explicit March 6 order to the interdepartmental State-War-Navy Coordinating Committee (SWNCC): begin a careful and detailed study of the aid requirements of countries other than Greece and Turkey.[11] The evolving Truman Doctrine thereby provided a move to deal with one particularly troubling situation, and also consciously started the mood toward dealing with wider matters.

If the geographical locus of policy makers' concerns in early 1947 was clearly beyond the eastern Mediterranean, just what was the target of their worries, and what was it there that troubled them?

Early concern regarding critical situations developing outside the eastern Mediterranean was almost immediately set into an economic context. Significant statements and discussions by policy makers in these months tended invariably to zero in on commercial and financial problems of sweeping nature. For example, although frequently overshadowed by his dramatic appearance before Congress six days later, President Truman's address to a commencement audience at Baylor University in Texas on March 6 provides excellent insight into the general trends of thought among key American policy makers at the time. After the usual polite comments on his hosts and their award to him of an honorary doctor of laws degree, Truman hastily established his theme. The world was yearning for "peace and freedom," he said, and in the very next sentences declared, "These objectives are bound up completely with a third objective—reestablishment of world trade. In fact, the three—peace, freedom, and world trade—are inseparable." It was to world trade and the dangers of severe economic dislocations and rivalry that the president devoted the entire balance of his address. He recited the horrors of the depression decade's international economic autarchy, stating emphatically, "We must not go through the thirties again"; he outlined plans for the International Trade Organization and upcoming negotiations in Geneva; he marshaled arguments in behalf of the reciprocal trade agreements program. In particular, Truman emphasized what he saw as a "turning point in history" that confronted leaders of the world:

> National economies have been disrupted by the war. The future is uncertain everywhere. Economic policies are in a state of flux. In this atmosphere of doubt and hesitation, the decisive factor will be the type of leadership that the United States gives the world.
> We are the giant of the economic world. Whether we like it or not, the future pattern of economic relations depends upon us. The world is waiting and watching to see what we shall do.[12]

As the president gave voice to his concerns for the "atmosphere of doubt and hesitation" pervading the international economy, other prominent policy makers were doing likewise. Secretary of the Navy Forrestal, for example, began on March 3 a steady series of meetings with numerous high officials that culminated in a forceful and meaningful statement at a cabinet meeting four days later. He began by lunching with Secretary of the Treasury John Snyder and outlining his impressions of what he saw as a developing crisis. *"I said I felt very strongly that the world could only be brought back to order by a restoration of commerce, trade and business, and that would have to be done by businessmen,"* he told Snyder (italics added). At lunch the next day, he repeated his ideas to Secretary of State Marshall, Secretary of War Patterson, Averill Harriman, and others, emphasizing to Marshall the "need for avenues of communication between government and business." The same was repeated the next day to Truman's special counsel Clark Clifford and to John Taber, chairman of the powerful House Appropriations Committee. In Taber and other congressional leaders, Forrestal was happily finding a tendency to do "more serious thinking on the subject of the United States position as the great stabilizer in international affairs." With this kind of momentum behind him, Forrestal attended a cabinet meeting on the morning of March 7, the day of Truman's return to Washington from Texas. With Acheson ostensibly beginning a discussion of specifically Greek and Turkish problems, others quickly broadened the focus to other struggles. Forrestal confided to his diary:

> In my remarks I said that what was occurring was simply the manifestation of what had been in the process of development in the last four years; that if we were going to have a chance of winning, we should have to recognize it as a fundamental struggle between our kind of society and the Russians' and that the Russians would not respond to anything except power. I said that it would take all the talent and brains in the country, just as it had taken all of them in the war. . . . *By that I meant that we would have to turn to business if what we were talking about is in reality holding out the hope of people in stricken countries that they again may make a living, and the way to provide a living for them will have to be opened up by business.* [italics added][13]

Forrestal might have felt satisfied by the end of the meeting, since the specific commitment to action of the day was the formation of a cabinet-level committee delegated "to lay out a program of communication with leaders throughout the country" concerning developing crises, "and particularly of the plan for laying the facts before a selected group of business people."

Although these particular statements by Truman and Forrestal express generalized concerns regarding developing international economic problems, it was already obvious by early March, and became increasingly so thereafter, that there was a fairly specific focus to these concerns. It was in Europe, in particular, that the floodwaters seemed to be rising, and it was clearly to that continent more than to any other area that Washington officials were looking in early 1947.

Shortly before his departure for a Council of Foreign Ministers meeting in Moscow, for example, Secretary of State Marshall met with Republican foreign policy adviser John Foster Dulles. Their exchange of ideas well reveals the direction of concerns. As an

international lawyer with a long career of work in Europe, Dulles
dealt frequently with Continental issues in his public statements.
In January, 1947, particularly, he began an intensive development
of ideas concerning the interrelatedness of German and all-Euro-
pean economic problems. In one address citing the forthcoming
Moscow conference, he had said: "That Conference will deal with
Germany. Whoever deals with Germany deals with the central
problem of Europe." He suggested that the United States adopt
a policy calling for the economic unification of Europe, a process
which might begin by making the great industrial resources of such
German territories as the Saar and the Ruhr available to Germany's neighbors as well as to itself. A federal economic system
tying Germany's resources into those of Europe as a whole seemed
eminently desirable to Dulles, and seemed to offer a solution to
the recurring cycle of wars that had shaken the Continent so
grievously.[14] His ideas along these lines came to Marshall's attention as he was preparing for the Moscow meetings on Germany,
and the two men met in Washington on February 24. The secretary began by asking Dulles to express his views "on various matters, principally the European situation." Dulles wrote immediately
after:

> I did so, emphasizing my belief that the European settlement
> must seek to strengthen economically western Europe; that that
> was the area of vital importance to us; that we had fought two
> wars to keep political freedom alive in that area, and that in
> essence we would have lost those wars if it fell under a Soviet
> type dictatorship which suppressed human liberty. I pointed out
> that the economy of Central Europe, including Scandinavia, was
> being integrated into, and drained into, that of the Soviet Union,
> and that if this tendency extended on into Western Europe,
> western civilization and personal freedom, as we had known it,
> would be impossible. I went on to say that I therefore felt it
> essential that the German economic potential, at least as repre-
> sented by the Ruhr and Rhineland, should be fully developed
> and integrated into Western Europe. . . .

When Dulles had finished, Marshall demonstrated his agreement
by immediately asking him to come to Moscow as an adviser.
Dulles was apparently surprised by the offer, but accepted.[15]
    Evidence of unfolding crises in Europe was, in fact, abundant,
and Dulles's fears for the collapse of Western civilization itself

do not seem so stark when the mood of the day is considered. A series of British government White Papers had cataloged that country's ever-mounting difficulties. For example, a coal shortage crisis was looming in the midst of the most severe winter in decades; electricity was being rationed; and financial resources were extremely thin as previously obtained credits from the United States and Commonwealth members were exhausted. As the financial editor of Reuter's put it, "The biggest crash since the fall of Constantinople—the collapse of the heart of an Empire—impends."[16] Across the Channel, conditions appeared no better. The severe winter of 1946–47 there compounded the problems of economic recovery, and on every hand there were serious food and fuel shortages. Millions who were starving and cold were not likely to remain completely idle, and rumors were rife concerning the possible actions of the European masses. Large Communist voting blocs were seen in distinctly Western states like France and Italy; prominent Communist members were seen in the Paris and Rome cabinets and "Communist-inspired" general strikes were easily envisioned as leading to the collapse of orderly life and business.

During March and April, signs of serious American concern over such European dilemmas increased. On March 22, for example, Senator William Fulbright and Representative Hale Boggs introduced concurrent resolutions in both houses of Congress calling for United States support of a drive for the federation of the Continent within the framework of the United Nations. Present crises demanded a positive policy toward Europe, the two congressmen argued, Fulbright in particular declaring, "Something must be done or the Western World, including ourselves, will commit suicide or be absorbed by the East."[17] The next day, March 23, former President Herbert Hoover publicly released one of a number of reports that had emerged from a mission to Europe undertaken at Truman's request. While in this particular report, Hoover focused on the German economic situation, "These problems," he made clear (as Dulles had earlier) "also involve economic stability and peace in Europe." Hoover's tone was as depressed as it might have been in 1932. *"We desperately need recovery in all of Europe,"* he told Truman and the public. He described a series of recommendations for policy as "based upon the stern necessities of a world involved in *the most dangerous economic crisis in all history"* (italics added).[18]

The men in Washington's executive offices hardly needed congressmen or former presidents to convince them of the gravity and the urgency of the European economic situation. On April 21, the State-War-Navy Coordinating Committee (SWNCC) completed a preliminary report in accordance with Dean Acheson's earlier instructions. Its pages were blocked out like a commercial and financial primer, and the lesson was a grave one. The report surveyed conditions in twelve "critical" countries, predominantly European, estimating reserves of food and fuel, gold and foreign exchange; it attempted to divide political tensions that might emerge from troubled economic conditions; it appraised the probable United States balance of payments through 1949; it tallied United States and United Nations aid commitments to crisis areas; it began mapping out a massive new foreign aid program. SWNCC put particular emphasis on the necessity of hastening German industrial recovery in order to alleviate the grievous economic problems of Europe as a whole.[19]

A week later, the message of this study was dramatized by the reports made by George Marshall and John Foster Dulles on the completed Moscow session of the Council of Foreign Ministers. The secretary of state, speaking over national radio, disconsolately described the failure of the assembled allies to deal with the crucial problems of Germany and Austria, two states at the "vital center of Europe." Continued uncertainty concerning the former enemy states posed serious dangers, Marshall told the public. "The German negotiations involved not only the security of Europe and the world, but the prosperity of all of Europe. . . . The recovery of Europe has been far slower than had been expected. Disintegrating forces are becoming evident. The patient is sinking while the doctors deliberate." If something was not quickly done to firm up the situation in Central Europe and to allow Germany especially to contribute to the recovery of the continent as a whole, "Problems which bear directly on the future of our civilization" were likely to have a tragic denouement.[20] Marshall's adviser Dulles spoke the following evening, and gave a no more optimistic presentation. He too grieved at the lack of success on a German peace settlement, also emphasizing the economic problems thus created for all of Europe. In assaying future policies, Dulles looked particularly to joint Anglo-American action in those areas which they fully controlled.

Our joint area includes the Ruhr, which is the economic heart of Europe. Today that heart is barely beating. The situation gives us a great responsibility and a great opportunity. If our joint administration can pump vitality into western Europe, that will bring about more competent administration elsewhere. . . .[21]

The impact of awareness of impending crises in Europe, evidenced in the SWNCC preliminary report and in the secretary of state's reaction to events in Moscow, was soon felt. Within days, it became clear that a major policy initiative was gestating. One of the clearest indications of this came in a crucial May 8 policy statement by Dean Acheson. Speaking in Cleveland, Mississippi, the undersecretary of state concentrated exclusively on the economic dilemmas he saw everywhere. At the beginning of his address, he drew on his superior's experiences to set the mood of the day: "When Secretary of State Marshall returned from the recent meeting of the Council of Foreign Ministers in Moscow, he did not talk to us about ideologies or armies. He talked about food and fuel and their relation to industrial production, and the relation of industrial production to the organization of Europe, and the relation of the organization of Europe to the peace of the world." Acheson proceeded to follow that example. He described the "state of physical destruction or economic dislocation" which afflicted most countries of the world; the continuing failure to allow recovery in Germany and Japan, "two of the greatest workshops of Europe and Asia"; the awful impact of storms and floods, blizzards and droughts on the European economy. He was not dealing with esoterica. Such "grim developments," such "basic facts of life," he saw as having major implications for the United States, and he proceeded explicitly to evidence the sense of self-interest involved in earlier statements by policy makers. Using figures marshaled in SWNCC's report, he estimated that American exports in 1947 were likely to total sixteen billion dollars, "an all-time peace-time high." Unfortunately, the devastation being experienced elsewhere in the world suggested that the United States was likely to be able to import only about eight billion dollars worth of goods and services. There were no signs of a change in this disparity for future years. "How," Acheson asked, "are foreigners going to get the U.S. dollars necessary to cover this huge difference?" Failure to find an answer to such a question could have disastrous and immediate effects on the American economy itself.

A number of remedies were suggested, prophesying the policy moves of days to come: in fact, President Truman has called Acheson's speech the "prologue to the Marshall Plan." First and most important, Acheson urged the necessity of continuing and expanding existent United States assistance to devastated and troubled countries, assistance that would allow them to maintain their purchases of American goods. Such aid, Acheson was quick to say, was "only in part suggested by humanitarianism." It was, in fact, "a matter of national self-interest. For it is generally agreed that until the various countries of the world get on their feet and become self-supporting there can be no political or economic stability in the world and no lasting peace or prosperity for any of us." Second, Acheson urged, the United States should prepare itself to accept an ever-larger quantity of imports to allow for a truly sound handling of the balance of payments problem on a long-run basis. Again, he added: "There is no charity involved in this. It is simply common sense and good business. We are today obliged from considerations of self-interest and humanitarianism to finance a huge deficit in the world's budget." "Human beings and nations exist in narrow economic margins," Acheson concluded, and it was obvious that he saw the United States being seriously endangered by the suffocating commercial and financial dilemmas that made up those margins.[22]

Acheson's call for a continuation of emergency aid by the United States, particularly his statement that "we are going to have to concentrate our emergency assistance in areas where it will be most effective in building world political and economic stability," was a clear signpost of the direction of evolving American policy. If any further impetus to a major new initiative was necessary, it came quickly, and definitively mobilized policy makers within the following few weeks. Perhaps most influential in this regard was the report on European conditions given to Truman and key policy makers by Undersecretary of State Will Clayton after his return to Washington on May 23. Clayton had been attending meetings in Geneva for the negotiation of multilateral trade agreements, and had had a chance to observe at close hand the European situation, which had already been worrying those at greater distances. In a succinct memorandum, elaborated on in personal conversations, he seems to have added the final plumb to the policy scales. "It is now obvious that we greatly underestimated the destruction to the European economy by the war," he began his memorandum. "Europe is steadily deteriorating. The political position reflects the economic. One political crisis after another merely denotes the existence of grave economic distress. Millions of people in the cities are slowly starving." Quoting precise figures, he proceeded to describe the serious financial conditions of the Europeans, estimating that even the existent low standard of living could not be maintained beyond the end of the year. ("If it should be lowered," he added ruefully, concerning that standard of living, "there will be revolution.") As Acheson and others had indicated earlier, Clayton proceeded to argue that substantial American aid was vitally necessary, and was called for by both humanitarian and selfish motives.

> Without further prompt and substantial aid from the United States, economic, social and political disintegration will overwhelm Europe.
> Aside from the awful implication which this would have for the future peace and security of the world, *the immediate effects on our domestic economy would be disastrous; markets for our surplus production gone, unemployment, depression, a heavily unbalanced budget on the background of mountainous war debt.* [italics added]
> *These things must not happen.*[23]

Scarcely two weeks later, the secretary of state stood before an audience at Harvard University and enunciated what has become known as the Marshall Plan, bringing to a climax months of deliberations among American policy makers. His words clearly reflected the nature of those deliberations. "The world situation is very serious," he said at first, but his focus quickly narrowed to the continent of Europe. It had become obvious, he explained, that the destructive damage of the war years had brought about a continuing "dislocation of the entire fabric of European economy. . . . The breakdown of the business structure of Europe during the war was complete . . . and the rehabilitation of the economic structure of Europe quite evidently will require a much longer time and greater effort than had been foreseen." Europe, in short, was going to require vast assistance in order to lift itself from the economic morass of wartime destruction—and it was only to the United States that it could look for such aid. There was no doubt in George Marshall's mind that the United States should undertake such a responsibility.

> Aside from the demoralizing effect on the world at large and the possibilities of disturbances arising as a result of the people concerned, the consequences to the economy of the United States should be apparent to all. It is logical that the United States should do whatever it is able to do to assist in the return of normal economic health in the world, without which there can be no political stability and no assured peace.[24]

The stage was set for an invitation to European leaders to meet and coordinate plans for cooperative economic recovery and requests for American assistance that would help bring it about. "The Fifteen Weeks" had ended, and a massive new venture in American foreign policy had begun.

What does all this reveal about the basic objectives toward which American foreign policies were directed? What, in the end, do the major pronouncements and deliberations by American policy makers during the crises of 1947 make it possible to say about United States motives in the early years of the Cold War? That something can be said is undoubted: the men in Washington talked freely and frequently about what they were trying to do and why they were trying to do it. Precisely what can be said, however, has sharply divided historians and political scientists for years, and the end of the battle is hardly in sight.

At base, it can be suggested, first, American policy makers were most fundamentally preoccupied with economic matters during early 1947. The glasses through which they viewed the world situation, though their specific lenses may have varied from man to man, were all heavily tinted by an awareness of commercial and financial problems. From the very beginning of the Fifteen Weeks, this was most obvious. It was a British financial crisis that served as an initial catalyst for rapid action; it was the economic difficulties of Greece and Turkey that created serious problems for those states; it was an awareness of the proximity of Greece and Turkey to both the vast oil resources of the Middle East and the economic heartland of Europe that made their situations seem so pressing; it was an appreciation of industrial inertia, food and fuel shortages, and currency difficulties that led policy makers to sight evolving crises on the general European landscape. Virtually all the policy statements of the day bespeak this basic preoccupation. Harry Truman told Congress on March 12, "I believe that our help should be primarily through economic and financial aid which is essential to economic stability and orderly political processes." James Forrestal told all who would listen that "the world could only be brought back to order by a restoration of commerce, trade and business." George Marshall described economic conditions in Europe which bore "directly on the future of our civilization." Will Clayton bemoaned the dangers of revolution on a continent experiencing basic economic "disintegration." No significant policy statement, in fact, or any episode of deliberation among policy makers failed to take into account the fundamental economic crises of the day.

Besides a fundamental appreciation of the economic nature of developing crises, American policy makers seem to have had no doubts that fundamental dangers of a likewise economic nature were specifically confronting the United States. The eastern Mediterranean dominoes were important precisely because they threatened to topple those in far more crucial areas like the Middle East and Western Europe. And the Middle East and Western Europe were seen as crucial because of the vital economic relationship which American policy makers felt it essential to maintain with those areas. As sources of raw materials, as the locus of extremely significant markets, and as arenas for vast potential investments, their importance was explicitly recognized by the men in Washington. John Foster Dulles could tell George Marshall, who hardly needed convincing, that "the European settlement must seek to strengthen economically western Europe; that that was the area of vital importance to *us*." Herbert Hoover, who had appreciated the nature of the problem as early as 1918, could declare that "*We* desperately need recovery in all of Europe (both italics added)." Dean Acheson, in an early discussion of what later became the Marshall Plan, could put his finger squarely on the necessities dictated by what he called "national self-interest." Will Clayton could survey the European landscape and postulate, first and foremost, that if disintegration continued, "the immediate effects on our domestic economy would be disastrous." George Marshall, speaking at Harvard, could be so sure of the awareness of this that he could say tersely that "the consequences of the economy of the United States should be apparent to all." What key policy makers never tired of saying, in other words, was that the major policy initiatives they were undertaking in early 1947 were designed to thwart fundamental economic threats to the United States itself.

This is of course not all that policy makers were thinking and saying during the critical days of early 1947. Other motivations were clearly evident. A streak of sheer idealistic humanitarianism is frequently obvious, for example. Men like Harry Truman and George Marshall did not hesitate to express their basic emotional and ethical concern for the fate of the Greeks and other Europeans. They frequently thought, in fact, that their audiences would be so convinced that this was the basis of their proposed actions that it was necessary to constantly remind listeners that more than humanitarianism was at stake. In addition, the all-purpose category of "security" was not absent by any means. Harry Truman's reaction to the Greek and Turkish situation, for example, was that the United States had two alternatives: to get involved in a forceful and meaningful way, or to make the decision to keep hands off an area of the globe that might be seen as insignificant. The latter alternative, he argued, "would be disastrous to our security and to the security of free nations everywhere."[25] Likewise, policy makers seem to have kept a keen eye on political as well as economic developments in Europe and the Mediterranean. Clayton, for example, spoke of the dangers of European political as well as economic disintegration; policy makers in general were greatly worried about what they saw as the internal political instability of countries like France and Italy.

It is important to recognize, however, that while such varying preoccupations and motivations may have been evident in early 1947, they were invariably dominated by economic concerns or dealt with in a specific fashion in an economic context. There was, in other words, a whole range of motives present in early 1947—economic, humanitarian, political, strategic, among others. Further, there exists an interconnectedness among these motives which makes it difficult to categorize precisely. But what seems evident from the words of policy makers themselves is that the dominant theme—the one which gave rise to, or colored, all others significantly—was an economic one. It was a basic awareness of an evolving economic crisis in Europe during 1947 that led policy makers to envision a whole range of problems: commercial and financial catastrophes for the United States, political instability on the Continent, vaguely discussed strategic dangers, and others. There existed an interconnectedness of concerns, to be sure, but there was one which was dominant. Policy makers appreciated the complexity of varying problems and crises, but likewise felt a fine awareness that there was a primary one (in the sense of first and original). As Will Clayton so accurately put it in his May 23 memorandum on the European situation: "Europe is steadily deteriorating. *The political position reflects the economic. One political crisis after another merely denotes the existence of grave economic disasters*" (italics added).[26] Or, as Dean Acheson described George Marshall's attitude upon returning from Moscow: "He did not talk to us about ideologies or armies. He talked about food and fuel and their relation to industrial production. . . ."[27] Or, yet again, as George Kennan significantly phrased it in a late May memorandum to Marshall, "It must be made clear that the extension of American aid is essentially *a question of political economy* in the literal sense of that term . . ." (italics added).[28] Webster's *New International Dictionary* provides such a "literal sense" when it defines "political economy" as "the art of regulating the politics or policy of government for the promotion of the wealth of the community and the government."

American foreign policy during early 1947, then, amounted to so many variations on a basic theme. That theme, as policy makers themselves clearly revealed, was one of international and specifically European economic crises and their potentially catastrophic impact on United States self-interest. In that theme were to be found the basic motivations behind evolving American foreign policies.

It might be added, considering the relatively narrow chronological scope of the preceding discussion, that there is no reason to doubt that the "art" of "political economy" dominated the making of American foreign policy both before and after the crises of 1947 as well. As a number of historians and political scientists have amply demonstrated, for example, the years encompassing World War II and its aftermath saw similar motivations setting the course of United States policy makers as they grappled with the widest range of decisions: evolving relations with Great Britain and France, particularly concerning crucial commercial policies in former empire regions; the future status of defeated Germany; the matter of access to large areas of Eastern and southeastern Europe; contentions with the British, French, and Russians concerning the openness of the Middle East; the potential of Japan in the Far East; the quandaries of civil war in China. In any and all cases, political economy seems to have formed the bedrock foundation for the making of United States policies.[29]

Suggesting what substantive motivations have provided the impetus to American foreign policies has been the primary goal of this essay. There is a refinement of this question, however, which has not yet been dealt with and which deserves at least brief attention because of what it may say about the essence of the Cold War era as a whole. United States policies in early 1947 provide ample indication of the way in which historians and political scientists have become prisoners of a Cold War rhetoric and mythology that are still reaching out of the past to define the way in which our work is done. In particular, the reaction of American policy makers in 1947 to what they deemed to be crises in Europe suggests how simplistic our notion of an all-pervasive single Cold War conflict has been. Almost invariably in the past, scholars have allowed the image of an American-Soviet hostility to dominate the work on international relations since the 1940s. Virtually every significant event and policy is placed in the context of this Cold War hostility; each is likewise deemed to have absorbed its very being from it. Sooner or later, every major aspect of world affairs following the Second World War has been seen as being rooted in the portentous free world versus Communism power struggle.

There is much evidence to indicate that the significance of Soviet-American relations as a determinant of world affairs after 1945 has been exaggerated. In particular, the importance of the fears of, and hostility toward, the Soviet Union on the part of American policy makers has been greatly overstated. Much that took place in early 1947 demonstrates that what the Soviet Union was and what it might do at the time had less of an impact on the making of United States policy than other, far more traditional American concerns.

The preceding discussion of crises in 1947 suggests a number of things. First, it is undoubtedly true that most of the individuals significantly involved in the formulation of such policy initiatives as the Truman Doctrine and the Marshall Plan were aware of and discussed Mediterranean and European problems in the context of United States–Soviet relations. Acheson's February description of falling dominoes, Truman's crusadelike March message to Congress, Clayton's late May predictions of revolution on the Continent—all seem to bespeak some preoccupation with the Communist "menace." But, second, there is also evidence which indicates that this was not at all the primary impulse leading to the enunciation of the Truman Doctrine and the Marshall Plan, and that other, non–Cold War factors were on the scene and played a far more meaningful role. A reading of two such major statements as Truman's March 6 address at Baylor University and Dean Acheson's May 8 speech in Cleveland, Mississippi, for example, offers clear evidence of this. Both men on both occasions dealt at great length with serious economic problems of major concern to themselves and other policy makers. In Acheson's speech, the outlines of the forthcoming Marshall Plan were clearly discernible. Yet neither he nor Truman mentioned in any way, direct or indirect, either the Soviet Union or Communism.

Indeed, to go further, on any number of occasions, policy makers took specific pains to make clear to each other that what has come to be thought of as the basic ingredient of all Cold War policy decisions was not really involved in the crises of the day. On May 23, for example, George Kennan submitted to the secretary of state the results of a major Policy Planning Staff study on European problems which Marshall had requested. Its concluding remarks well reveal the lack of relevancy of standard Cold War imagery:

> Steps should be taken to clarify what the press has unfortunately come to identify as the "Truman Doctrine," and to remove in particular two damaging impressions which are current in large sectors of American public opinion. These are:
> a. That the United States approach to world problems is a defensive reaction to Communist pressure and that the effort to restore sound economic conditions in other countries is only the byproduct of this reaction and not *something we would be interested in doing if there were no Communist menace*. . . . [italics added]

Kennan's *Memoirs* further reveal that as his staff surveyed European economic dislocations, it "did not see Communist activities as the root of these difficulties." It further informed Marshall that "American effort in aid to Europe should be directed not to the combatting of communism as such but to the restoration of the economic health and vigor of European society."[30]

Further, Will Clayton's influential May 27 memorandum on the immediate seriousness of European conditions made precisely the same point. In formulating a recommendation, Clayton argued, "It will be necessary for the President and the Secretary of State to make a strong spiritual appeal to the American people to sacrifice a little themselves, to draw in their own belts just a little in order to save Europe from starvation and chaos (*not from the Russians*) and, at the same time, to preserve for themselves and our children the glorious heritage of a free America" (italics added).[31]

What is suggested is that the objectives of American policy makers would have been almost exactly the same if the Soviet Union had not even existed in 1947. If hoary Communists had been nowhere in sight, and the policy makers had still been able to implement their ideal programs, the Truman Doctrine and the Marshall Plan could still have been forthcoming. As the above discussion of the actual deliberations of policy makers in 1947 reveals, what was involved first and foremost was the crucial relationship between the United States and Europe. The economic condition of the Continent and the resulting political dangers that seemed to threaten were *the* great menace to substantive American interests. Soviet policies and Communist activity might exacerbate the situation, and did seem to do so as far as many policy makers were concerned, but they clearly had not given rise to, and were not the primary reasons calling for, major American action.

That this is true, it might be mentioned, is the result of some of the deepest urges in all the history of American foreign policy. More than any other area of the globe, Europe held a great traditional priority for the makers of American foreign policy. As long ago as the war for independence, French assistance was recognized as having proved decisive in bringing victory, for example, and the gaining of access to European and European-controlled markets was to be a primary objective of the founding fathers' foreign policies. Primary commercial ties with Europeans were a major characteristic of the growing American economy in the nineteenth century. Even as areas like Latin America and the Far East began to attract great attention for their potential commercial significance, few policy makers ever lost sight of the bird in hand. While there are serious debates still raging concerning the precise reasons for American participation in World War I, there is no doubt that in some way—political, economic, ideological—American interests were seen as most vitally involved in that basically European conflict. The end of the struggle brought no diminution of concern. In fact, the deliberations of the Paris Peace Conference gave rise to some of the most explicit evidence of fundamental United States policies. When Americans expressed concerns over the instability and unsettled condition of Europe's economy after 1919, they were prophesying the feelings of a later generation. The words of many policy makers could easily have been uttered in the 1940s. Thomas Lamont, for example, bemoaned the failure of Congress to approve the appointment of an American delegate to the Reparation Commission in 1919:

> This whole question, however, in my judgment, will never be properly and finally settled—nor will the adjustments be carried out in a manner to bring about world restoration—unless, and until, America has an official share in these discussions. America is already in the situation. She cannot disentangle herself. Europe is her greatest customer, her greatest purchaser of grains, cotton, copper, and all other raw materials. If our own industry and commerce are to be restored, if we are to get back to former prosperity, then, indeed, must we lend our efforts to European restoration.[32]

Such sentiments subsequently found their way into the policy deliberations of such key figures as Herbert Hoover, Charles Evans Hughes, Henry Stimson, Cordell Hull, Sumner Wells, and Franklin Roosevelt during the 1920s and 1930s. So long, indeed, had policy makers seen significant American interests involved in Europe that an astonishing thing to have happened in 1947 would have been the lack of the Truman Doctrine and the Marshall Plan.

This all—to repeat—suggests how inadequate are the usual images of the Cold War era. Much of American foreign policy after 1945, even in such crucial instances as the formulation and execution of the Truman Doctrine and the Marshall Plan, did not exclusively or even primarily revolve around the free world's response to a Communist menace. As far as policy makers were in reality concerned, this concept is far from the mark. Other historians have now extensively explored the way in which traditional impressions of what the early Cold War years were all about emerged from the political maneuvering of these same policy makers. Faced with a doubting Congress and a basically apathetic public, the men in Washington's executive offices not infrequently resorted to a melodramatic rhetoric to gain support for programs they saw as vitally necessary to serve traditional American interests. Once reluctant senators, representatives, and ordinary citizens were stirred by the call to an anti-Communist crusade, they believed and—more important—they paid. Arthur Vandenberg put it well when he advised Harry Truman that if authorization was to be forthcoming for aid to Greece and Turkey, the administration would "have to scare hell out of the American people."[33] If Truman and his advisers needed the lesson—which is doubtful—they learned it well. Like medieval clerics, they proceeded to stir emotions for an assault on the infidel.[34]

As a result, of course, the policy makers of the early Cold War years fashioned a legacy that still lingers. A public and a Congress whose emotional fervor was roused soon produced a mass antiradical, anti-nonconformist hysteria in the United States. McCarthyism—and all that it stood for—has yet to have its mark on American society erased, the 1968 elevation to the presidency of a central figure in that rabid phenomenon being a case in point. Furthermore, for the public and for scholars too, an image of the Cold War has been created that is in significant ways out of touch with the realities of past years. Although the gothic visions of harsh, sharply defined Cold War conflicts have served to some extent as self-fulfilling prophecies as the decades have passed, they were clearly not totally real and substantive for many policy makers in the 1940s. Men who were practicing the art of political economy in 1947 were not basically concerned with the dangers of Communist conquest of Western Europe—and, what is more, they said so. Fundamentally economic motives moved them to action, as they had in days long before the beginning of the Cold War.

Such a conclusion, finally, is usually associated with a revisionist approach to the history of the Cold War. The label "revisionist"—perhaps like all labels—is innately unsatisfactory because it lends itself too easily to simplistic and misleading definitions and summaries. It is said far too often, for example, that revisionist historians concentrate exclusively on conspiratorial economic objectives and ignore the complexities of men's actions in the past. Any serious reading of so-called revisionist work belies this conclusion. What these historians have variously described is a complex early Cold War environment in which many personalities and many motives played roles. Economics, politics, strategy, ideology, ethics, religion, a yearning for power—all are observable among the men formulating American foreign policy. In addition, such concerns almost invariably overlapped within particular individuals, so that it is seldom possible to say that a Mr. Z was acting for precisely such and such a reason. In the end, however, the words and deliberations of policy makers themselves, in a period like early 1947, indicate how dominant a preoccupation was the economic. More often than anything else, it was concern for economic interests which gave rise to a crisis perception, which colored the way in which problems were discussed and which determined emergent solutions. When the revisionists argue in this fashion, they are offering a far more real description of American foreign policy in the early Cold War era than weary clichés will ever allow.

NOTES

1. There are numerous surveys of American foreign policy and international relations during these early years of the Cold War. Among the most valuable are Walter LaFeber, *America, Russia, and the Cold War, 1945–1966* (New York: John Wiley & Sons, 1967); John Spanier, *American Foreign Policy Since World War II*, 2d rev. ed. (New York: Praeger, 1965); Gabriel Kolko, *The Politics of War: The World and United States Foreign Policy, 1943–1945* (New York: Random House, 1968); and Joyce and Gabriel Kolko, *The Limits of Power: The World and United States Foreign Policy, 1945–1954* (New York: Harper & Row, 1972).

2. See, for example, Athan Theoharis, *Seeds of Repression: Harry S. Truman and the Origins of McCarthyism* (Chicago: Quadrangle Books, 1971); and Joyce and Gabriel Kolko, *The Limits of Power*.

3. Joseph Marion Jones, *The Fifteen Weeks* (New York: Harcourt Brace Jovanovich, Inc., 1955).

4. Joyce and Gabriel Kolko, *The Limits of Power,* p. 228; Walter Millis, ed., *The Forrestal Diaries* (New York: Viking Press, 1951), p. 210.

5. Jones, *The Fifteen Weeks,* pp. 4–7.

6. *Ibid.,* pp. 138–42.

7. Frederick J. Dobney, ed., *Selected Papers of Will Clayton* (Baltimore: The Johns Hopkins University Press, 1971), pp. 198–201.

8. Quoted in Barton J. Bernstein and Allen J. Matusow, eds., *The Truman Administration: A Documentary History* (New York: Harper & Row, 1966), pp. 255–56.

9. Jones, *The Fifteen Weeks,* p. 24.

10. *Ibid.,* pp. 136–37.

11. Ibid., pp. 199–201.

12. *Public Papers of the Presidents of the United States: Harry S. Truman, 1947* (Washington: United States Government Printing Office, 1963), pp. 167–72.

13. *The Forrestal Diaries,* pp. 247–53.

14. See, for example, John Foster Dulles, "A New Year's Resolve," address before the National Publishers Association, January 17, 1947, in John Foster Dulles Papers, Princeton University Library, Princeton, New Jersey.

15. John Foster Dulles, memorandum, "Re: Council of Foreign Ministers Meeting in Moscow," February 26, 1947, Dulles Papers.

16. Quoted in Jones, *The Fifteen Weeks,* p. 80.

17. *New York Times,* March 22, 1947.

18. *New York Times,* March 24, 1947.

19. Jones, *The Fifteen Weeks,* pp. 203–5.

20. *New York Times,* April 29, 1947.

21. John Foster Dulles, Report on Moscow Meeting of Council of Foreign Ministers, radio broadcast, April 29, 1947, Dulles Papers.

22. The text of Acheson's speech is printed in Jones, *The Fifteen Weeks,* pp. 274–81.

23. *Selected Papers of Will Clayton,* pp. 201–4.

24. The text of Marshall's address is printed in Jones, *The Fifteen Weeks,* pp. 281–84.

25. Harry S. Truman, *Memoirs: Years of Trial and Hope* (New York: New American Library, 1956), p. 124.

26. *Selected Papers of Will Clayton,* p. 201.

27. Jones, *The Fifteen Weeks,* p. 275.

28. George F. Kennan, *Memoirs, 1925–1950* (New York: Bantam Books, 1967), p. 359.

29. It should clearly be indicated that this concept of motivations before, during, and after 1947 is only a first step toward a full understanding of the reasons for American foreign policies. While it has been possible to focus on broad economic impulses in this essay, the specific composition of those impulses has not been adequately described. Particular issues, such as the balance of payments dilemma and the multilateral versus bilateral trade pattern struggle, which are most important for an exact understanding of United States policies, have only been fleetingly mentioned. For a full and significant elaboration, see Joyce and Gabriel Kolko, *The Limits of Power.*

30. Kennan, *Memoirs,* pp. 358–63.

31. *Selected Papers of Will Clayton,* p. 203.

32. Thomas Lamont, "Reparations," in Edward Mandell House and Charles Seymour, eds., *What Really Happened at Paris: The Story of the Peace Conference, 1918–1919* (New York: Charles Scribner's Sons, 1921), p. 289.

33. Quoted in LaFeber, *America, Russia, and the Cold War,* p. 45.

34. See note 2, above.

3
The Origins of the Cold War in Asia

EDITORS' NOTE. If, as Professor Pruessen suggests in the preceding chapter, the headlines of most newspapers in the early Cold War years were strident signposts of basically Atlantic and Mediterranean community problems, inside pages were likely to tell other stories as well. There the baroque complexities of a civil war in China were receiving ample coverage even before 1945. After the defeat of Japan too, one might have read of new struggles in an exotic and remote area called Indochina. With seeming suddenness in 1949, the headlines were grabbed by such stories. By far the greatest attention was paid to the headlong flights of Chiang Kai-shek, which paved the way for the establishment of the People's Republic of China in Peking on October 1, 1949.

To policy makers at the time, it may have seemed that a whole new arena for the waging of the Cold War had been opened. Communist success in China grated harshly on a United States which had always demonstrated a degree of concern for the Far East. While that concern might have seemed to lie beneath the surface in the early years of the Cold War, it had been there all the same. Too much had gone before to allow a complete abandonment of Asia in the face of preoccupations with European problems. The sailing of the New England clipper *Empress of China* in 1784 had been perhaps the first substantive sign of American interest in the Far East. From that beginning, a sometimes fruitful economic relationship had grown up in the nineteenth century. Annexation of the Philippines at the end of the Spanish-American War and John Hay's Open Door notes subsequently marked a vigorous assertion of United States intentions in the area. When in the 1930s Japan attempted to carve out for itself an exclusive Asian preserve, American concern had been great enough to lead to eventual war in the Pacific. All this history was dramatically underlined by the events of 1949 and after. There ensued an intense commitment of American policy makers to the Far East, a commitment involving something qualitatively and quantitatively different from the past. The prophecies a half-century earlier by Brooks Adams and Frederick Jackson Turner, that Asia and the Pacific were to be the fruits for which future powers would struggle, seemed to be coming true. Such a man as General Douglas MacArthur could call the area America's "new frontier."

Harrison Salisbury has been a journalist of such experience that he has frequently come into direct contact with the evolution of the Cold War in Asia. In the chapter which follows, he attempts to step back and survey the overall contours of some of the most significant events since 1949. His overview is not an optimistic one. He describes a gradually developing drama: the response to the end of the civil war in China; the acceptance of the challenge of Korea; the slow fruition of involvement in Indochina. Each is like the unfolding of a new chapter in a gothic novel. To that unfolding, he argues, the United States has responded in a continuously inflexible and unrealistic fashion. Through it all, policy makers in Washington have insisted on mounting crusades against what Salisbury calls the "vision of an international plot directed against the United States—a plot, a conspiracy which, when analyzed bit by bit and piece by piece from its origins twenty-five years ago to the present day, is shown to be based on false impressions, false images, and false assumptions." The road so littered through the years has led unmistakably to a tragic involvement in Vietnam.

As a particular example of the way in which Americans have developed a mythology of the Cold War, Salisbury deals with the origins of the Korean conflict. The Truman administration's interpretation of the nature of the Communist challenge in Korea was widely accepted by the American people at the time. While the war generated a great deal of controversy in many quarters, it is ironic that virtually none of that controversy disputed the administration view that the attack on the South was directed by the Kremlin as a challenge to the American position there and elsewhere in Asia.* Rather, as the war raged on, the great domestic

* There were a few important voices who argued that, even so, the administration had overreacted to the challenge by committing American troops.

dispute came to focus on America's goals and conduct of the war.
The conviction that the attack from the North constituted an act
of unmitigated Soviet (or Sino-Soviet) hostility to the United
States led more extreme anti-Communists to the view that the administration's first goal of a restoration of the cease-fire line at
the 38th parallel was insufficient punishment of the aggressors. At
the fanatical extreme of this viewpoint, Senator Joseph McCarthy
and his followers hinted darkly that such a "no win" policy revealed the sinister influence of Communist sympathizers at the
highest levels of the American government.

When the president moved beyond his original goal, and
ordered troops to cross the 38th parallel and to proceed into the
North, massive numbers of Chinese troops did intervene in the
conflict, with the eventual result that the American government
was forced to retreat once again to the goal of merely "containing"
the would-be aggressor. Soon the domestic debate came to be
reflected symbolically in the growing public differences over the
conduct of the war between General Douglas MacArthur and his
commander in chief. When Truman relieved the general of his
command, in April, 1951, it caused a political flap of the first
order in the United States. With that, the war dragged on to its
stalemated conclusion, and it was not until 1953—with a new
president in the White House—that an armistice was achieved.

For most Americans who lived through that period—regardless
of the stand they took in the domestic controversy aroused by the
war—mention of the Korean conflict probably still evokes an
image of the United States responding defensively to an unpro-
voked attack from a hostile power. It is, however, a measure of
the changes that have occurred in international politics that we
are now beginning to see that thesis challenged in fundamental
ways. Salisbury offers one of the newest and most unorthodox hy-
potheses as to the reasons for the attack in Korea. Much of its
plausibility obviously derives from a historical experience that became evident only some ten years after the war in Korea—the
so-called Sino-Soviet split that was finally manifested to the outside
world in the early 1960s. The split is now clearly so deep and
pervasive as to encourage commentators to look more deeply into
the past for explanations about what caused it, somewhat in the
way that the friends of a couple, supposedly happily married, who
are suddenly divorced are able to recall all sorts of indications

that the marriage was, in fact, going badly for some time, even though they didn't notice those signs earlier. To Salisbury, false assumptions and false impressions of the Soviet Union, the People's Republic, and Communism in general served in the early 1950s as blinders on American policy makers, limiting their vision of the complexities of the Korean conflict to a narrow range. Through succeeding decades as well, the blinders were not removed, and American foreign policy was less than brilliant as a result.

Perhaps the present offers hope that the United States may at last be waking from what Salisbury calls the "dream of the Cold War." Richard Nixon's much-heralded visits to Peking and Moscow; increasing trade relations between the United States, the People's Republic, and the Soviet Union; the establishment by the United States and the People's Republic of "liaison" offices in each other's capitals; and the negotiated termination of a direct American military role in the Vietnam war—all can be taken as signposts on a road toward more peaceful and satisfactory relations between formerly bitter foes.

If I had been writing about the Cold War ten years ago, I probably would have minimized its relationship to Asia. But the more I've turned to Asia, the more I feel that in Asia the Cold War, in its deepest aspects, has been preserved and continued right up to the present day, as is manifested in Indochina.

The question is, how did this come about? Without doubt the outstanding traumatic event of the Cold War in Asia—and perhaps the Cold War in general—was the victory of Mao Tse-tung in the Chinese civil war. It is difficult today to realize the deep, largely emotional commitment which Americans once felt toward China. I think in this attachment are to be found the emotional origins of the very deep trauma that arose when China was "lost."

I think quotation marks belong around that word "lost." For surely any intelligent analysis shows that we did not lose China. We never had China to lose. We had a rather false conception—a misty conception, an emotional conception—of our relationship with China which had very little meaning to the Chinese themselves. One can say that the American conception arose at least in part from the long missionary effort undertaken by thousands of Americans in China. In contrast to the European powers, whom we perceived as responsible for virtually dismembering the Chinese empire while pursuing predatory commercial and economic interests, the American missionaries believed that they were doing China great good and felt spiritual and emotional satisfaction in their work. Moreover, Americans saw themselves as superior to the mercenary interests of other great powers because of the Open Door policy. The term had such nice connotations, and made us feel good. In reality, of course, it was simply our insistence that we share in all the commercial and trade privileges which had been obtained at the point of a gun by the British, the French, and others.

This brief background allows some appreciation of the concept of China which most Americans had in 1949. Without this awareness, it is almost impossible to look back to what happened in that year and the later McCarthyite use of the China disaster and

HARRISON E. SALISBURY is currently editor of the editorial page of *The New York Times*. For many years he was the Moscow correspondent of *The New York Times*. The recipient of a Pulitzer Prize in journalism, his recent books include *The 900 Days: The Siege of Leningrad, War Between Russia and China,* and *The Many Americans Shall Be One.*

to understand why the country reacted as violently as it did. It is quite clear to me that it was the emotions of Americans that were touched—not logic and reason.

Indeed, in considering the Cold War in the context of Asia, we find again and again that emotion and image, often distorted and often false, play extraordinary roles. Efforts have been made to trace, for example, the tortuous path of our involvement in Indochina. It is interesting to go back to World War II and see what was in Mr. Roosevelt's mind so far as Indochina was concerned. This leaves a trail which runs all the way to the present time—a trail of misconception. It was, for one thing, Mr. Roosevelt's conceit that Indochina and the French role there were major factors in causing the Japanese aggression in the Pacific which led to Pearl Harbor. I don't know where he got the idea that if the French policy in Indochina had not been so oppressive, the Japanese would not have succeeded with their "Co-Prosperity Sphere" in east Asia or the military policy which led them from the occupation of China down into Southeast Asia. But he had that idea fixed firmly. As a corollary, he felt that France should be punished for her bad policy in Indochina and for turning the Japanese loose on the world. The logical penalty envisioned was that Indochina should not be returned to France at the end of the war.

That the colonial powers should not persist in their rule over Southeast Asia and Asia after World War II became firm Roosevelt policy. This was a forward-looking concept. Unfortunately, it had a corollary which is harder to appreciate—that is, while Roosevelt was convinced that France should not regain control of Indochina, he did not know what should happen to it. He didn't really believe that it was ready for nationhood. In casting about, he thought that it would perhaps be wise to put it under the guardianship of the Chinese. Chinese guardianship was sound, Roosevelt argued, because the Indochinese, after all, were the same kind of people as the Chinese. This was one of those great illusions. To say that it is reasonable to put Indochina under the Chinese because they are the same kind of people is like saying it is reasonable to put the Poles under the Russians because they are the same kind of people. The Poles and the Russians are not the same kind of people. All we can say about the Indochinese is that they happen to inhabit the same continent with the Chinese. For 1,500 years, these two peoples have fought. The first thing that happens when you go to Hanoi is that they take you on a visit to the Museum of Revolution. In the first room of the museum, the guide shows you maps, artifacts, pictures, bits of Indochinese history. About what? About the 1,500 years of war against the Chinese, about the great national heroes of Vietnam who won laurels and, sometimes, sainthood by leading the Indochinese people in these wars, which were always successful, according to the Vietnamese. (It's curious that with all these successes in 1,500 years, the Vietnamese were driven from south China, where they originally lived, into the peninsula that they now occupy.) You quickly understand that there is permanent hostility formed out of history which sets Vietnam against China. Any idea that they are Chinese puppets or are likely to put themselves into a position from which they will fall under Chinese influence goes against the grain of these people.

The misconception which underlay Mr. Roosevelt's policy is typical of the misconceptions concerning Asia which have persisted. In the immediate postwar period, Southeast Asia was not important to Americans. No major decisions were made. The French came back and immediately faced a civil war in Indochina. We stood by not much interested because our attention was riveted on the great drama being played out on the China mainland. There we watched the effort of Mao Tse-tung to take over the rotting empire, to drive Chiang Kai-shek off the mainland. We tried, first, to conciliate the irreconcilable—the Nationalists and the Communists—demonstrating our idealism and naiveté concerning China. When that failed, as it was bound to, schemes, plans, proposals were drafted for massive American intervention in that civil war—the intervention of American manpower and American military forces. Of course this was wild talk and nothing more.

This was the American mood in 1949 when Communism triumphed in China. In those first few months after October 1, 1949, when Mao Tse-tung proclaimed his regime, President Truman and Secretary of State Dean Acheson perceived what had happened in China accurately and realistically as a civil war which had been won by the Communist side. They did not call it a Soviet victory. They did not call it a victory for international Communism. They saw it for what it actually was—the triumph of one side in a hard and bitterly fought civil war.

American policy in the autumn of 1949 is often described as

one, in Acheson's phrase, of letting the dust settle. We had not chosen up sides. We were not for the Chinese Nationalists on Formosa, and indeed we refused Chiang Kai-shek an American blanket of protection. As a matter of stated policy by President Truman, we withheld military support from Formosa, and we canvassed our diplomats on the subject of recognizing and entering into diplomatic relations with Communist China.

This policy was followed through the autumn of 1949. It was, perhaps, still an elaboration of that policy, when in January, 1950, Secretary of State Acheson made his famous speech defining the American line of defense in the Pacific. It resounds to this very day. He defined the line of defense as running from the Aleutian Islands southward to Japan and then on southward to the Philippines. He omitted Korea from that perimeter. We had withdrawn the forces we had had in South Korea about a year previously; the Russians had no organized forces in North Korea in early 1950.

This perception of events in China was not to last long. Within months, in June, 1950, came the Korean War. This was to be the second great traumatic event which defined the course of the Cold War in Asia, and which continues to define it to the present time. It brought in its train new policies based on perceptions less wise and founded all too often on illusion and misconception.

Following the invasion of South Korea, President Truman immediately committed troops to the defense of that area. At the same time, certain auxiliary measures were decided upon: the Seventh Fleet was ordered into Formosa Strait, and Chiang Kai-shek, so recently refused a firm commitment of American protection, won a total reversal of United States policy; additional military assistance was channeled into the Philippines. These auxiliary measures reveal much concerning the new perceptions of the Asian scene by American policy makers in mid 1950. They make it clear, above all, that Truman and Acheson were responding to the attack on South Korea on the predication that this was indeed a Chinese Communist threat. Chiang needed protection from the Chinese Communists; the Philippines needed strengthening to prevent a possible Chinese incursion. Clearly the "waiting until the dust settled" attitude had given way to a harsh evaluation of Mao Tse-tung's government and a determination to act swiftly and powerfully to halt ongoing Communist expansion.

But the Korean War was not alone responsible for these changing perceptions. In the months preceding June, one could sense
the growing atmosphere of Cold War in Washington. The Cold
War in Europe had already reached its peak—the Berlin crisis.
Tensions between the Sovet Union and the United States were at
boiling point. Likewise, during these months of the spring of 1950,
the Republicans in Congress began aggressively to attack the Truman administration for the "loss" of China. Republican critics now
began to couple China with the Soviet Union. By March, Senator
Joe McCarthy was talking about Mao's success as part of a Kremlin plot aided by sympathizers installed in the State Department.
He began pointing his accusing finger at Secretary of State
Acheson.

A significant contribution to tension was the signing of the
Sino-Soviet Treaty of Alliance, Aid, and Mutual Assistance in
February, 1950. This was to have a great effect on American
policy. I was in Moscow at the time. Mao Tse-tung came in mid
December, having left China for the first time to make the great
pilgrimage and sit down with Stalin. He spent almost seven weeks
negotiating the treaty. The fact that he had spent so long should
have caused some suspicion as to what was actually going on. But
we did not pay much attention. According to the analysis of the
treaty by State Department experts, it demonstrated clearly that
the Chinese regime was in fact a puppet of Moscow.

Events in Europe, the mood of Congress, and the Sino-Soviet
Treaty were not without effect on the Truman administration. The
president and the secretary of state began to reanalyze what had
happened in China. They emerged with a new scenario of a worldwide Communist conspiracy that had expanded from Moscow and
the Soviet Union to Peking and mainland China. The administration became convinced that the Chinese Communists were aggressively probing a whole new perimeter ranging from Korea in the
north to Indochina in the south.

To repeat, assistance to South Korea and increased aid to
Chiang and the Philippines indicated the kind of response flowing
from this new perception of the Asian scene. Significantly, however, changing American attitudes were evident even before June,
1950. It is a curious fact that more than a month before the
Korean attack, on May 8, 1950, Truman and Acheson approved
the first financial aid to the French in Indochina. The first small

dribble of aid—about ten million dollars—indicates that even before the outbreak of war in Korea, the administration viewed the forces fighting the French in Indochina as directed by the Soviet Union. Rather than seeing Ho Chi Minh as a typical Asian amalgam of Communism and nationalism, we began to see him as part of a worldwide conspiracy. Depending on the specific moment, the headquarters of that conspiracy was seen as either Peking or Moscow.

I have already mentioned the problem of American misconceptions. The changing American attitude toward China and Asia during the first half of 1950 was permeated with them. We now know this from the statements of Mr. Khrushchev, Chou En-lai and Mao Tse-tung in the polemics between the Soviet Union and China. We know that the idea of the Sino-Soviet alliance as an amalgam of two great Communist forces, as well as the idea that the Chinese were puppets of the Russians, was utter nonsense. The plain fact was that in those months leading up to that treaty, China and Russia almost came to a complete breaking point. In Mr. Khrushchev's words, had it not been for common fear in Peking and Moscow of the United States, they would have come apart at that time rather than ten years later. A split would have occurred because the hostility between Mao and Stalin was so intense. Stalin insisted on treating Mao as a semicolonial figure of power. Through the Sino-Soviet Treaty, he imposed on the Chinese provisions of a colonial nature. Joint-stock companies were created for the exploitation of Chinese natural resources in which the Russians had the deciding vote; most of the old imperial Russian military positions and concessions in north China and Manchuria—including of course the vital ports of Dairen and Port Arthur—were secured. Stalin acted exactly as the imperial tsarist government would have acted vis-à-vis the Chinese. Mao was a newly risen nationalist—Communist to be sure—but a man who made it on his own in a movement which had its own ideology, based on the peasant and the rural countryside rather than on the urban proletariat. He was a man who had resisted being purged by the Comintern and who had constantly engaged in private conflict with Stalin. Early in 1950, compelled by circumstances, he was forced to accept an unequal treaty. He accepted it only because the United States did not have the wisdom to do what we had planned to do, what we were talking about doing, in the autumn of 1949—establish normal diplomatic relations with the new regime in Peking. Had that happened, in all probability China and Russia would have split, the treaty would never have been signed, and the story of the past twenty years would be a far different one.

It is important to know of the Sino-Soviet hostility in order to understand what I think happened in Korea at the time. Most Americans assume that the Korean attack was a clear challenge to American power—that Stalin was ringing the alarm bells in the East as he had earlier done at Berlin in the West.

I offer a different hypothesis—not one which can be proved but one which I think fits the circumstances and casts an eerie light on the origins of the Cold War in Asia. Here is an event which we perceived either as a move by the Chinese in Korea, a definite threat to us, or, alternatively, a move by Stalin to challenge our position in the Far East and possibly threaten our relationship with Japan. Indeed, we often had the two perceptions at the same time. What was the reality behind them? I suspect that we were not the objective of that attack at all. It can be proved—I think, conclusively—that Stalin was the instigator and initiator of the attack in Korea. Further, he initiated it for his own ends and purposes. But those purposes were not connected with the United States. We may have provided an ancillary objective, but not the primary one. The primary objective was not the United States—it was Mao Tse-tung. Why do I make such a statement? Primarily because of the history of hostility between the two governments.

Stalin's policy vis-à-vis China insisted upon a restoration of the military position of the Russians in north China and Manchuria. He had resisted—and this has come out again in more recent times—a demand by Mao Tse-tung that Outer Mongolia be returned as a protectorate of China. Both the Chinese Nationalists and Mao Tse-tung always considered Outer Mongolia within their sphere. The Russians had had control of it since 1911. Each Chinese leader acquiesced—Chiang Kai-shek in 1945, and Mao Tse-tung in 1949—to continuance of the Russian supremacy in that country. But neither liked it. Mao Tse-tung asked for it back; Stalin refused. The Soviets had a powerful position in Outer Mongolia, and by the terms of the Sino-Soviet pact, their position in Manchuria also was reinforced.

Stalin had another card up his sleeve which no one knew at

that time, and it was an important one—a man named Kao Kang, chairman of what was called the North China Autonomous Region, which embraced Manchuria, the most important industrial region in China. Kao Kang went to Moscow in the summer of 1949 and signed economic and political pacts with the Soviet regime. Although he was obviously there at the designation of Mao Tse-tung, we now know he was also acting on his own. After Stalin's death, after the execution of Chief of Police Beria, Kao Kang suddenly committed suicide. Following his suicide, the Chinese issued a cryptic, but extremely interesting announcement. They said that Kao Kang was a traitor to his country because he had taken his own life before he could be executed for high crimes and misdemeanors.

What were Kao Kang's high crimes? Conspiring to set up an independent kingdom in Manchuria. Who was he conspiring with? It was not said. Nevertheless, it is obvious, in view of his intimate and close relations, that he was conspiring with the Russians— with Stalin or with Beria or with their agents. The evidence strongly suggests that Kao Kang was, in fact, a secret agent of Stalin, that Stalin had already placed himself in an extraordinarily strong position to exert military pressure against Mao Tse-tung.

If we go back to 1948–49, we see that this was the year in which Stalin, deeply troubled by the split with Tito, fearful of new Titoist movements everywhere, launched his terrible purges in Eastern Europe. In Moscow, he purged several leading Chinese specialists—people whose contacts and associations in China he feared. Is it logical to suppose that he would have done this without making some move against Mao Tse-tung himself? What I am arguing is that when we fortuitously declared Korea outside our perimeter of defense, it opened an opportunity for Stalin to strengthen himself vis-à-vis Mao Tse-tung. A move into Korea would place the Soviet Union in a position even stronger than that held by Japan when she launched her assault on north China from Manchuria during the 1930s. To add to Outer Mongolia, Manchuria, and north China, a strong position in Korea would put Peking within a Soviet nutcracker.

It is, I think, this Soviet desire—to avoid the repetition of a Titoist independence movement in the Far East—that explains most logically the origin of the Korean War. It is much more satisfactory than the simplistic notion that Stalin thought he could jangle American nerves by moving against a pawn in the Pacific. The United States of course never considered the motives behind the outbreak of war in Korea. We quickly amalgamated into our Cold War psychosis the idea that the attack on South Korea was one more maneuver by a massive Communist conspiracy seeking to dominate the world.

There are other bits of evidence that one can cite in examining American misconceptions concerning Asia. One favorite theory was of course that the Chinese had much to do with the outbreak of the Korean War. We supposed that because the Chinese came crashing over the Yalu River when we marched up to the frontier, they were really behind the whole thing. President Truman and Secretary of State Acheson, for example, demonstrated such a conviction when they addressed polite appeals to the Russians to try to use their influence with the North Koreans and with the Chinese to bring the war to an end. Yet the truth is that there were no Chinese in North Korea. The Chinese had not participated in the liberation of North Korea; that had been a Russian operation. Kim Il Sung, who came into power, was Russian-trained and a Russian puppet; there were Russian advisers in every department of the Korean government, particularly in the armed forces. There were no Chinese. In fact, the Chinese did not even open a diplomatic mission in North Korea until August, 1950, two months after the war had broken out. The chances that the Chinese had anything to do with Korea are slim indeed. I would venture to say that the attack on Korea was as great a surprise and as great a shock for Mao Tse-tung as it was for President Truman.

Of course this kind of misconception has marked the Cold War in every one of its aspects, but nowhere, I think, more profoundly than in Asia. The Korean War, with its deep effects on American opinion; the quick acceptance by the public and by the government, Democratic or Republican, of the theory that we were confronted with a combined Communist threat all along the perimeter in Asia—these led us to where we are today. By the time the Korean War ended, John Foster Dulles was secretary of state and Dwight D. Eisenhower was president. At about the time the Korean War was coming to an end, the Indochinese war was entering a new phase. Mr. Dulles viewed the war in Indochina as one end of the long front against international Communism in the Pacific. As the French got into more and more trouble, as the terrible days of Dien Bien Phu came closer and closer, and as disaster loomed over the French effort, Dulles—and some of the military—tried to respond to the desperate French pleas for American aid. But President Eisenhower turned them down. He refused the French in their hour of need. He refused to allow Admiral Radford and others to fly air missions from the Philippines—refused to allow anything to save the French.

This blunt refusal did not end our Cold War in Asia. The Geneva Conference came and went. We participated, but we didn't participate. We were there, but we didn't sign. We were on the scene and we accepted the results, but we really did not. Hardly was the ink dry on the Geneva protocols before we became the direct supporter of the Diem regime. Significantly, we moved in, as stated by Dulles, because of the Chinese and the Communist threat.

What has happened since that time has been little more than a constant expansion. Our protective blanket remains around Formosa. We are in a state of armed truce in Korea. And I do not have to go back over the history of the Vietnamese struggle. It is well known that after 1954 every year saw us somehow getting deeper and deeper and deeper into Indochina. As long as Mr. Dulles was in office, this was our "crusade," the open front which we were maintaining against international Communism. I am sure there was no conception in his mind that it was possible that there could be a split in the Communist world, that, indeed, what we were confronting in Asia and Indochina were far more nationalist movements than parts of an international conspiracy. Few would have believed that behind the lines between Moscow and China or Korea or Vietnam were rising tensions, conflicts so great that they have built up almost to open warfare.

Even today, patterns of thinking and emotion inculcated during the long years of the Cold War persist. Even today, people in this country and elsewhere are, I think, convinced that our involvement in the Indochinese war has entailed holding the line against Chinese Communism in Southeast Asia. Even today, I think Americans are convinced that if we do not continue to protect and support the Chinese Nationalists, we ourselves will be threatened in some fashion. We have still not come to the point of looking at Indochina and seeing the elements there—the origins of the war, the roots of the conflict—as being between the peoples of one country. Nor are we able to look at Taiwan and Peking and see remnants of a civil war. We have continued to interfere in the internal affairs of these countries.

As such policies have continued, what has been the justification offered by our policy makers? What has been the American goal? It has consistently been the notion that somehow or other we must intervene to protect our interests. But protect our interests against what? Against the vision of an international plot directed against the United States—a plot, a conspiracy which, when analyzed bit by bit and piece by piece from its origins twenty-five years ago to the present day, is shown to be based on false impressions, false images, and false assumptions. These continue even now.

I am not saying that there are no conflicts in national interests between the People's Republic of China and the United States. Nor am I saying that there are no conflicts of national interest between the Soviet Union and the United States. Such conflicts obviously exist.

Every nation, ourselves included, has its own particular posture and motivation. Each has its own security considerations. What is required is a more realistic study of those postures and consider-ations. We cannot even begin to do this until we wake from what might be called the dream of the Cold War.

Walter LaFeber

4

Crossing the 38th:
The Cold War in Microcosm

EDITORS' NOTE. The following chapter by historian Walter La-
Feber focuses in depth on one specific policy decision in the gamut
of American responses to the Cold War in Asia which Harrison
Salisbury has broadly discussed—the September, 1950, resolution
of the Truman administration to seize the offensive in the Korean
War and to cross the 38th parallel separating North and South
Korea.

The year 1950 had brought the first overt military test of the
United States policy of "containment" of the Soviet Union. The
arena, Korea, had long been a pawn in the competition for influence between regional powers in the Far East, and from 1910 until
the close of World War II, it had been under the direct control
of Japan. When Japan surrendered Korea at the end of the war,
the peninsula quickly became a testing ground between the Soviet
and American governments, which had divided it "temporarily"
at the 38th parallel into northern and southern occupation zones.
Rival Korean governments were established in the two areas, each
dependent upon the backing of its great power ally. Both the
superpowers and their client governments in Korea professed to
seek a reunification of the country as their goal, but none of the
parties—each fearful of losing the dominance it had achieved in
half the country—could agree with their rivals on the terms of
reunification.

In June, 1950, North Korean troops crossed the armistice line
into the South and were quickly followed by tanks supplied by
the Soviet Union. President Truman's response has usually been
described as based on the administration's view that the attack
constituted a massive challenge to the interests of the United States
in Asia and called for the use of American power to repel the

invasion. As the president came to describe it, the attack was Russian-directed—although he did not immediately say so publicly—and might be intended as the opening chapter in a concerted Sino-Soviet attempt to seize virtually all Asia. To meet such a challenge, Truman immediately ordered: General Douglas MacArthur to dispatch supplies from his headquarters in Japan to South Korea; the Seventh Fleet to enter the Formosa Strait in order to forestall an attack by the Chinese Communists on Taiwan; and additional assistance to the anti-Communist forces of the Philippines and Indochina. Shortly thereafter, United States military units were ordered into action, and the first of several United States–sponsored Security Council resolutions was passed (the Soviets were boycotting the council at the time), calling for a cessation of hostilities and a return to the 38th parallel.

For several months, the United States–United Nations forces were on the defensive, and by September 15, they had been forced back within a small perimeter around Pusan at the southern end of the peninsula. But on that same date, American troops were able to resume the offensive, and by early October, General Mac-Arthur was directed to move beyond the 38th parallel, if the success of such an offensive seemed likely, and into the North. That was done, and United States troops swept nearly across North Korea before they were stopped by the addition into the enemy ranks of large numbers of Chinese soldiers.

In a number of ways, Walter LaFeber sees American actions in the Korean War as crucial components in the evolution of the Cold War. He argues particularly, for example, that the American decision to mount a crusade across the 38th parallel had implications that ranged far beyond the specific geographic and chronological area involved. In addition to the specific relevance of the decision to fight in Korea, so many policy threads fed into the September, 1950, decision that it offers to LaFeber a microcosmic model of the Cold War as a whole. European defense problems and the overall reintegration of Germany; a deepening commitment to Chiang Kai-shek; a changing relationship to the United Nations; a developing concern for Indochina; worries over the fate of budget proposals in Congress and the political storms swirling around Senator Joseph McCarthy—all, according to LaFeber, were interrelated with the problem of Korea in 1950, and played a role in the decision to cross the 38th parallel. With repercussions in Europe, the United States, and the Far East as a whole, the conduct of the Korean War was thus truly global in its impact.

The American response to this global problem, in turn, becomes for LaFeber a major turning point in the history of the Cold War. At the most fundamental level, the decision stretched the containment doctrine into a new and offensive shape. Communist forces were not simply to be prevented from successful aggression, but were to be driven back, if possible, from territory they occupied before the outbreak of hostilities. Here was the first dramatic demonstration of the ambiguities that result from containment's purportedly defensive goals and the opportunities for offensive action that can arise during military engagements. (The Indochina war has of course raised these ambiguities to an even more obvious level.) More specifically, in Professor LaFeber's view, the decision to cross the 38th parallel goes far to explain the American involvement in Vietnam in the 1960s. Events surrounding that decision involved the United States in Asia more heavily than ever before, and that involvement has persisted to the present day. It was in the context of that decision that the United States first committed itself militarily to the support of Chiang Kai-shek on Taiwan and to the French in Indochina. It was also at that point that suggestions were first made for the creation of a multilateral alliance for Southeast Asia. More immediately, however, the decision brought Communist Chinese troops into the battle on a massive scale, producing both the threat of a much wider war and a United States–Chinese enmity so deep as to prevent any kind of normal relations between them for more than twenty years.

There is irony in the fact that as a result of the Chinese intervention in the conflict, the war dragged on to a stalemate and an armistice that only slightly redrew the 1945 boundary between North and South Korea. The original, more modest goals of containment were thus, in effect, confirmed, if by default. Meanwhile, however, in LaFeber's words, "the decision to cross the 38th . . . put us on a Cold War footing and gave us the Cold War ideology which we still confront today."

During the summer of 1941 the editor of Time-Life, Inc., Henry Luce, confidently predicted the coming of the American Century. That same summer, President Roosevelt and Prime Minister Churchill signed the Atlantic Charter, which pledged the two powers to follow the principles of an open world and free elections. With some reservations, the Soviet Union shortly after agreed to sign the charter. Thirty years later, Americans look back upon a quarter-century of Cold War, a trillion dollars spent on arms, and a tragic involvement in Indochina which, instead of bringing about an American Century, threatened to bring about a second American civil war, or a series of civil wars, worse than anything the United States had endured in more than a century.

The discovery of how Americans headed for the American Century and ended up mired in the Big Muddy is the purpose of history. Margaret Mead and her ideas of a post-figurative culture to the contrary, this and every other generation will have to discover from its ancestors how it got where it is, which historical processes shaped its present life, and how those processes can be perceived accurately. In tracing the course of the American Century, several guideposts loom as of special importance. One appeared in 1943–44 when President Roosevelt began to discard his "Three Policemen" (the United States, Great Britain, and Russia) concept, which would have allowed special spheres of interest for each of the policemen, to a view developed by Cordell Hull which held that no blocs could be allowed to develop in the postwar world. When the United States and the Soviet Union clashed over the Russian attempt to construct a Communist bloc in Eastern Europe and the Middle East, the Cold War formally began. A second guidepost appeared in 1946 when in response to supposed Soviet incursions into the Middle East and Eastern Mediterranean, the United States developed a policy which in March, 1947, would be called the Truman Doctrine.

A most important milestone in the Cold War was passed between mid July and October, 1950. During these months, the United States decided not only to roll back invading North Korean troops to the 38th parallel but to move beyond the parallel itself. This historic decision marked the moment when the United States

WALTER LAFEBER, Professor of History at Cornell University, is a diplomatic historian best known for his books *The New Empire* and *America, Russia and the Cold War*.

decided to move from a policy of "containment," as defined by President Truman in 1947, to a policy of "liberation," or the rolling back of Communism. In this decision, as in most others, Dean Acheson and Harry Truman practiced what John Foster Dulles would be blamed for preaching several years later.

Truman's decision to move beyond the 38th was obviously taken partially to punish the North Koreans for their effort in June to destroy American interests in South Korea, but to examine the president's action in this context is misleading. When Washington officials took the initiative to move into North Korea, they radically changed the course of the Cold War. The world that went into the autumn of 1950 and the world that emerged from that autumn were very different, and nowhere was the change more marked than in the United States. Americans went into that season with a contained war in Asia, a Europe-first foreign policy, considerable unity at home, and a confident if (as usual) beseiged administration in power. The nation emerged in December with: the threat of a third world war hanging in the balance; the possibility of using atomic weapons against the Chinese not being excluded by the president;[1] a new and long-lasting emphasis upon such non-European areas as Formosa and Indochina; and an administration enduring vitriolic attack at home, an onslaught led by Senator Joseph McCarthy.

The turn in the autumn occurred when the United Nations forces crossed the 38th parallel during the first week of October and then, some six weeks later, encountered the massive armies of Communist China. The decision to cross the parallel, however, was not made in October, nor was it concluded after General Douglas MacArthur's magnificent success at Inchon on September 15 enveloped the North Korean forces and reversed the military fortunes of the war. One of the most striking aspects of the decision was that it was made during July and August, when the military situation in South Korea was exceedingly grim for the United Nations forces. Those were the days of the Pusan Perimeter, when it still seemed possible that the North Koreans might push the United Nations forces into the sea. Yet paradoxically, this was also the time when Washington officials laid the plans to cross the 38th.

One root of the resulting crisis goes back to March, 1949, when General MacArthur defined South Korea as being beyond the bounds of direct American military responsibility.[2] By that time, the Soviet forces, which had occupied Korea to the 38th in 1945 in order to accept the Japanese surrender in the area, and the American forces, which for similar reasons had marched north to the parallel, had largely moved out of the country. The Russians had left behind military advisory groups to aid a strong Communist government in the North; the American military similarly helped a considerably weaker and faction-torn government, led by Syngman Rhee, in the South. On January 12, 1950, Secretary of State Acheson reiterated MacArthur's sentiments when he defined Korea as being outside the American defense perimeter. The secretary of state carefully noted, however, that any aggression in Korea would be a matter for the United Nations,[3] although that was hardly a threat which would keep either Stalin or North Korean Premier Kim Il Sung awake nights.

In April, 1950, the president announced that John Foster Dulles would head an American team which would sign a treaty giving Japan her independence from American occupation but, it was hoped, would also maintain United States bases in Japan for the indefinite future. Stalin probably perceived Dulles's mission as an attempt to create an anti-Soviet military alliance on Russia's eastern flank, just as Acheson had built the North Atlantic Treaty Organization during the preceding months on the western flank. Because the Rhee regime was tottering, and since MacArthur and Acheson had defined South Korea as being beyond unilateral American defense responsibilities, Stalin might well have thought he had no reason to block Kim Il Sung's plan to unite Korea by force. Little evidence exists that Stalin encouraged the invasion, but if it proved to be successful, the Russian-built North Korean army and regime could be a useful pawn to play against Mao Tse-tung—already emerging as a threat to Stalin's control of the Communist bloc; and more immediately, the Communists would control all Korea and thereby hold the "dagger" which pointed at the Japanese home islands. A quick military victory would go far in neutralizing the power of American bases in Japan.

Within seventy-two hours after the North Koreans pushed across the 38th, the Truman administration committed American naval and air forces to helping the retreating South Koreans. Within another seventy-two hours, American ground troops were fighting in the area.[4] The rapidity of these decisions can be explained in part by the shock suffered by Acheson and Truman. For the secretary of state, the invasion must have been particularly traumatic. Six months before, he had declared that South Korea was not of primary importance to the United States. Acheson was already in some political trouble because he had happened to be in office when China fell into the hands of the Communists. He had also remained loyal to Alger Hiss when Hiss was being convicted for former Communist affiliations. Of perhaps equal importance, Acheson's impeccable mustache and attire, his brilliant mind and cutting tongue, his Yale Law School background and wealthy Washington law practice—these did not endear him to people, who noted that Hiss had also been an Ivy Leaguer, that so-called eggheads made the world seem more complicated than did down-to-earth people like Joseph McCarthy, and that Acheson's remarks in January about Korea left him open for those who had been waiting long and angrily for just such a mistake.

The secretary of state had prided himself on basing his diplomacy on so-called situations of strength—that is, negotiating from a favorable basis of power. The North Korean invasion exposed one grave weakness in that approach, for the United States was not dealing from strength in Korea in the summer of 1950. Acheson would never repeat such a mistake; in the future, his rhetoric would seldom be as restrained as it was on January 12, 1950. Instead of defining defense perimeters, he began to take the offensive. His determination to do so was reinforced by his perception of the source of the personal attacks. In his memoirs he calls the onslaught the "Attack of the Primitives."[5] He certainly did not consider such "primitives" worthy of influencing the course of American foreign policy. An interesting counterpart to Acheson's view was the president's refusal to obtain congressional approval before sending American men to Korea and Truman's reluctance to explain the crisis to the public until July 19. Aside from how these actions reveal Truman's and Acheson's concepts of policy making, the two men doubtlessly believed that a diplomatic offensive resulting in new situations of strength would be a splendid ameliorization for remedying the growing assortment of domestic political problems.

The administration went on the offensive in a series of moves during the summer and early fall of 1950. The decision to cross the 38th was part of this offensive, but that move cannot be studied in isolation. Acheson launched a series of diplomatic maneuvers around the globe. Diplomatically it was the most active and important series of months in the history of the Cold War, with the possible exception of the period which led to the Truman Doctrine formulation in 1946–47.[6]

The secretary of state first went to the United Nations to gain that organization's support for the American commitment in Korea. The key resolutions were passed on June 25 and 27. On June 25, the UN asked the North Koreans to retreat behind the 38th parallel. When they did not do so, the organization passed a new resolution two days later requesting its members to help repel the aggression so that "peace and security" could be restored "to the area." The word "area" was not defined. The president would later use the term as meaning all Korea, not merely Korea to the 38th, as the resolution on June 25 had stated. From available records, it seems impossible to find any official, moreover, who, during the days following the passage of the resolution, referred to the "area" as meaning all Korea.[7] The meaning of the term assumes even more significance given its authors, for Acheson and a few close aides drew up the resolution in Washington and then telephoned it to the United Nations. In this, as in General MacArthur's military effort, the United States controlled the planning and used the UN as a front.[8]

The president believed that the American response to the North Korean invasion had saved the United Nations from the fate of the League of Nations. Having rescued it, the administration proceeded to transform the organization. In September, Acheson proposed the Uniting for Peace Resolution. This resolution stated that when the Security Council could not deal with an international crisis, the General Assembly could vote and commit its members to solving the crisis. Since 1946, the United States had been trying to devise a method to weaken the force of the Soviet veto in the Security Council. The problem was driven home in June when the council had been able to act on the Korean crisis only because the Soviet delegate had absented himself as a display of his alleged displeasure over the UN exclusion of Communist China. Acheson and Truman did not want to be dependent upon such good fortune again. The Uniting for Peace Resolution passed the General Assembly overwhelmingly—53 to 5—on November 3. With this vote, the power of the Russian veto in the Security Council was theoretically severely limited, and much of the power of the UN flowed into the General Assembly, where the United States enjoyed a majority of the members' votes on nearly all important issues.[9]

Another part of the American diplomatic offensive during the summer of 1950 involved Formosa. That island has become so thorny an issue, and has loomed so large as an obstacle to the formation of Sino-American diplomatic relations, that one forgets how close Washington came to giving up on Formosa in 1949 and early 1950. Throughout those months, United States military leaders told Truman that Formosa could not be defended given American political priorities. The State Department fully expected the Communists, who were massing large numbers of troops across the strait from Formosa, to take the island sometime in 1950. On January 5, 1950, Truman publicly announced that although he would continue to allow low-level economic aid to flow to Chiang Kai-shek on the island, the United States would not provide either military personnel or assistance to Formosa.[10] When North Korea struck on June 25, however, the president placed the Seventh Fleet between the mainland and Formosa to contain any possible struggle in that area and also, in Assistant Secretary of State Dean Rusk's words, to protect the flank of the Korean struggle. The major change occurred in August when MacArthur's recommendations that the United States send military advisers and assistance to Chiang were accepted by Truman. The policy of January 5 was reversed. In August, 1950, the United States bedded down with Chiang.[11]

A similar policy transformation occurred in American relations with Indochina. The military involvement of the United States in Vietnam, indeed, dates from 1950. Acheson had made a commitment to give France financial aid for her Indochina venture as early as May, 1950, one month before the Korean War broke out. But not until after June 25 did American personnel become involved. On June 27, in the same announcement in which he announced American support for South Korea, Truman revealed he had "directed acceleration in the furnishing of military assistance to the forces of France and the Associated States in Indochina and the dispatch of a military mission to provide close working relations with those forces."[12] Within a month, the first glimmerings of the Southeast Asia Treaty Organization (SEATO) ap-

peared when Representative Jacob Javits of New York, a member
of the House Foreign Affairs Committee, suggested a NATO for
Southeast Asia.[13] By September, Dulles was openly talking about
such an alliance, in large part, no doubt, because of his work in
Japan on the peace treaty. He had become convinced, as he told
a private dinner at the Council of Foreign Relations in October,
that Japan could move in only one of two directions if she hoped
to become prosperous and stable: either toward her traditional
markets in China, now Communist, and thus form relations with
Mao's government; or find markets in Southeast Asia. Because
Japan was key to the entire American position in the Pacific,
Southeast Asia had to remain open for Japanese exploitation.
Dulles never dropped this theme, and, significantly, Southeast Asia
was again mentioned as a market for Japan's continued economic
viability in 1954 when President Eisenhower made his famous re-
mark about falling dominoes in the Far East.[14]

At the same time American policy was becoming transformed
in regard to Korea, Formosa, and Southeast Asia, Acheson also
opened a summer diplomatic offensive on the European front, the
area which he and the president considered to be of greatest significance throughout the Korean conflict. They used the crisis of
the Korean War as an opportunity to achieve goals in Europe
which had theretofore not seemed possible of accomplishment because of opposition in both the United States and Western Europe.
These goals included the integration of West Germany firmly into
the Western alliance and the arming of the West German army.
The American commitment to this policy was sealed in September
when the president announced, much to the consternation of Congress, that he was stationing American troops for a long period
of time on Western European soil. Acheson had assured Congress
in 1949 that the United States did not want Germany armed, and
that American men would not be stationed in Europe by the president without consultation with the legislature. Truman, however,
bypassed Congress in this as in other matters during the summer
of 1950, and, as have many of his successors, used his constitutional powers as commander in chief to order the troops into a
most sensitive theater without bothering to consult the Senate or
the House. In September, the secretary of state informed the British and French that the United States was now determined to
rearm Germany. At the same time, Truman committed American

troops to the NATO command and, in cooperation with the West-ern Europeans, established a unified command structure under General Dwight D. Eisenhower. By late September, the United States commitment to Western Europe was fixed for at least the next twenty-two years.[15] The final nails which sealed this new com-mitment had been hammered down quickly, without consultation with the parties stuck with paying for the tools, and as part of a hasty carpentry job which Truman and Acheson were perform-ing in the Far East as well as in Europe.

One other aspect of the Western European situation also be-comes clearer when placed in this context of the American deci-sion to unite Korea. Acheson and West German Chancellor Kon-rad Adenauer explicitly discussed the relationship of Korea to Germany, for the secretary of state knew that the American re-sponse in Korea removed doubts that the United States would re-spond the same way to aggression in the more vital area of Central Europe.[16] Or at least almost in the same way, for, as Truman told columnist Arthur Krock privately in late June, 1950, if there is to be a confrontation with the Russians directly, "We want any showdown to come in Western Europe 'where we can use the bomb.' " This comment explains why, as part of his summer offen-sive, Truman asked Congress on July 7 for supplemental appro-priations of $260 million so that the Atomic Energy Commission could "build additional and more efficient plants" to accelerate its work on "all forms of atomic weapons, including the hydrogen or fusion bomb."[17]

This presidential action also further reveals a most important dimension of Truman's and Acheson's policies in 1950. The presi-dent ordered such a sharp rise in defense spending that by the end of the year military expenditures rocketed upward to the levels where they have remained—or gone above—ever since. Until June, 1950, Truman had planned on a $13.5 billion defense bud-get, and had done so despite the warnings of National Security Council Memorandum No. 68 (NSC-68)—one of the most crucial documents in the history of the Cold War and one that remains classified twenty-three years later—that to protect the free world, the president would have to spend at least $50 billion annually on armaments. By mid July, Truman's arms budget had been raised to approximately $30 billion. By December, after the crossing of the 38th had brought into action the armies of China, defense spending was planned for the $50-billion level. In this, as in many other matters, the administration's reaction to the Korean crisis metamorphosed the theories of NSC-68 into reality.

The decision to cross the 38th during June (when, without consulting Congress or explaining the reasons to the public, Truman made the historic decision to have American troops fighting on the Asian mainland) can be fully understood only when placed alongside these administration initiatives in Formosa, Indochina, and Central and Western Europe. Taken together, these commitments provided Acheson with new and exceptionally strong situations of strength from which he supposedly could deal profitably with the Communists. The decisions also rendered him less vulnerable to criticism from hard-liners in the United States—that is, if the plans worked, particularly if crossing the 38th succeeded; if it did, the United States for the first time would have rolled back Communism—and, to boot, in Asia, the area which most critics of Acheson treasured above all but their home electoral districts.

The State Department files on Korea should be opened after the elapse of more than twenty years, but the peculiar sensitivity of some officials, as well as of some congressmen, who refuse to appropriate the necessary monies so that their constituents might know why their sons are dying in foreign wars, has prevented the release of the 1950 records. We consequently do not yet know exactly how the decision to cross the 38th developed, although from good circumstantial evidence historians can come to some tentative conclusions.

The origins of the specific policy decision apparently date from about mid July. In a speech to Congress on July 19, Truman implied that the United States would attempt to restore security to all Korea. The boundaries were undefined in his speech.[18] Two days later, as George Kennan relates in his *Memoirs,* two staff officers told Kennan they were concerned over rumors that plans were being made in the State Department to advance beyond the 38th. During the next several days, Kennan attempted to discover the source of the reports, and, in doing so, apparently had rather intense arguments with Dulles and Secretary of State Acheson. Kennan did not, as he put it so neatly, want Douglas MacArthur to have permission to go to "the gates of Vladivostok. The Russians would never under any circumstances agree to this."[19] Kennan left the department shortly thereafter, but the emerging policy was revealed in a private letter from Dulles to a close friend who was the editor and publisher of the *Arizona Daily Star*. Dulles wrote that he did not want to get too close to Vladivostok or to Port Arthur either. "On the other hand, I quite agree that if we have the power to do otherwise, it would be folly to go back to the division of Korea at the 38th parallel."[20] As in so many things, Acheson and Dulles apparently agreed on this policy. The secretary of state took the lead in August in formulating the directive ordering MacArthur to move above the parallel.

This decision was finally based upon an evaluation of possible Soviet reaction—would Stalin retaliate if the United States moved above the 38th? Less concern was felt about China, in part because Acheson increasingly believed that Russia controlled Chinese movements and also because the Chinese, after a long civil war, did not seem capable of effectively fighting the awesome power of the United States. If China did decide to strike, it would probably be into Formosa rather than through Manchuria and Korea. Russia was the main worry. As Secretary of Defense Louis Johnson later commented, the decision to counter the North Korean invasion in June had been a "calculated risk," because no one knew what Stalin might do. But in early July, the Soviets officially called the conflict a "civil war" in which Russia was not involved.[21] By August 23, Secretary of Defense Johnson could tell an executive session of the Senate Foreign Relations Committee that an attack by the Soviets, especially in Europe, where it was most feared, was no longer likely, "because Russia was probably aware of the fact that at the present time we had a greater supply of atomic bombs than she had, and also our steel capacity was way above that of Russia's."[22]

During the days when this assumption was forming, the United States defense in Korea began to hold. On July 20, MacArthur wired Washington that the enemy had lost its opportunity to win a complete victory. As Kennan relates, talk began to circulate in the State Department about crossing the parallel at precisely this time. UN forces continued to hold in August, and the course of American policy became apparent in two speeches. On August 17, American Ambassador to the United Nations Warren Austin announced that North Korean forces should surrender so that the country could be reunited by elections held throughout Korea under UN auspices. The only significant objection to Austin's proposal apparently came from George Kennan, then no longer in the State Department.[23] Shortly after Austin spoke, Secretary of the Navy Francis Matthews told an audience of 100,000 that Americans should fight a "war to compel cooperation for peace." This speech was the closest thing to urging preventive war which any Washington official advocated publicly during the period. It was a frightening address. Truman privately tongue-lashed Matthews, but the president would not publicly repudiate his secretary of the navy—although Matthews shortly found himself on the high seas en route to his new post as ambassador to Ireland. During the week of Matthews's speech, the Chinese began to warn with increasing frequency that UN forces should not cross the parallel.[24]

The American response to the Chinese statements was most interesting and instructive. On September 1, Truman publicly assured China that the United States wanted no territory in Korea, but only a united nation.[25] Acheson emphasized this point throughout September and October, assuring Peking that UN troops on the Yalu would pose no security problem or danger to Chinese interests just across that river, interests which included plants providing much of the power for Chinese industries in Manchuria.

On September 1, the directive allowing MacArthur to move beyond the 38th was completed by the National Security Council. On September 11, the president signed the directive. Four days later, on the morning of the Inchon invasion, the directive was sent to MacArthur. With the success of that invasion, the directive was sharpened on September 27. MacArthur was told to move troops north of the parallel if such movement did not encounter Chinese or Russian resistance and if he was certain of success in the field.[26] Given MacArthur's temperament, this instruction was an open invitation for him to drive to the Yalu. When, in late November, he met Chinese troops, the general refused to admit that his UN armies were in trouble until it was too late.

The United Nations faithfully followed the American initiatives. The United States desire for a truly international organization resembled Augustine's prayer: "Lord, give me chastity, but do not give it to me yet." On October 7, the General Assembly, in another resolution written by Acheson and his staff in Washington, authorized the UN forces to move above the 38th. This action had been preceded by a speech of Ambassador Austin's which announced that Korea would now be used as a laboratory for other newly emerging areas; as the UN developed a united Korea, so the organization would raise up other nonindustrialized areas (perhaps Indochina or Africa or the Middle East).[27] It was a magnificent vision from the American point of view—nothing more.

Thus UN forces moved beyond the parallel and met Chinese armies in overwhelming numbers in late November; on December 26, the Chinese and North Koreans recrossed the 38th, this time going south. Acheson once again was shocked. On November 15, the secretary of state, usually so sensitive and debonair in his public appearances, became incoherent, even ludicrous, in explaining why the Chinese should not fear an American encampment on the Yalu. "Everything in the world" was being done to reassure the Chinese that their interests were not in jeopardy, the secretary of state declared, "and I should suppose that there is no country in the world which has been more outstanding in developing the theory of brotherly development of border waters than the United States." As examples of this brotherly concern, he listed the Rio Grande and Colorado River settlements with Mexico and the St. Lawrence and Great Lakes treaties with Canada. "So we really are the people who have led the world in international development of border waters," and would like "to bring about a constructive adjustment of Chinese-Korean interests in the Yalu River" if Peking would only agree. Such an American "brotherly development" of the Yalu was of course precisely what the Chinese were determined to prevent. Yet Acheson's statement brightly illuminates the American perception of such less-developed areas as North Korea and China.[28]

The American decision to cross the parallel had proved to be exceptionally costly by the time a truce was arranged in 1953. Four-fifths of all American casualties in the Korean War occurred after the UN forces crossed the 38th. This was a high price to pay for abortive "liberation," particularly when an agreement based on the status quo ante bellum might have been worked out with North Korea in late September.

The cost in blood and treasure greatly escalated in the longer run. The war froze the United States into the Cold War posture in which it has stood since the winter of 1950. The confrontation with the Red Chinese troops especially paralyzed American-Chinese relations. At one point in early 1950, some possibility existed for diplomatic contact between Washington and Peking.[29] Such possibilities were diminished in June, but they were eradicated by December. The great China market, so long sought by Americans from the 1780s through the time of Henry Luce, disappeared behind the Bamboo Curtain, and, as one observer summarized, "700 million potential customers had turned into the apparition of 700 million dangerous adversaries."[30] At home, the enlarged war and the resulting two-year stalemate brought on the worst years of McCarthyism and witch-hunting. This, in turn, severely weakened the Foreign Service, which carried out American policy.

The Truman administration paid a high political price for deciding to cross the 38th, but then that decision had been a political decision made by civilians and not primarily a military decision.[31] Although it is convenient to blame the military-industrial complex for many of our problems, both public and personal, in 1950 the civilians in the State Department formulated the decisive policies. The 38th parallel, after all, was significant for its political, not its military, importance, and no one understood that better than Acheson. At the same time, these civilians also made the new commitments in Indochina, Formosa, and Europe which fixed the American view of these areas for two decades.

The problem in Korea was seen by Truman and Acheson as an opportunity for action in the Far East and Europe. The crisis was used as a lever for global diplomacy. The secretary of state revealed the fundamental approach that had been used when he declared on November 17, 1950, that the American "purpose and its direction, in its relations with other countries, have been to create and to maintain the environment in which the great American experiment in liberty could flourish and exist." He continued:

> This is all we have asked of the world. We have no special interests that we want to achieve. We don't want to dominate anyone. We don't want territory. We don't want any of the things for which empires in the past have fought. We want only a world in which we can be free and in which everyone else can be free.[32]

This speech could be viewed almost as a shining page in the history of so-called American idealism, except of course that most

American historians and political scientists have declared that only Woodrow Wilson and his intellectual descendants should be thought of as idealists, and that Acheson was of course a realist, not an idealist. The absurdity of such a dichotomy in American diplomatic history becomes evident when Acheson's words of November 17 are placed within the context of his actions since June. Acheson resembled Wilson in his idealism, an idealism that could quickly become transmuted into realism, whether this required declaring war on Germany in 1917 or sending American troops to help cement Germany to the United States in 1950.

The decision to cross the 38th, combined with the related policies adopted during the summer and autumn of 1950, demonstrates this continuity of American history. That continuum did not of course slow down or stop in 1953.[33] In its most important sense, the summer of 1950 marked the point of acceleration which hurled the United States not into an American Century but into a more dangerous era and which fixed the nation's Cold War ideology for more than twenty years.

NOTES

1. *Public Papers of the Presidents of the United States. Harry S. Truman . . . 1950* (Washington, 1965), pp. 726–27; Press release from U.S. Mission to UN, Conference Dossiers (UN-Korea), November 30, 1950, Papers of John Foster Dulles, Princeton.

2. Allan Whiting, *China Crosses the Yalu* (New York, 1960), p. 39; Martin Lichterman, "To the Yalu and Back," in Harold Stein, ed., *American Civil-Military Decisions: A Book of Case Studies* (Birmingham, Alabama, 1963), especially p. 577.

3. Dean Acheson, "Crisis in Asia," *Department of State Bulletin* 22 (Jan. 23, 1950), 111–18.

4. Glenn D. Paige, *The Korean Decision* (New York, 1968), pp. 185, 250.

5. Dean Acheson, *Present at the Creation: My Years in the State Department* (New York: W. W. Norton & Co., 1969), p. 354.

6. Paige, *The Korean Decision*, pp. 303–4. Coral Bell has critically explained the assumption in *Negotiation from Strength* (New York, 1963). On the effect of domestic opinion on Acheson's and Truman's decision to move beyond the 38th, James Reston later had an interesting column in the *New York Times*, Nov. 16, 1950.

7. Harry S. Truman, *Memoirs: Years of Trial and Hope* (Garden City, N.Y., 1956), pp. 341, 346; Lichterman, "To the Yalu and Back," p. 580. During hearings in 1951, the following exchange occurred: Senator Harry

F. Byrd, Democrat of Virginia: "Well, the fact is then that you were actually in conflict with the North Korean units [on June 26] one day before the resolution was passed by the United Nations." General Omar Bradley, Chairman of the Joint Chiefs of Staff: "By air and naval, yes. Probably the naval had not reached there yet, but the orders had been given." U.S. Congress, 82nd Cong., 1st Sess., Senate Committee on Armed Services, *Military Situation in the Far East* (Washington, 1951), p. 993. When President Truman later decided to go beyond the parallel, he believed that the UN resolution had been "very broad." *Public Papers of the Presidents . . . 1950,* p. 658.

8. *Military Situation in the Far East,* p. 20.

9. *Department of State Bulletin* 23 (Oct. 2, 1950), 523–29; *Ibid.* (Oct. 23, 1950), 651–55; *Military Situation in the Far East,* p. 1722, for an interesting Acheson interpretation of the resolution; Dulles to Jean Chauvel, September 28, 1950, Conference Dossiers, Uniting for Peace, Dulles Papers; Dulles to Senator Arthur Vandenberg, October 20, 1950, Dulles Papers; Memorandum from Leonard C. Meeker to James Hyde, November 10, 1950, Dulles Papers.

10. H. B. Westerfield, *Foreign Policies and Party Politics: Pearl Harbor to Korea* (New Haven, 1955), pp. 109, 368–69.

11. *Military Situation in the Far East,* pp. 999–1001; *Public Papers of the Presidents . . . 1950,* pp. 626; 679; Burton Crane to H. Alexander Smith, August 6, 1950, unmarked file. Foreign Relations Committee, Box 100, H. Alexander Smith Papers, Princeton.

12. *Public Papers of the Presidents . . . 1950,* p. 492.

13. *New York Herald Tribune,* July 12, 1950; Department of State Bulletin 23 (Oct. 30, 1950), 704; "Memorandum: Conversation with Mr. Dallas Coors," August 8, 1950, unmarked file, Foreign Relations Committee, Box 100, Smith Papers.

14. Council of Foreign Relations Study Group Reports, October 23, 1950, meeting, Conference Dossiers, Draft of Japanese Peace Treaty, Dulles Papers. In his January 12, 1950 address, Acheson had also expressed concern about the future of the Japanese economy: "Crisis in Asia," p. 117. The Eisenhower comment is in *Public Papers of the Presidents . . . 1954* (Washington, 1960), p. 383.

15. Paige, *The Korean Decision,* p. 147; Lawrence W. Martin, "The American Decision to Rearm Germany," in Stein, ed., *American Civil-Military Decisions,* especially pp. 651–52.

16. "Aide-Memoire," received by Allen Dulles and sent to J. F. Dulles, who forwarded it to Henry Byroade in the State Department on September 11, Correspondence, 1950, Dulles Papers; Acheson, in *Department of State Bulletin* 23 (Oct. 16, 1950), 612, and *Department of State Bulletin* 23 (Nov. 20, 1950), 818; H. Alexander Smith to Austin, October 6, 1950, and Austin to Smith, October 10, 1950, Correspondence, 1950, Dulles Papers.

17. From Arthur Krock, *Memoirs* (New York: Funk & Wagnalls, 1968), p. 260. Copyright © 1968 by Arthur Krock. With permission of the publisher, Funk & Wagnalls Publishing Company, Inc. *Public Papers of the Presidents . . . 1950,* p. 519.

18. *Ibid.,* pp. 528–31.

19. George F. Kennan, *Memoirs, 1925–1950* (Boston: Little, Brown and Company, 1967), p. 488. Copyright © 1967 by George F. Kennan. Reprinted by permission of the publisher.

20. Dulles to William R. Mathews, July 24, 1950, Correspondence, 1950, Dulles Papers; but Dulles's enthusiasm waned after Chinese troops appeared in large numbers in North Korea. Dulles to Mr. Ferdinand Lathrop Mayer, November 9, 1950, Conference Dossiers (UN-Korea), Dulles Papers.

21. Max Beloff, *Soviet Policy in the Far East, 1944–1951* (London, 1953), p. 186; Paige, *The Korean Decision,* pp. 117–18; David S. McLellan, "Dean Acheson and the Korean War," *Political Science Quarterly* 83 (March, 1968), 36.

22. Memorandum of "Executive Meeting of the Foreign Relations Committee on Wednesday, August 23, 1950," Foreign Relations, 1950, Secretary Louis Johnson, Box 101, Smith Papers.

23. Kennan, *Memoirs,* pp. 488–89; also *New York Times,* Nov. 16, 1950.

24. David Rees, *Korea: The Limited War* (New York, 1964), p. 75; John W. Spanier, *The Truman-MacArthur Controversy and the Korean War* (Cambridge, Mass., 1959), pp. 84–85.

25. *Public Papers of the Presidents . . . 1950,* pp. 612–13.

26. Lichterman, "To the Yalu and Back," pp. 584–85; Spanier, *Truman-MacArthur . . . ,* p. 95; the September 15 message is in *Military Situation in the Far East,* pp. 718–19. After the American decision to cross the 38th had been made, Truman was asked what American troops would do when they reached the parallel. The President replied solemnly that he had not yet decided, for "That is a matter for the United Nations to decide. . . . It will be worked out by the United Nations and I will abide by the decisions that the United Nations makes." *Public Papers of the Presidents . . . 1950,* p. 644. Richard T. Ruetten had detailed MacArthur's military errors in the drive to the Yalu: "General Douglas MacArthur's 'Reconnaissance in Force': The Rationalization of a Defeat in Korea," *Pacific Historical Review* 36 (Feb., 1967), 79–94.

27. *Department of State Bulletin* 23 (Oct. 9, 1950), 580–81; *Military Situation in the Far East,* pp. 361–62.

28. *Department of State Bulletin* 23 (Nov. 27, 1950), 855. The confusion in the State Department was caught by Rusk's remarks on November 15 (quoted in *Ibid.* (Dec. 4, 1950), p. 890): "Why this new phase in Chinese intervention? May I say that we do not know what Chinese intentions are, and when I say that I do not mean to imply that we do not have a good many ideas. But we do not know, in the sense in which you have to know, if you are a government, as a basis for action which you yourself might have to take. In other words, not to know may mean that you are not certain. I suggest that it does not always mean that you are simply ignorant."
One of the more dangerous errors in assessing Sino-Russian policies is committed in Maxwell D. Taylor, *Responsibility and Response* (New York: Harper & Row, 1967), pp. 34–35: "I personally have never felt

that this danger of possible escalation is something that should make us timid or reluctant to do the right thing. There seems to be a conclusion, borne out in our past relations with the Communist world, that one never provokes Communists to do anything—they will do what suits their purpose in their own time, when it is to their interest. They will not withhold doing us a bad turn because we are nice to them." This view is flatly contradicted by the American acts which provoked the Chinese to intervene in North Korea.

29. Westerfield, *Foreign Policy and Party Politics,* pp. 360–61; McClellan, "Dean Acheson and the Korean War," pp. 16–17.

30. A. T. Steele, *The American People and China* (New York: Mc-Graw-Hill, 1966), p. 60.

31. Richard E. Neustadt, *Presidential Power* (New York, 1960), pp. 123–46; on the military insignificance of the parallel, General Lawton Collins made the pertinent comment that "The thirty-eighth parallel has absolutely no military significance of any kind whatever." *Military Situation in the Far East,* pp. 1303–4.

32. *Department of State Bulletin* 23 (Nov. 27, 1950), 840.

33. Gaddis Smith has noted how, for Acheson, Rusk, Richard Nixon, and other policy makers and their generations, the Korean War is a "golden age," in that it represented a "grim but deeply satisfying experience. For them the war represented the triumph of courageous leadership over uncertainty and lethargy in the American people." Smith, "A History Teacher's Reflections on the Korean War," *Ventures* 8 (Spring, 1968), 59, 63–64.

Norman B. Hannah

5
The Asian Boundaries of Coexistence

EDITORS' NOTE. In the following chapter, Norman B. Hannah presents an overview that is quite different from that of the other articles in this collection. He does not, for example, present a revisionist interpretation of the Cold War, in the sense of questioning the propriety of the American response to Communism during the past twenty-five years. Nor does he share the skepticism toward American policy that characterizes the positions of other contributors to this volume. And yet from his own particular vantage point, Hannah too reaches significant conclusions concerning the nature of the Cold War experience.

Hannah's overview is one which basically contends that for all its incredible intricacies and difficulties, for all its bloody and torturous moments, the past twenty-five years of Cold War have yielded certain tangible results. The confrontation between the free world and communism is described as a "manifestation of a deeper process of reorientation, working toward a new equilibrium." In significant ways, that equilibrium has been partially achieved. If it is a fact that the world is inhabited by real nations which are conglomerates of power, self-interest, and occasional idealism, and not by hypothetical agencies of altruism, this has been no mean accomplishment.

In Europe, for example, the Cold War has been characterized by a certain amount of symmetry in the bipolar competition for influence, and a clearly demarcated boundary—the Iron Curtain, in the familiar phrase—between antagonists. It was in response to the Communization of Eastern Europe that the United States formulated its containment policy, which announced America's intention to hold the line against what was viewed as nearly unlimited Soviet expansionism, but not to act offensively against the Communists to remove them from areas in which they were already established. In spite of frequent rhetoric, especially during the Eisenhower administration, that sounded as if a rollback of Soviet power was America's goal, the United States has adhered scrupulously to the defensive, hold-the-line stance in Europe. When unrest in Eastern Europe with Soviet domination has reached crisis proportions—as in Hungary in 1956 and in Czechoslovakia in 1968—the West has made no attempt to prevent Moscow from using force to bring her allies back into the Soviet fold.

In contrast, the boundaries of the Cold War in Asia have never been so clear-cut. At least two factors account for the difference. First, with the triumph of Communist forces in mainland China in 1949, a third important actor entered the Asian contest and, in doing so, virtually eliminated the possibilities for a symmetrical competitive balance such as has existed in Europe. (The United States, it is true, was long inclined to discount the independence of Peking from Moscow's influence and, hence, to regard the Cold War in Asia as essentially bipolar too; this misperception itself undoubtedly contributed to the great ambiguity and complexity of the Asian struggle.) Second, as Hannah reminds us, the East-West competition in Asia became inextricably bound up with the anticolonial movement there. As a result, the United States has had great difficulty in distinguishing national liberation movements from pro-Communist uprisings.

Hannah concludes his sweep over Asian Cold War experiences, not surprisingly, by indicating the major arena of confrontation in which tolerable boundaries for coexistence have not yet been established. In Southeast Asia, thirty years of strife, involving the anticolonial struggle, the Chinese Communists, local rivalries, and fundamental Cold War hostilities, have yet to be resolved.

Since World War II, the Cold War has been the archetypal symbol of international politics. The term "Cold War" has been stretched to cover everything and depreciated by excessive and indiscriminate use until—like inflated money—it covers nothing. At one extreme, it has been used to force all manner of phenomena into a cataclysmic struggle between good and evil. At the other extreme, more recently, some observers have overcorrected, appearing to say that at best the Cold War was ideologically meaningless or irrelevant and, at worst, an instrument for the pursuit of sinister ulterior purposes.

As we approach the end of it, it is clear that the Cold War was neither of these but rather a complex amalgam of ingredients in varying proportions in different areas. The term was first used in Europe to describe the confrontation between Soviet Communist power and Western non-Communist power, in a controlled framework where all the elements of power could be used as counters but without exploding into military hostilities. The term stuck, and was simplistically extended around the world to cover any situation in which Communist and anti-Communist elements interested themselves competitively, despite the fact that many such situations bore little resemblance to the European prototype.

It may be too late to change the vocabulary, but it is useful to review the history. The phrase "boundaries of coexistence in Asia" does not unveil a new theory, but suggests two views which underlie this chapter. First, that we should distinguish those situations bordering directly on some Communist power from those occurring some distance away; second, that the Asian phenomena lumped under the term "Cold War" are parts of a prolonged many-layered process whereby the forces bearing on Asia, gravely unbalanced after World War II, have been gradually working toward equilibrium.

In Europe, the Cold War burst forth starkly as a confrontation between those who only lately had been allies. The locus of the cleavage was set by large Russian occupation armies and was dramatically engraved the "Iron Curtain" by Winston Churchill. The shock was deepened by the sudden realization that, contrary to the expectations fostered by Yalta, these Russian forces were being

NORMAN B. HANNAH is a career officer in the United States Foreign Service with a wide diplomatic experience in various parts of the globe. At present, he is U.S. Consul-General in Sydney, Australia.

used to establish satellites in the ancient countries of Eastern Europe.

The dichotomy of ideology, superimposed on this military division, deepened the wound further. The violation of the integrity of peoples sharing common cultural, religious, and ethnic heritages heightened outrage in the West. In short, everything, including Western response, conspired to etch the Cold War bifurcation on the minds of men as deeply as on the strategic, political, and social geography from the Baltic to the Aegean.

Not so in Asia. Apart from the northeast Asian lands lost by Japan, the role of Soviet forces outside their own territory was limited to Iran, from which they withdrew belatedly and under pressure. The Cold War developed in Asia piecemeal, in a series of different kinds of tests in various countries whose cultures and politics are separated from Western patterns by a conceptual gulf most difficult to bridge. The ideological confrontation so total in Europe was diluted and blurred by the colonial question in Asia. Nor did Asia provide a neatly circumscribed arena for a balanced military standoff. Whereas the vast bulks of the USSR and China abut directly on most of the smaller and weaker countries from Turkey to Korea, there was a breathtaking withdrawal of European imperial power from the southern rim of Asia, while the United States was on the opposite side of the world. Where the colonial withdrawal occurred early and amicably, as in the Philippines and India, the Cold War overtones were muted. In Indochina, where the colonial power resisted, the war of independence was exploited by the Communists, and the Cold War was intensified.

Another factor interwoven in the process has been underdevelopment, political, social, and military, as well as economic. The relationship of development to the Cold War has varied widely from country to country. In Indonesia, Russian exploitation of Sukarno's appetites led to heavy debt burdens for unproductive military equipment and to near bankruptcy. In Burma, after experimenting with aid from both sides, the government virtually cut off both, and turned in on itself in a new experiment in what amounts to negative economic growth. The almost total lack of political and economic development in Laos has seriously undermined its potentiality as a unified nation-state, as reflected by North Vietnamese domination of the eastern part, Chinese penetration of the northwest, and the neutral government's heavy dependence on aid from abroad, chiefly from the United States. The size and isolation of India and Pakistan, below the Hindu Kush and Himalayas, coupled with the interlocking relationship of their rivalry to the Sino-Soviet split, have made it possible for them to benefit from assistance from both sides in the Cold War without the same risks that affect others. Iran and Thailand, having never been colonized, hence lacking political inhibitions against alignment, have used the time purchased by their alignments to remedy many of the political and economic weaknesses they faced at the end of the war. The experience of Afghanistan, utilizing aid from both sides, despite its sensitive location, is an encouraging omen of the future possibility of expanded peaceful coexistence on the basis of neutrality where there is agreement on all sides. In the long term, these aspects of change are more significant than the bipolar Cold War competition, and are leading toward a new equilibrium. But the road to this equilibrium leads through the Cold War.

How did it happen that the European Cold War concept was extended so literally to Asia? One factor is that despite all the special Asian complexities, the issue was most often joined in a response to an actual expansionist move supported by the USSR and/or China. Another factor which seems to me to have received too little attention is the manner in which the Cold War started in the middle 1940s.

In one sense, the Cold Wars of both Europe and Asia began in 1944 in Greece, at the critical corner where the future north-south boundary of the European Cold War would later meet the east-west Asian boundary. In April, 1944, a Communist mutiny in the Greek navy signaled the commencement of the guerrilla war in which the Russians and Yugoslavs would provide external support to an assault on the Greek government which, in turn, was supported first by Britain and later by the United States. This early split between the wartime allies began the process by which the main political environment of the world changed from a division between the allies and the Axis powers to a cleavage between the Soviet orbit and those outside it. Once the issue was joined in Greece, it led eastward through Turkey and Iran to the subcontinent. The actual situations arising in this long sector were complex, differing in many ways from the stark showdown shaping up in Central Europe. This complexity, however, was obscured because the issue was joined in the form of a response to actual Soviet expansionist pressures. This is the essence of the Cold War, which erupted in Greece before it did in Central Europe.

Greece is in Europe, a member of NATO, occupying an anchor position in European defense. But its entry into the Cold War resembled the later Asian pattern more than it did the European. Unlike the countries to the north, Greece was not dragged into the Cold War by Russian occupation forces, but was liberated by the British as the Germans withdrew. In Greece, as in Asia, the war brought about a consolidation of massive Communist power to the north, followed by the withdrawal of European imperial power to the south, creating a need for some offsetting outside support, which was eventually provided under the Truman Doctrine.

Communist tactics in Greece resembled more closely the guerrilla-type "war of liberation" later so familiar in Southeast Asia, than the Red Army's brutally direct methods displayed in Czechoslovakia and Hungary. Greece presented internal problems of political, social, and economic underdevelopment, as did the countries of southern Asia. Finally, the security of an independent, non-Communist Greece both required, and was required by, the security of Turkey at the western end of Asia. The guerrilla attack on Greece was accompanied by overlapping Soviet pressures on Turkey and Iran. In 1945–46, Turkey was subjected to a Soviet effort to gain joint control with Turkey over the defense of the Bosporus, in effect superseding the regime existing since 1936 under the multilateral Convention of Montreux. In March, 1945, Moscow denounced its neutrality treaty with Turkey, and offered to negotiate a new one on condition that the convention be modified to give Russia what it wanted in the Bosporus, and that Turkey meet territorial demands on its eastern provinces of Kars and Ardahan. Simultaneously, Soviet Armenia and Azerbaijan launched propaganda campaigns supporting their desire to annex these areas. It was against this background that the Truman Doctrine was based on the indivisibility of Turkish and Greek security.

Next door in Iranian Azerbaijan, a more ominous scenario was working itself out. There the USSR was seeking to use its occupation forces in a manner similar to that used in Eastern Europe. Blocking Iranian access to the province, while organizing and arming an "autonomous" puppet regime, the Soviets held their forces in Azerbaijan two and a half months beyond the March 2, 1946, deadline imposed under their treaty with Iran and Britain.

That Azerbaijan was not detached from Iran, or the government in Tehran overthrown, resulted from an extraordinary series of circumstances. The crisis came too soon after the war to permit the USSR to use the full panoply of techniques it subsequently used in Europe. They were more sensitive then to international and UN pressure than they were four and a half years later in Korea; they were preoccupied in Europe, where they had not yet staged their Hungarian and Czech coups d'état; they were uncertain how far the United States would go militarily to support Iran—they had to act hastily. Under the klieg light of UN publicity and already overdue on the treaty-fixed deadline for withdrawal, they felt obliged to leave even though the puppet regime was not firmly entrenched and its army not tightly disciplined. Relying on this jerry-built "autonomous" structure, they departed, hoping its weaknesses would be offset by an Iranian government and army unable to pick up the challenge.

They were disappointed. The Iranian army entered Azerbaijan and within two days the puppet regime had dissolved, the leaders fleeing to Russia. Without a stronger reed than this to lean on in Iran, Moscow wisely chose not to intervene and accepted the inevitable, while shifting to a longer-range, more sophisticated political strategy.

An opportunity to apply such a strategy was not long in coming, and it nearly succeeded. In the early 1950s, the failure of Iranian Premier Mossadegh's government to make a postnationalization settlement with the Anglo-Iranian Oil Company shut off oil revenues and brought near bankruptcy. As Mossadegh became progressively isolated, he relied increasingly on the Iranian Communist party (Tudeh), which was receiving political, financial, propaganda, and organizational support from Russia. Nevertheless, in its new sophisticated posture, the Soviet government adopted a cautious official position and did not threaten direct intervention. At the very last moment, the Iranian Communists lost out through their own tactical error, which enabled pro-shah elements, supported by the army, to regain control of the streets of Tehran and to establish a new government, to which the United States promptly gave economic and military aid.

After losing out twice in Iran in less than ten years, the USSR has concentrated on cooperation with the existing government, and today enjoys good relations, even providing some development assistance. The case history of Iran illustrates how what is called the Cold War can lead, albeit circuitously and abrasively, to a new equilibrium. There were three stages: first, the direct military threat across a land frontier; second, a covert attempt to exploit an internal crisis by political means without military threats; and third, the present, more balanced relationship.

This was a multifaceted process running from Greece to Iran, not a single massive confrontation such as occurred in Central Europe. It included a proxy guerrilla war, diplomatic pressure on international agreements, incipient irredentism, the spawning of a puppet regime, UN pressure, and covert political operations, not to mention a tactical blunder for which we must occasionally thank the Communists. The result was to mark a well-defined political boundary along the southern edge of the Communist world. Although coinciding with the northern frontiers of Greece, Turkey, and Iran, it became a boundary with a new political significance because, under pressure, it had become a watershed between Communist and non-Communist nations.

Complex problems of culture, history, social and economic development, former imperial dependence, and continuing regional rivalries were obscured by the drama of unconcealed expansionist pressure from the USSR, halted and turned back with United States support. Because of this, attention has focused on the Baghdad Pact (later CENTO) as a manifestation of a United States–Soviet bipolar Cold War, whereas in fact it was more closely related to other regional problems. Turkey, convinced that the United States would take no initiative, went ahead on its own to stimulate a regional defense organization. The then government of Iraq sought support to strengthen itself relative to Egypt. The British sought a means of maintaining their role in Iraq and the Middle East. Pakistan sought regional support vis-à-vis India. Iran sought to bolster its position in the difficult post-Mossadegh period while it undertook major internal reforms. The United States never joined and sought to avoid an unnecessary provocation to the USSR.

The stabilization of this Greek-Turkish-Iranian boundary of coexistence has actually tended to limit the Cold War. There is no question that it could be crossed militarily. But the crossing would have to be calculated in terms of stakes and risks higher than the intrinsic cost of the crossing itself. More important, the result was to buy time until an amelioration of Soviet strategy came about in the name of coexistence under the aegis of Khrushchev.

One must not exaggerate. It is possible to vault such a frontier with political or economic weapons or to circumvent it with military ones. But pole-vaulting is different from a football line charge. There is a difference between power transmitted by remote control over an insulator and power exerted directly by land. Indeed, the existence of the insulator may make it safe for small states to risk involvement with a more powerful but distant force with which it would be foolhardy to dally were it next door. Thus, Egypt could risk a degree of involvement with the USSR which would have been unthinkable for Turkey, Iran, or Afghanistan.

Afghanistan provides an interesting example of how the Cold War can lead to a less abrasive pattern of coexistence. British withdrawal from India left Afghanistan without an effective counterpoise on the south to offset Russian power in the north. This imbalance was worsened by the appearance in the south of a larger more powerful Muslim state—Pakistan—in some ways more ominous for the Afghans than was the British raj. Feeling isolated and less developed than its neighbors, Afghanistan sought economic and military assistance from the United States. In the late 1940s and early 1950s, some economic help was given, but military aid was refused, to avoid provoking a Cold War competition with Russia. This refusal, coinciding with our favorable response to a similar request from Pakistan, which also joined SEATO, caused the Afghans to risk heavy dependence for both military and economic aid on Russia, which was not as shy as we were about risking a Cold War competition in Afghanistan.

The Afghans considered the risk worth taking as the price of reducing their great disadvantage relative to their neighbors. They kept seeking United States aid, particularly in the education field, and belatedly (late 1950s and early 1960s) the United States responded with an economic program about half the size of Russia's. Germany also became a significant source of aid. The Afghans have sought to prevent conflicts among the programs. In recent years, relations with Pakistan have improved greatly, which is essential if Afghanistan would emulate Switzerland in maintaining neutrality while surrounded by three much larger nations. The large Russian programs have apparently not so far resulted in divisive political agitation in Afghanistan. Meanwhile, with concentration of aid, the Afghans hope to close the gap between themselves and their neighbors.

In this way the Cold War has led to a more stable balance, which, in effect, operates as an extension of the Middle Eastern boundary of coexistence, linking it with the mountain boundary which insulates the subcontinent. Afghan neutrality works because the country is internally unified and because its neighbors agree on this neutrality and do not violate it. This is a useful contrast to Laos, whose neutrality has not been so happy.

Before turning to Southeast Asia, however, something must be said of two other sectors—the Pacific Far East and the Indian subcontinent. In the former, the Chinese Communists had, by 1950, conquered the mainland. With more time available, the Russians had been more successful in fostering a Communist regime in partitioned North Korea than in the hasty Azerbaijan attempt. The spectacle of both the USSR and China supporting an outright armed attack by North Korea could not have been better calculated to engrave the image of polarization. This impression was heightened by contrast with the rather low posture adopted by the United States in the preceding year. In 1949, we had retained consular representation in the Communist-ruled cities of Mukden, Peking, and Shanghai in a transparent experiment in maintaining relations with the Communist regime. Money appropriated for military assistance to Nationalist China was used elsewhere. A few months before the North Korean attack, we had publicly excluded Korea from the perimeter of United States essential interests.

Our response to the North Korean attack had to be supported on its flank in Okinawa and Taiwan. One wonders what would have happened to Taiwan in the chaos of the flight from the mainland if the Korean attack had not thrown down a gauntlet that had to be picked up all the way from the Sea of Japan to the South China Sea. The Cold War in the Pacific Far East was "hot" and even more polarized than in Europe because it was born of violent aggression. By contrast, the progressive definition of a political watershed in the Middle East was a delicate pas de deux.

Nevertheless, it resembled the Middle East sector in drawing a line which established a kind of standoff running from the 38th parallel in Korea through the Formosa Strait and South China Sea, west of the Philippines to mainland Southeast Asia. Here, as elsewhere, this is the essence of the Cold War—it has drawn lines which, even if not bridged by goodwill, provide a practical rough-and-ready instrument for sorting out competing interests, while it buys time until changing circumstances create new opportunities for further amelioration. This is illustrated by recent events in Sino-American relations, including President Nixon's Peking visit and the cooling of the Taiwan tension.

"Coexistence" has sometimes been misrepresented as the opposite of "Cold War," but in fact it is the fruit of successfully waged Cold War. "Coexistence" is not the same as "coalition." It does not mean the dissolving of ideological differences or the abandonment of national interests or ambitions. When two opposing sides reach the stage at which they decide to put certain differences provisionally "on ice," they can implement this decision in the form of a geographical line defining the limits of their respective control. They then may be said to coexist. They maintain their ideological differences, national interests, and ambitions. They do not sink their differences in a coalition of ideological opposites. Such coalitions fail, as has been shown many times, most recently in Laos, post-Geneva, 1962. As Khrushchev used to emphasize, coexistence is no love feast. It is a hard row to hoe, abrasive and sometimes bristling, but it provides an operational rule of thumb— "your side, my side"—for avoiding conflicts. This is not the millennium, but it is better than either World War III or capitulation. In a way, coexistence and Cold War are opposite sides of the same coin.

The Indian subcontinent has played a special role—special because, unlike in the Middle East, Pacific Far East, and Southeast Asia, the standoff line in the subcontinent was not defined primarily by direct confrontation. There, an effective boundary of coexistence was provided by nature in the form of the ocean on the south and the most forbidding mountain range in the world on the north. The subcontinent was fortunate to have this element of insulation, given the grievous internal divisions which were uncovered when the British imperial tide withdrew. Or, stated conversely, perhaps this very insulation created a lee in the Cold War which allowed other local problems to rise to the surface. It is hardly necessary to do more than mention Kashmir, the Indo-

Pakistan war and detachment of Bangladesh, the instability of the North-West Frontier between Afghanistan and Pakistan, the Naga agitation in eastern India, and the arm's-length relationship with Burma turned in on itself. Perhaps the reduction of external pressure by topographical insulation makes these regional problems less tractable because of the reduced need to compromise so as to find strength in unity against an external threat. Interestingly, only the Sino-Indian war of 1962 came even a small way toward generating a real sense of shared interest between India and Pakistan.

The impact of the Cold War in the subcontinent has accordingly been less bipolar and more complex than elsewhere. As the largest and most secure of the south Asian countries, India has been able to pursue a more consistent course, continuously neutralist, despite internal and regional problems. The Communists are sometimes their own worst enemy, and, as has sometimes happened elsewhere, Communist behavior has periodically subjected India to a dash of cold water, reviving her healthy respect for the dangers of exploitation. For example, the Indian Communist party's agitation after the war and the later experience of Kerala put Indians on their guard domestically. The Chinese take-over of Tibet and the Sino-Indian border war of 1962 served to engrave the northern boundary more deeply, one hopes. The Chinese-Pakistani relationship also has reminded India that opportunism is a greater factor than Pancha Sila is in the politics of Peking.

Pakistan, smaller than India, has had a harder time. Frustrated by partition, the intractability of the Kashmir problem, harassment in the tribal areas, and noting neutral India's progress in dealing with the USSR and China, Pakistan sought, in the 1950s, to bolster its position by seeking ties outside the subcontinent. This meant not only the United States but linkages with the Middle East and Southeast Asia through affiliation with the Baghdad Pact and SEATO.

These ties did not solve Pakistan's subcontinental problems. SEATO became increasingly absorbed with the distant problems of Thailand and Indochina. The United States did not join CENTO (the Baghdad Pact without Baghdad), and as quiescence spread along the Greek-Turkish-Iranian boundary, CENTO focused increasingly on economic projects. Accordingly, these alliances gradually took second place in Pakistan to an effort to compete with India in direct relationships with Russia and China. In retrospect, it would appear that for Pakistan the SEATO-CENTO association was not a mistake but rather a phase. In fact, these alignments may have played an important role in assisting Pakistan to bridge a difficult period. Now, with West and East Pakistan definitely divorced, each can concentrate its attentions on its natural neighbors—to the west or the east, respectively. There will be strains in the process of readjustment, but the relative insulation provided by the mountainous boundary of coexistence against direct Soviet or Chinese interference (coupled with the Sino-Soviet standoff) will continue to provide a lee behind which to resolve regional problems.

In sum, since nature has provided the equivalent of a boundary of coexistence, the Cold War has not been a dominating archetype in the subcontinent but a peripheral factor. As the United States as well as SEATO and CENTO have lowered their postures in recent years, the Cold War has receded, to be replaced by the Sino-Soviet split. There has been much speculation on the alleged steadying effect the Sino-Soviet standoff might have on many situations such as Southeast Asia, but India and Pakistan are better situated than any others to benefit from it. The size and relative geographic insulation of India and Pakistan, combined with their strategic relationships to Russia and China, make possible an interesting four-handed game, with shifting partnerships.

Last and most intractable of all has been the definition of a boundary of coexistence in Southeast Asia. Actually, there has been a boundary ready-made and sanctified in international agreements. It would include the northeastern frontier of Burma, a neutral Laos (Geneva Accords of 1962) and the Vietnam demilitarized zone (Geneva Accords of 1954). Such a boundary would have much in common with similar boundaries elsewhere—for example, Germany and Korea. Two international agreements have defined such a boundary and established machinery for its enforcement, but to no avail. This is what the Vietnam war was all about.

What was lacking? The missing ingredient was a mutual understanding, a real meeting of the minds as to the possibility and location of a line along which there could be coexistence. Failing an early agreement between North and South Vietnam leading to reunification after 1954, the 17th parallel might have been an instrument for at least preventing war, as did the ceasefire line in Korea and the zonal boundary of East Germany. This would have to have been predicated on a mutual understanding—which did not exist—that in the interest of peace, unification would have to be sought gradually, in a longer period of time and in the context of future historical political change. We see such a process well started in Germany and Korea. A Cold War line need not be permanent, but can develop into a boundary of coexistence and eventually provide a foundation for moves toward reunification.

Both Laos and Cambodia were neutralized under the Geneva Accords of 1954, and a special statute for Laos was negotiated in 1962. Juristically, the latter was a model of precision and balance, predicated on an internal troika coalition (a misapplication of coexistence), a neutrality recognized by all the great powers, the former metropolitan power, all Laos's neighbors, the leaders of both sides in the Cold War, both participants in the Sino-Soviet split, and neutral India. The International Control Commission had one Communist, one anti-Communist, and neutral India as chairmen. It reported to the cochairmen, Britain and Russia. The formula had all the symmetry of a Gothic arch.

The result is well known. North Vietnam retained some six thousand military in Laos, and after eight months the Pathet Lao withdrew from the coalition and set up their own administration in Khang Khay under protection of the North Vietnamese. In eastern Laos, a footpath called the Ho Chi Minh Trail was developed into a major corridor for attack down which nearly a million soldiers have passed en route to South Vietnam.

Three points are important. First, there was no real agreement that Laos should be neutral. Although Hanoi and Peking signed the Geneva Accords, there was evidently no meeting of the minds. It has been fashionable to explain that the problem of Laos was related to Vietnam, and would not be solved until the problem of Vietnam was solved. But if so, then what was the purpose of the Geneva Accords? Evidently, Hanoi signed on the unstated premise that the accords would not seriously interfere with their use of the routes through eastern Laos. The USSR may well have favored a neutral Laos, as Khrushchev told President Kennedy, but was unable to induce North Vietnamese and Chinese agreement. This lesson is that a small landlocked buffer state must depend on a real meeting of the minds among its neighbors, as in Switzerland and Afghanistan.

Second, the Communist side was not ready for a full-scale genuine coalition in Laos. Given Pathet Lao dependence on Hanoi, it is not surprising that they withdrew from the coalition. However, the failure of coalitions, including Communist ones, has assumed a familiar pattern around the world for the past fifty years. This bears on the question of what forms of coexistence are possible. Considerable success has been had with coexistence on the basis of lines which separate the two sides. No particular line is valid in perpetuity but, for the time being, it needs only to be accepted tacitly on the understanding that any effort to change it will be sought only gradually in the context of future political change—not immediately through the use of military force. We see this kind of line all the way from Stettin to India. In a sense, the Cold War was the process by which this equilibrium was worked out while simultaneously the Soviet policy was being ameliorated and the United States and USSR moved toward negotiation on broader issues. But nowhere along this line has coexistence been based on a successfully imposed coalition regime.*

The lesson here is that the concept of coexistence has not progressed far enough in Communist theory to admit of accepting a minority position in a government indefinitely, because this would imply the abandonment of ideological purity and political expansion as well as the acceptance of heresy. This is the advantage of coexistence on a "your side, my side" basis. The Communists can tacitly agree to live and let live if not obliged to compromise their political principles as they would be required to do in a genuine coalition.

The third point is that this lesson is an important point in considering what the prospects would be for an imposed coalition in South Vietnam. This does not exclude the possibility that a stabilized boundary of coexistence in Vietnam might eventually create the conditions for coalition as well as reunification.

As for Cambodia, although not saddled with a coalition government, its neutrality came under the same threat that destroyed Laos's neutrality—the necessity for North Vietnam to use Cambodian territory to pursue its war against South Vietnam. Prince Sihanouk's problem was that while he wanted to preserve neutrality, he was convinced of the inevitability of a Communist victory

---

* Austria was neutralized in 1955, but not on the basis of an internal political coalition.

and ultimate Chinese domination of the whole region. Trimming his sails to this prospect, he allowed Hanoi, bit by bit to use ever greater parts of his eastern provinces. Finally, he tried to call a halt in the autumn of 1969, but it was too late. He had lost control of the game. First, Hanoi refused to meet his requests, and then his own government deposed him. Neutrality, to be effective, must be integral and thorough, not an umbrella for a more devious, less neutral position.

What has been needed all along is to focus the military aspects of the conflict on a geographical line which could become an extension of the "your side, my side" frontier which has been established from the Baltic to Southeast Asia and in Korea. Progress was made toward this by the military actions in Cambodia in 1970 and in Laos in 1971, both of which brought the reality of the external aggression from the north out into the open and cleared the way for military operations to oppose that aggression at the border.

Since 1969, the progressive withdrawal of United States ground forces has served further to rectify the alignment of the conflict, substituting a clear pattern of forces and responsibilities for the old, ambiguous miasma of counterinsurgency. We took our ground forces out of the internal role, which properly belongs to the South Vietnamese, and concentrated our military effort on stopping the external aggression.

But it was Hanoi that put the finishing touch on this rectification by launching the April 1, 1972, offensive which for a while created a true more or less conventional front below the DMZ and at the same time provided the occasion for an effective aerial and naval line of interdiction between North Vietnam and its principal external suppliers.

With patterns of war thus straightened out to conform more nearly to the Cold War territorial axis, the president's proposal of a cease-fire led to the negotiations of October, 1972, and eventually to the agreement signed later in Paris. If this agreement fills in the final sector in the long Eurasian Cold War frontier, the way will be open for the fading of the Cold War in Indochina into coexistence, just as it has faded elsewhere in Europe and the Pacific Far East.

It may be objected that this view of the process overemphasizes geographical lines to the exclusion of deeper political and social processes. It might be desirable of course to eliminate or solve all the deep issues which agitate and divide the world, but it strikes me that we, like people since the beginning of time, have to work at our problems little by little, not rejecting half a loaf simply because it is not a whole loaf. If some tacitly accepted lines can be established—as they have been in many areas—which reduce the chance of war and limit the parameters of international competition, then that is progress. Indeed, it is just this kind of insulation that many countries need in order to devote themselves to the deeper problems they face. International politics is at best a rough kind of process for managing many disparate forces and problems—not necessarily solving them but keeping them within certain bounds until they may be solved or, more likely, until they fade away, having been replaced by other forces and other problems.

It is in this gross sense that despite everything, the Cold War is a manifestation of a deeper process of reorientation, working toward a new equilibrium. Coexistence is a way station, not the end. There is no end. As the Cold War changes into coexistence, so the new equilibrium will be followed by a new metamorphosis with its own problems.

Barton J. Bernstein

6

The Cuban Missile Crisis

EDITORS' NOTE. For a few days in October, 1962, the world seemed poised on the brink of a nuclear apocalypse. The president of the United States had threatened to take direct military action against the Soviet Union in the event that the Russians refused to accede to his demand to dismantle the missile bases they were then installing in Cuba. Once the Soviets did agree to the president's terms, a sigh of collective relief swept over the world, and postmortem analyses of the crisis began. Almost immediately, the Cuban missile crisis was perceived as a major landmark or turning point in the Cold War—if only because of its magnitude—although any determination of what it proved or did not prove still remains very much in dispute.

At the core of contention, myriad knotty problems await resolution. Historian Barton Bernstein deals with some of these in the following chapter. In addition to the vast quantity of materials already published on the crisis, which have mounted steadily as each participant in those October days has told his version, Professor Bernstein draws on documentary sources only recently made available by the Department of State and the John F. Kennedy Library.

Among the many questions concerning the missile crisis which have engaged the attention of analysts in the past decade are those concerning the motivations of the protagonists in the crisis. Why, it has often been asked, did the Soviet Union risk the emplacement of "offensive" missiles on an island ninety miles from Florida? And why, in turn, did the United States choose to respond in the dramatic and risky way it did? As to the Soviet decision, Bernstein describes a variety of possible factors: he views Premier Khrushchev's decision to place the missiles as a relatively cheap attempt to satisfy militarists at home and Maoists abroad by slightly increasing Soviet nuclear flexibility while seeming to support a revolutionary regime.

On the American side, Bernstein finds the motives beneath the Kennedy administration's policies equally complex—but more disturbing. In his quarantine speech of October 22, President Kennedy argued that the Soviet moves were a clandestine attempt to upset the nuclear balance of power, by providing Russia with offensive weapons in the Americas. In other words, he implied that the Soviets had failed to adhere to the only acceptable rules by which nuclear politics could be played, which were designed to prevent any sudden imbalance between the nuclear actors. It was on these grounds that the president rationalized the uncompromising American response. Yet, as Professor Bernstein seeks to demonstrate, the president's statement was more than a little misleading, and deliberately so, for "the Soviet missiles in Cuba . . . did not offset American superiority. Nor did the Cuban missiles make a Soviet first strike more likely."

If this was the case, then the reasons for the United States response were more deceptive than they generally appeared to Americans at the time. Bernstein adduces three sets of factors as having been principally responsible for the American position. His analysis of these suggests that the "courage" and "determination" of American policy makers, usually viewed in the abstract as fine and admirable qualities, can be taken quite differently. Bernstein's argument, for example—that United States domestic pressures contributed to the administration's taking a hard line with the Kremlin—is reminiscent of Walter LaFeber's discussion of the pressures that prompted Dean Acheson and Harry Truman to plunge across the 38th parallel in Korea twelve years earlier. Both Bernstein and LaFeber question in a most fundamental way what they see as a general characteristic of American foreign policy in the Cold War—an acquired habit in which policy makers take more extreme and dangerous action than an objective analysis of the situation seems to require.

Whatever forces pushed or pulled the United States and the Soviet Union to that 1962 precipice, something might also be said, before turning to Professor Bernstein's essay, about what happened after they drew back. At the most obvious, general level, the missile crisis demonstrated in the most dramatic terms imaginable the enormous dangers inherent in a bipolar competition for power whose stability was premised ultimately upon the threat of nuclear deterrence. The paradox of such a premise, long understood in theory, was awesomely revealed in practice: it might be necessary to destroy what each country sought to protect in order to prove their determination to protect those things. Such a revelation, in and of itself, no doubt encouraged much soul-searching and a new determination in many quarters to try to prevent the recurrence of conditions that could lead to such a confrontation again. Thus it is plausible on a number of counts to trace the greater Soviet-American detente of recent years directly to the missile crisis. The "hot line" linking Washington and Moscow, the limited Test Ban Treaty, the Nonproliferation Treaty, and the Outer Space Treaty—all were generated in the aftermath of the crisis as attempts to defuse, albeit in very limited ways, certain areas of at least tangential relevance to the nuclear balance of terror. And it would be possible to argue that the 1972 Moscow summit's nuclear arms limitation agreement represents a continuation of a decade's momentum.

But there is another side of this coin as well. As Richard J. Barnet argues in a subsequent chapter, expenditures for armaments took a quantum leap in the Soviet Union and the United States after the missile crisis, and the upward spiral continues to the present day. How can this be explained in light of the tendency of the superpowers to cooperate more fully in some areas since 1962? One explanation argues that Premier Khrushchev's handling of the missile crisis lost him a crucial struggle with the militarists in his own government. His eventual demise threw power to these very same domestic rivals, and the larger military budgets which they had been advocating became a reality. In other words, not only improvements but also more complex problems in the relationship of the United States and the Soviet Union followed the Cuban missile crisis.

More than a decade has passed since that eventful October, 1962, when the two great powers approached the abyss of nuclear destruction while the citizens of most nations fearfully awaited the resolution of the conflict. It was a time, as Khrushchev later said, "when the smell of burning hung in the air."[1] Had there been nuclear war, probably a hundred million Americans and a hundred million Russians, as well as millions of Europeans and Latin Americans, would have been "incinerated"—to use Dean Rusk's choice word.[2] Previous wars and national disasters, by contrast, would have seemed insignificant—like a death in the family compared to genocide. At the time, President John F. Kennedy placed the probability of disaster at "somewhere between one out of three and even."[3] The potential tragedy alone—the capacity of a government or two to kill so many—renders the events awesome and certainly demanding of analysis.

Even now, after some memoirs and inside reports as well as published surmises and conjectures,[4] many facts are still in dispute, most sources are still closed, and the basic questions remain unsolved: Why did the Soviets place missiles in Cuba? Did Khrushchev intend to challenge Kennedy? Why did the Soviets back down? Did the missiles constitute an imminent military threat to the United States? Did domestic and international concerns influence Kennedy's choice of tactics? Were Kennedy's tactics essential to protecting American security?

It was on Sunday, October 14, that an American U-2 reconnaissance plane photographed the uncamouflaged sites of medium-range missiles (MRBM) in Cuba. The next day the rolls of film were processed, and that evening some of the president's top Washington advisers learned of the news. McGeorge Bundy, the president's special assistant for national security affairs, concluding that the president would need his sleep and that official action required more intelligence work, delayed until the following morning (Tuesday) to inform the president.[5]

For seven days, the crisis advisers—later known as the Ex Comm (Executive Committee of the National Security Coun-

BARTON BERNSTEIN, Associate Professor of History at Stanford University, has published widely on the subject of recent American foreign policy. He is perhaps best known for his editorship of *Towards a New Past: Dissenting Essays in American History.*

cil)—held numerous secret meetings while trying to conceal their feverish activity from the rest of Washington. Included within the group were those with a formal responsibility for national security as well as those whose duties were remote from this problem but whom the president respected.[6] In their meetings, seldom attended by the secretary of state and only sometimes by the president, who continued his campaigning, comparative freedom and openness prevailed—in contrast to the deliberations leading to the debacle at the Bay of Pigs. The discussions ranged broadly, with various participants taking different positions at different times. The range of possible tactics (even allowing for plausible combinations) was quite narrow: private negotiations with Khrushchev without a public announcement of the presence of the missiles; a public announcement and then negotiations in the United Nations or between the two states; an invasion and air strike; a surgical air strike against the missiles; a quarantine or blockade; or a private approach to Castro.

Almost from the first, the president made it clear that doing nothing was unacceptable. He "could not accept what the Russians had done," his brother Robert Kennedy later explained. "There were those, although they were a small minority," recalled Robert Kennedy, "who felt that the missiles did not alter the balance of power and therefore necessitated no action," but they soon backed away from that position—partly under the subtle pressure from the president. The president, while not wanting to inhibit what he regarded as useful discussion, had in effect given the committee a mandate: devise a strategy for removing the missiles.[7]

The joint chiefs (JCS) favored an invasion, seizing upon the missiles to achieve what the Bay of Pigs had not: the elimination of Castro's government. A blockade, they stressed, would not be effective because it would not force withdrawal of the missiles. A surgical air strike was ruled out on military grounds: it could not be simply surgical, for the JCS considered the risks unacceptable, and therefore wanted to extend the operation to include bombing air fields, surface-to-air missles (SAMs), and ammunition dumps. Later the JCS, Paul Nitze, and Dean Acheson lined up in favor of an air strike. At a critical juncture, when a surprise air strike against the missiles was being warmly endorsed, Robert Kennedy, the president's closest adviser, indignantly declared that his brother would not go down in history as another Tojo. America's moral position in the world would be destroyed, he contended. A technical impediment soon appeared to buttress his moral objections: an air strike might miss some missiles and therefore, like the blockade, would not accomplish the task of promptly removing the missiles; moreover, Cubans, as well as Soviets tending the missiles, would die. To many it seemed that such a disaster might provoke a strong Soviet response. While most members of the Ex Comm were prepared to risk war to remove the missiles, they sought to devise tactics which in the early stages would be less dangerous than an air strike or an invasion.[8]

By Thursday evening, the president declared his tentative choice: a quarantine. According to its advocates in the Ex Comm, the quarantine would be a bold, threatening act, but it would be less dangerous than war, and in theory would allow the United States to control the pattern of escalation by using force and the threat of force in gradual stages—while keeping open the options of an invasion or air attack. On Friday, while the president was again away campaigning, the advisers continued to discuss the possibilities and perils; once more they considered an invasion or air strike, but, under pressure from Robert Kennedy, Theodore Sorensen, Robert McNamara, and Roswell Gilpatric, moved back to a quarantine and a discussion of the details. The first three, the president's most trusted advisers in the group, triumphed temporarily. On Saturday, October 20, the fifth day of intensive and intense meetings, after the Ex Comm reached tentative agreement on a quarantine, the president returned hurriedly to Washington from the campaign trail, with his press secretary explaining that Kennedy had an "upper respiratory infection" and a slight fever. On Saturday, and again on Sunday, the debate on tactics was renewed, each time with the bulk of opinion renewing support for the quarantine.[9]

On Monday, the administration released the news of missiles in Cuba. Calling in high-ranking congressmen of both parties, Kennedy informed them privately of the missiles in Cuba and of his proposed tactics—which most, including Senator J. William Fulbright, opponent of the Bay of Pigs invasion, considered too weak. On that same day, American officials were scurrying around Washington and the world—with even Dean Acheson journeying to France to inform de Gaulle of the problem and of Kennedy's action.[10]

On Monday evening, October 22, on a nationwide broadcast, the president delivered his speech announcing the presence of Soviet missiles in Cuba and the establishment of a quarantine (blockade) of the island. He emphasized a number of themes: that the missiles were emplaced clandestinely; that the Soviets had lied when promising not to take such actions; that the missiles upset the balance of power; and that their purpose could be "none other than to provide a nuclear-strike capability against the Western Hemisphere," thereby emphasizing the dangers to Latin America and implying that the United States would also be endangered.[11]

In fact, since there was no camouflage, the missiles were not emplaced clandestinely. Second, though the president accused the Soviets of lying when they stated that the armaments sent to Cuba were "designed exclusively for defensive purposes," it is clear that the Kennedy administration's own distinctions between offensive and defensive weaponry were arbitrary, unilateral, and somewhat self-righteous. After all, when is a missile offensive, and when is it defensive? For America, it turned out, her missiles in Turkey were defensive, but Russia's missiles in Cuba were offensive. The distinction, at least for the United States, did not always seem to rest upon the nature of the weapon—all surface-to-surface missiles can be used for aggression—but sometimes upon the administration's presumptions about the intention of the possessor. To other interpreters, however, a nation's likely intention is judged, and also influenced, by its overall strategic capabilities, as well as those of its potential adversary. The distinction employed by the United States was never accepted by the Soviets, who continued throughout the crisis, as before, to call the weapons in Cuba defensive. Also, Kennedy wrongly cited a Soviet statement to establish that the Soviets had promised not to place missiles on foreign soil, particularly in Cuba. What the Soviets had actually said was more limited: there was "no need" to place missiles outside the Soviet Union in order to maintain a second-strike capacity. These Soviet statements were not false; perhaps, given possible Soviet judgments of American knowledge and understanding, the statements were not even deceitful.[12]

Kennedy also unfolded his plans: a quarantine on all "offensive" military equipment, with the American navy starting at 2 P.M. (Greenwich time) on Wednesday searching all ships and turning back those carrying such equipment. He also warned that "further action will be justified" if "offensive military preparations continue" and that there would be a "full retaliatory response upon the Soviet Union" if any missiles were launched from Cuba against any country in the Western Hemisphere. In addition, the United States reinforced the naval base at Guantánamo, Cuba, evacuated the civilian personnel, and called for action by an emergency meeting of the UN Security Council and by the Council of the Organization of American States.[13]

While UN Ambassador Adlai Stevenson confronted the Soviets at the Security Council and Dean Rusk won unanimous support for American policy at the OAS,[14] the administration waited uneasily for the Soviet response. In the first days, high-ranking Soviet officials in the United States—Valerian Zorin, Ambassador to the UN, and Anastas Mikoyan, Deputy Premier, perhaps themselves uninformed—denied the presence of missiles in Cuba even after Khrushchev had privately admitted their presence.[15] To anxious Ex Comm members, many of the Soviet actions were troubling, perhaps even portending war. On Tuesday, Anotoly Dobrynin, Soviet Ambassador to the United States, asserted privately that he knew of no orders for Soviet ships to turn back[16]; a high-ranking Soviet general at a Washington party said that Soviet ships would defy the blockade; and a press officer of the Soviet UN delegation told his American counterpart: "This could be our last conversation. New York will be blown up tomorrow by Soviet nuclear weapons."[17] Thirteen hours after Kennedy's speech, a more official Soviet response (from *Tass*) condemned the United States for "sabre rattling" and "piratical actions," warned Kennedy that he was "playing with fire," and declared that Russia "would not use nuclear weapons against the United States unless aggression is committed."[18] In a private letter an hour later, Khrushchev was less sharp. Though warning that the quarantine "would lead to catastrophic consequences for peace," he did not explicitly threaten to test the quarantine.[18a] The question of whether the Soviets would respect the quarantine could not be answered until Wednesday.

That morning the quarantine went into effect, and it looked for a few anxious hours as if the Soviet ships headed to Cuba would test the quarantine. While awaiting the news, the president told his brother, "It looks really mean, doesn't it? But then, really, there was no other choice. If they get this mean on this one in our part of the world, what will they do on the next?" The brothers agreed that the president had not had a choice, and, if he had not acted, he "would have been impeached." While they waited, the situation became more tense when they learned that a Soviet submarine had joined the two leading freighters, and the JCS was predicting a shoot-out at sea. "These few minutes were the time of gravest concern for the President," his brother later wrote. "We had come to the time of fatal decision," Robert Kennedy thought. But then, sudden good news arrived: the six Soviet ships nearest the quarantine line had stopped dead, and the navy soon reported that the other fourteen had also stopped or turned around.[18b] The events of that morning might have seemed even more menacing, and the subsequent relief greater, if policymakers had then known that Khrushchev, just a few hours before, had told William Knox, vice-president of Westinghouse who was visiting in Moscow, that if American ships stopped any Soviet ships, the Soviets would sink the American ships—which, he warned, would mean World War III.[19]

By the afternoon, policymakers had some reason for guarded hope. Khrushchev had obviously decided not to challenge the blockade that day, and perhaps he was preparing to accede. In the afternoon, he also replied to Bertrand Russell's letter by calling for a summit meeting and peace and promising not to take any "reckless" actions. But there was also reason for continuing fear. Khrushchev warned "that our efforts may prove insufficient," for if the United States insisted upon carrying out its program of "piratic actions . . . , we shall have to resort to means of defense against an aggressor. . . ." He went on to say, "We have no other way out. It is well known that if one tries to mollify a robber by giving him at first one's purse, then one's coat, etc., the robber will not become more merciful, will not stop robbing . . . Therefore it is necessary to curb the highwayman. . . ."[20] The message implied that he would not respect the quarantine. In the evening, policymakers received a private communication that restated the same themes more forcefully. Khrushchev branded the quarantine "outright banditry," warned Kennedy that the president was pushing mankind "towards the abyss of world missile-nuclear war," and indicated that the Soviet ships would not accede to the quarantine. If the United States tried to halt the Soviet ships, "we will then be forced . . . to take the measures which we deem necessary and adequate in order to protect our rights."[20a]

Despite the premier's strong language in that late-evening message, the possibility of avoiding a naval confrontation improved. On Thursday, the Soviets eagerly accepted Secretary-General U Thant's proposal that the Soviets suspend arms shipments to Cuba and that the United States suspend the quarantine in order to allow negotiations.[21] (The United States rejected this proposal, as Arthur Schlesinger explains, because "it equated aggression and the response," did not deal with the missiles in Cuba, allowed work on them to continue, and neglected provisions for inspection.[22] Kennedy responded that the crisis was "created by the secret introduction of offensive missiles into Cuba and the answer lies in the removal of such weapons."[23]) While insisting on removal of the missiles and refusing to relax the quarantine, Kennedy had also let a Soviet tanker through the blockade, and hoped to delay having the American navy board any ship until Khrushchev "had more time to consider."[24]

On Thursday, about a dozen Soviet ships turned back, thereby avoiding the blockade. So far, despite the Soviet respect for the quarantine, the main United States problem was unsolved: the MRBM missiles were in Cuba, and the work on them continued; some were already operational, and all were expected to be ready by Sunday.[25] The quarantine, while devised to avoid a shooting confrontation and reckless escalation, was inadequate itself as a tactic for removing the missiles. Unless the Soviets soon retreated and agreed to withdraw the missiles, the president was prepared to attack Cuba. Given his definition of the challenge and the appropriate response, the course of events would soon seem inevitable, and the careful crisis management would lead the nation to (undeclared) war against Cuba, and perhaps to nuclear war.

But on Friday, there were new rays of hope. That afternoon, John Scali, a newsman for the American Broadcasting Company, was invited to a meeting which Aleksander Fomin, the top Soviet intelligence officer in the United States, who had his own channels of communication to Khrushchev. Fomin offered a possible deal: removal of the so-called offensive weapons; United Nations verification of their removal; and a Soviet promise not to restore the weapons. In return, the United States was to issue a public pledge not to invade Cuba. Scali, reporting first to Roger Hilsman, State Department director of intelligence, and then to Dean Rusk, who discussed the matter with other members of the Ex Comm, was instructed to inform Fomin that the "highest levels" in the government were interested in the bargain but that time was short.[26]

Fomin, seeming pleased by the news after being assured that the "very highest" people were favorably disposed, then tried to raise the terms by suggesting inspection of the bases in Florida as an additional requirement for an agreement. Scali strongly objected, arguing lamely that the situations were not comparable since American missiles were not aimed at Cuba, and warned that Kennedy would probably reject this additional proposal. He also stressed the need for speed—lest there be "a disaster for Cuba, for the Soviet Union, and for the world." ("John," Rusk told Scali in the characteristic rhetoric of the New Frontier, "remember when you report this that eyeball to eyeball, they blinked first.")[27] While Scali was conferring with Fomin that evening, the United States was receiving the so-called first Khrushchev message—described variously as excited and even rambling—which suggested (but did not offer explicitly) a similar bargain.[28] Together, the premier's message and Fomin's offer seemed to be part of a strategy of accommodation in crisis. To most of the Ex Comm, the suggested bargain seemed attractive, though Acheson and apparently Robert Lovett, two of Truman's former cabinet members, felt that the United States should put more pressure on Khrushchev and force more concessions.[29]

On Saturday, when the Ex Comm convened to draft a reply to the first Khrushchev message, the optimism of the night before quickly collapsed. Robert Kennedy announced that the FBI reported that Russian officials in New York were destroying sensitive documents, thereby suggesting that hostilities might be imminent. Also, a Soviet ship had left the convoy outside the quarantine line and was headed to Cuba, apparently to test American determination. During the discussions, the Ex Comm also learned that the crisis had claimed its first victim: the pilot of a U-2 reconnaissance plane reporting on the missile sites in Cuba had been shot down. Worse yet, the committee confronted a more serious problem: there was another letter from Khrushchev, this time apparently a committee effort, which increased the terms of the bargain by also demanding withdrawal of American missiles from Turkey in return for removal of Soviet missiles from Cuba.[30]

"It was the blackest hour of the crisis," reports Hilsman.[31] This was the time, participants later admitted, when the nations were closest to war. Kennedy, fearing rash action or errors by men in the field, ordered all atomic missiles defused.[32] The committee faced two problems—how to respond to the pilot's death, and to the second note. The Ex Comm had decided earlier that the United States would bomb the offending antiaircraft SAM site if a U-2 was shot down, and that all the SAMs would be destroyed if a second U-2 was shot down. At first, the Ex Comm concluded that there would have to be an air strike on the Cuban surface-to-air missiles at dawn the next day (Sunday) in order to allow continued U-2 surveillance without risk to American pilots. In considering the second Soviet note, the president, while annoyed that the missiles in Turkey had not been removed months before as he had directed, was unwilling to offer them explicitly as part of the bargain, even though there were fears in the Ex Comm that the military was taking over in the Soviet Union and that the new terms reflected their demands. "He obviously did not wish to order the withdrawal of missiles from Turkey under threat from the Soviet Union," explained Robert Kennedy, even though they were obsolete, useless, and provocative.[33] The president's brother hit upon a strategy for dealing with the seemingly contradictory letters. Why not, he suggested, ignore the second letter and try what was later called the "Trollope ploy"[34]—that is, like the heroine in Anthony Trollope's novels, accept the offer that was not explicitly made. Adopting this deft strategy, the administration sent a message accepting the conditions advanced explicitly only by Fomin: dismantling and removal of the "offensive" weapons, inspection, and a no-invasion pledge.

This strategy required giving the Soviets time for a response, and therefore the Ex Comm dropped plans for the surgical air strike against the SAMs the next morning. The president, at the end of the Saturday meeting, when the great powers seemed so near war, remarked that the crisis could "go either way."[35] The administration was acting on various fronts to emphasize the dangers and to warn the Soviet leadership of imminent American action if the offer was not accepted speedily. Already publicized news of the buildup of American troops in Florida continued, and the administration further dramatized the dangers. Scali, meeting with Fomin at Rusk's behest, had already branded the Soviet attempt to improve the bargain a "stinking double cross" and warned that time was running out.[36]

Attorney General Kennedy told the worried Soviet ambassador that the United States would launch an attack on Cuba by Tuesday if the Soviets did not agree by Sunday to remove the missiles. ("We all agreed . . . that if the Russians were ready to go to nuclear war over Cuba, they were ready to go to nuclear war, and that was that. So we might as well have the showdown then as six months later," the attorney general later explained.)[37] The attorney general also told Dobrynin that while the United States would not make removal of the missiles in Turkey part of the agreement, these were long considered vulnerable and would be removed if NATO approved. In effect, then, the administration was also giving a guarded private—but not a public—pledge, and thereby conceding only part of what the Soviets had demanded in the second note. Would it be enough? The Kennedy brothers were not optimistic. The president "had not abandoned hope," the attorney general later reported, but it "was a hope, not an expectation."[38]

The next morning, on Sunday, Khrushchev conceded, as the Ex Comm had hoped. The premier declared:

> In order to eliminate as rapidly as possible the conflict which endangers the cause of peace, to give an assurance to all people who crave peace, and to reassure the American people, who, I am certain, also want peace, as do the people of the Soviet Union, the Soviet Government, in addition to earlier instructions on the discontinuities of further work on weapons construction sites, has given a new order to dismantle the arms which you described as offensive, and to crate and return them to the Soviet Union.

He went on to mention inspection and the no-invasion pledge. Looking ahead, he also wrote, "We should like to continue the exchange of views on the prohibition of atomic and thermonuclear weapons, general disarmament, and other problems relating to the relaxation of international tension."[39]

The week of crisis had ended—peacefully. Sticky problems

would linger: Castro became obstreperous, and refused to allow on-site inspection of the missiles; and the right wing in America sought to rekindle fears of a dangerous Soviet buildup in Cuba. But the great powers worked harmoniously, and their leaders exercised statesmanship in order successfully to avoid new misunderstandings and provocations. Having come so close to the brink of war and having seen the abyss, the two nations were able to move toward a detente in future months.

At the time, and long afterward, politicians and scholars would continue to speculate on why the Soviets placed the missiles in Cuba. Whatever the answer, the widely accepted explanation that they overturned—or even greatly altered—the *strategic* (military) balance of power is incorrect. Even John F. Kennedy, who suggested this interpretation during the crisis, later retreated to a more moderate position—that the missiles altered the balance of power politically, not militarily. "It would have appeared to [change the balance of power], and appearances contribute to reality."[40] As Theodore Sorensen later wrote, "To be sure, these Cuban missiles, alone, in view of all the other megatonnage the Soviets were capable of unleashing upon us, did not substantially alter the strategic balance *in fact*—unless these first installations were followed by so many more that Soviet military planners would have an increased temptation to launch a preemptive first strike."[41] At the meetings of the Ex Comm, Secretary of Defense Robert McNamara, who best understood nuclear stategy, had maintained for two or three days, in Hilsman's words, "that Soviet missiles in Cuba made no real difference." At best, putting missiles in Cuba simply allowed the Soviets "to begin to close the gap in 1962 rather than a few years later." "A missile is a missile," McNamara argued. "It makes no great difference whether you are killed by a missile fired from the Soviet Union or from Cuba." "The clear implication of McNamara's position," writes Roger Hilsman, "was that the United States should do nothing, but simply accept the presence of Soviet missiles in Cuba and sit tight."[42]

In fact, contrary to many assumptions and analyses, the missiles neither made a Soviet first strike more likely nor increased the capacity of a Soviet (retaliatory) second strike. Nor did the missiles in Cuba make an American first strike more difficult or weaker. The explanation of the last statement is easiest: Because the missiles in Cuba were "soft" and reasonably easy to locate, America's conventional weapons or short-range tactical nuclear weapons (not ICBMs) moved to the southern United States could have destroyed the Cuban missiles in a first strike without diluting the supply of American weaponry available for a synchronized first strike against the Soviet heartland. And the missiles in Cuba did not raise profound problems in the timing of an American first strike, for it was possible to synchronize strikes against the two targets—Cuba and the Soviet Union—so that the enemy in each case would spot the attacking missiles at the same time.[43]

Nor did the Cuban missiles make a Soviet first strike more likely.[44] The addition of forty-two missiles (only thirty-six could be fired in a single salvo)[45] in Cuba to the Soviet arsenal of weapons able to reach the continental United States was insufficient to make a Soviet strike rational or likely—assuming that the Soviets did not plan to commit suicide. Simple arithmetic justifies this conclusion. At most, the Soviets would have had about 120 ICBMs or their functional equivalents (about seventy-five in the Soviet Union[46] and thirty-six in Cuba) to direct against a United States arsenal of 177 land-based ICBMs and 144 submarine-based Polaris missiles. Since the wide-cruising, long-submerged American submarines were difficult—virtually impossible—to locate, the Soviet weaponry could not eliminate the 144 Polaris missiles and therefore, in theory, could be directed only against the American land-based ICBMs—fifty-four Titans (eighteen targets), seventy-two hardened Atlas F's (seventy-two targets), twenty-four Atlas D's (seven targets), and twenty-seven Atlas E's (twenty-seven targets)—which constituted 124 different targets.[47]

Assuming ideal conditions, including perfect (1:1) kill ratios, and that the Cuban-based missiles could reach United States ICBMs, they could have eliminated forty-two targets—say, all eighteen Titan I bases (fifty-four missiles) and twenty-four Atlas F bases (ten missiles). And the Soviet-based missiles, if one also assumes an unusually high level of accuracy, could have eliminated another forty-four targets—say, seven Atlas D bases (twenty-four missiles), twenty-seven Atlas E bases (twenty-seven missiles), and ten Atlas F bases (ten missiles). This would have meant that the United States, at minimum, would have retained thirty-eight ICBMs, 144 Polaris missiles, and 750 SAC bombers, as compared with the Soviet Union, whose second-strike capacity would have rested on about four hundred bombers and on eleven submarines with thirty-three missiles, which were easier to spot because their short-range missiles (launched from within four hundred miles) required that the ships surface. Obviously, if at least thirty-two SAC bases were added, the number of American targets would then be increased, and thus more ICBMs and fewer bombers would be available for a second strike. With the Polaris submarines added, the United States second strike would have been greater than the Soviet first strike, and would have been directed largely at Soviet cities, not weapons. Put bluntly, a Soviet first strike was equally implausible with or without the additional missiles—unless the Soviets were suicidal.[48] As Roswell Gilpatric, Deputy Secretary of Defense later admitted, "the military equation was not altered" by the introduction of Soviet missiles into Cuba. "It was simply an element of flexibility introduced into the power equation that the Soviets had not heretofore possessed."[49]

Some have admitted that the additional missiles in Cuba did not alter the balance of nuclear power, but have argued that these additional missiles made it easier for the Soviets to achieve parity or superiority in the short run. That statement is right in theory but misleading in actuality, for it neglects that the number of American ICBMs was being almost doubled in the next eight months and almost quadrupled within twenty months. More than twenty hardened Minutemen (ICBMs) became operational by December, and more than 120 others became operational in the first half of 1963. About 350 more were scheduled for fiscal 1964, as were fifty-four Titan II hardened missiles and at least five more Polaris submarines, with ninety missiles. Put simply, the American nuclear arsenal would continue greatly to outstrip the Soviet arsenal in the early and mid sixties, and the missiles in Cuba (even when all seventy-two were operational) would not redress the projected imbalance. The missiles in Cuba were not effective as a cheap "quick fix."[50]

The official Soviet explanation was that the missiles were placed there to protect Cuba from attack. This explanation has been dismissed on two counts—one political, and the other strategic. First, the United States was unlikely to attack Cuba, and the Soviets should have known this and therefore did know it. But the United States had already assisted in an attack on Cuba (the Bay of Pigs); Castro did seem to believe that another invasion was planned;

Kennedy had seemed at times to consider another invasion; and the Cubans did claim to fear one. Khrushchev, in his secret negotiations with Kennedy during the week of crisis, stressed the American threats to Cuba, and steadfastly maintained that the missiles were placed in Cuba only to protect her from the United States.[51]

On strategic grounds, it is more difficult to explain the missiles. Perhaps they were devised as a decentralized system that would be useful only to defend Cuba. By placing these weapons in the theater of likely attack, the Soviet Union may have been offering the possibility of limited war—not escalating from outside the theater. The Soviets, according to this analysis, were responding to the American doctrine of counterforce and America's overwhelming nuclear superiority. A limited capacity in Cuba might make it believable that the Soviet Union, perhaps at Cuba's request, could respond to an American invasion with something painfully unpleasant but perhaps not so unpleasant as to unleash all-out war. For example, the Soviets, if Cuba was facing an American attack, could have responded with a missile or two—with conventional warheads. Nuclear warheads lurking in the background might have deterred a United States attack inspired by petty reasons. In fact, this capability might serve to deter such an attack precisely because the Soviets could control the early levels of escalation. And a United States first strike against all the missiles would have involved a serious risk: missing a missile that might reach Miami or Atlanta. In this theory, the cost to the United States of attacking Cuba would far outweigh the likely gains. Obviously, Soviet-initiated conflict integrated into the Soviet missile system, and begun for any purpose other than defending Cuba, would have had no hope.[52] This theory is highly speculative—it rests upon intent, not just nuclear capacity—and was never tested, for the United States quickly raised the stakes because of the missiles in Cuba, and they were withdrawn. These events do not disprove this speculative interpretation of Soviet calculations, but events do indicate that the Soviets were wrong if these were their calculations.

There is an additional, and more likely, explanation which is compatible with, but does not depend upon, the notion that the missiles were actually designed to protect Cuba. They had an international political function. At a time when the Communist world was being torn by the Sino-Soviet dispute, and when one of the ideological issues was support for revolutions (liberation movements), the Soviets had devised a relatively cheap way (under a billion dollars) of seeming to support the Cuban revolution. Related to this is the substantial possibility that placing missiles in Cuba constituted a potential victory useful to the Soviets, who seemed to be stalled elsewhere. Blocked in Berlin and condemned by the Chinese as unduly conservative, the Soviet Union, by placing missiles in Cuba, could gain prestige in the Communist world and perhaps also be in a stronger position for the next round of negotiations on Berlin.[53]

Among another constituency—this one in the Soviet Union—the missiles also had political value. Khrushchev, long an advocate of peaceful coexistence, was under attack within the Kremlin leadership from a faction that wanted a larger military budget—and therefore less emphasis on consumer production—and the more militant foreign policy that greater armaments could support. Khrushchev, in response, was directing his de-Stalinization campaign against this faction. The emplacement of the missiles can be plausibly understood as part of Khrushchev's campaign against his enemies at home and within the bloc as well as those abroad.[54] In effect, he needed a victory in international affairs in order to be free of pressures at home and in the bloc pushing for bolder adventurism. It is unlikely that the plan was forced on him by his militant opposition or that they warmly endorsed it.

To Khrushchev, the deployment of missiles should have seemed politically attractive and comparatively safe. Perhaps he did not intend to keep them a secret after their arrival, and therefore left them uncamouflaged. It seems more reasonable to assume that this was part of the strategy, and not a terrible blunder or simply the product of low-level bureaucratic procedure.[55] Perhaps he intended Kennedy to discover them, but even if he did not, he undoubtedly was watching for strong signs of American displeasure or of acquiescence. The missiles—introduced into Cuba as early as about September 8, according to McNamara[56]—did not seem, to Khrushchev, to provoke from Kennedy public or private expression of disapproval. Kennedy's statement of September 13, warning that the United States would act if Cuba became "an offensive military base of *significant* capacity for the Soviet Union" or if "Cuba should possess a capacity to carry out offensive actions against the United States . . . ,"[57] was less than a clear-cut response (italics added). Cuba did not control (i.e., possess) the weapons, nor was Cuba "an offensive base of significant capacity."

Put simply, Khrushchev was probably awaiting signals that Kennedy never delivered—at least not in unambiguous fashion. To Khrushchev, Kennedy's response to the missiles may have seemed similar to the president's response in early September to about 3,500 Soviet troops in Cuba, whom Kennedy called simply "technicians."[58] Even when the Soviet military in Cuba grew to nearly 20,000,[59] there were no sharp challenges from the administration. The president's public statements on the subject of the buildup in Cuba seemed designed primarily to disarm his right-wing opponents and to allay anxieties at home. Kennedy, it probably appeared to Khrushchev, was avoiding a public admission of what was happening. Khrushchev, through intermediaries, assured Kennedy that Soviet purposes in Cuba were wholly defensive, and that he would not do anything to embarrass the president on the eve of the election.[60] Even Gromyko's visit to the White House on October 18, when the foreign minister communicated Khrushchev's desire for a summit meeting soon after the election, seems to have been part of the Soviet strategy of promising to delay issues until after the voters went to the polls.[61]

Whether or not Khrushchev assumed that Kennedy had discovered the missiles, the Soviet premier undoubtedly recognized that there were likely advantages and fewer likely disadvantages from this plan. Placing the missiles in Cuba could signify Khrushchev's support for Castro without publicly and irrevocably committing Khrushchev to this course—if Kennedy vigorously objected. Even then, private bargaining, not public confrontation, seemed most likely. The missiles might be traded for Cuba's security, and perhaps also a settlement on Berlin as well as the provocative missiles in Turkey. When Kennedy seemed to ignore the missiles privately and publicly, new options may have opened—even, as Adam Ulam has suggested, the possibility of a larger package deal, to be announced at the UN in November. The deal might have included a German peace treaty, with a prohibition on nuclear weapons for West Germany; a similar guarantee in the Far East, with a nuclear-free zone in the Pacific and a promise from China not to manufacture weapons. This is a highly ingenious theory, and probably assumes too much flexibility on the part of China, but it does suggest that the missiles, though not a rational military threat to the United States, had a value for bargaining.[62]

Khrushchev's adventurism, while bold, should have seemed comparatively safe to him. Undoubtedly, he recognized that Kennedy might act before the election rather than acquiesce. But he had every reason to anticipate that the action would be private, not public. That way Kennedy could have avoided the possibility of a political crisis at home. Presumably, depending upon the level and credibility of the threat or the value of the proposed bargain, Khrushchev would have quietly backed down and withdrawn the missiles.

But that is not what happened. Khrushchev miscalculated. Kennedy made the crisis public, established the quarantine, threatened more serious action, leaked warnings of an imminent attack on Cuba, and compelled Khrushchev to choose between armed conflict and public humiliation. Perhaps it was this aspect of Kennedy's policy that led the Soviet leader to complain bitterly to William Knox that under Eisenhower the crisis would have been handled more maturely.[63]

Why did the Soviets back down? Why didn't they challenge the blockade or, alternatively, refuse to remove the missiles and even warn the United States that some missiles were operational and could be launched against America? The evidence on these matters is sketchy and often indirect, but some tentative answers can be formulated on the basis partly of strategic theory and the assumption of Soviet rationality. To each question, the answer seems to be basically the same: overwhelming American nuclear superiority left the Soviets without the options and flexibility to maneuver in an area of vital interest to the United States. Challenging the blockade would have led to a shoot-out at sea and an American naval victory. Escalation of the conflict locally would have been costly to the Soviets, because the United States had control of the seas and greater weaponry. A Soviet move in Berlin, in turn, might have given the Soviets a temporary advantage, but at the risk of pushing dangerously close to a nuclear confrontation. Always lurking behind each scenario was America's overwhelming nuclear superiority, which constituted a restraint on Soviet boldness or daring.

Khrushchev later explained that he withdrew the missiles "to prevent an invasion of Cuba and to preserve the peace."[64] This simple explanation, while incomplete, is probably accurate. Certainly the premier wanted to prevent an attack on Cuba, for he wanted neither to go to war to support Cuba nor to remain aloof during an attack, thereby revealing that the Soviet Union would not support an ally and could not protect national liberation movements. What Khrushchev failed to explain is why the Soviets first offered one settlement, then raised the terms to include the missiles in Turkey, and then finally retreated to the first position.

Most analysts agree that Khrushchev was probably the prime mover within the Soviet high command in placing missiles in Cuba, and therefore that a retreat threatened his prestige, if not his power. The treatment of the issue in *Pravda* during the early days of the crisis made retreat quite painful politically, and there is also considerable evidence that the military was resisting a settlement on moderate terms. On Friday, for example, *Krasnia Zvezda,* the organ of the Ministry of Defense, declared: "History teaches that one must not give in to pirates. A policy of appeasement of an aggressor has always led to tragic consequences. . . . A decisive demand grows in all countries: destroy the criminal intentions of the warmongers."[65] Such counsel publicly dramatized the opposition to Khrushchev's emerging strategy of seeking accommodation in the crisis.

The famous, so-called first Khrushchev message, delivered in Moscow that same afternoon, took a more moderate tone than did *Krasnia Zvezda.* In his letter, the premier warned repeatedly of the dangers of war. He obliquely rebuked Kennedy for letting the forthcoming elections influence him ("we must not succumb to intoxication and petty passion regardless of whether elections are impending in this or that country"), urged the president to control his emotions, lectured Kennedy on the fact that the Soviet Union was not suicidal, and warned that an attack on Cuba could provoke war. But Khrushchev's emphasis was on seeking an accommodation to prevent war. "We and you ought not now to pull on the ends of the rope in which you have tied the knot of war," Khrushchev wrote, "because the more the two of us pull, the tighter the knot will be tied." To help untie the knot, he suggested the now-famous deal, which would guarantee the protection of Cuba—his sole purpose, he still maintained, in placing the missiles in Cuba.[66]

In examining this period, Michel Tatu concludes that Khrushchev actually lost control of policy after his first offer on Friday and was outvoted on Saturday, when the missiles in Turkey were added to the terms. The events on Saturday, Tatu contends, can be explained by understanding that the increased terms were "not a sign, or the sign, of stiffening . . . but merely an intermediate stage between a much more extreme stiffening and retreat."[67]

Tatu's thesis is based largely upon the handling of the crisis in Soviet papers. On Saturday morning, *Pravda,* for example, did not reflect the moderate strategy that Khrushchev had adopted on Friday, even though the paper presumably had ample time to fall in line. Instead, its headline was tougher than the day before. Nor was *Krasnia Zvezda* conciliatory. Its commentator proposed that the Soviet Union should withdraw the missiles only in exchange for American evacuation of troops and equipment "from the hundreds of bases that surround the Soviet Union." But soon the official Soviet position changed, and the second Khrushchev letter was issued, thereby leading to painful and revealing public contradictions for the Soviets when the press failed to conceal that the standards had suddenly been revised. *Izvestia* published the second message on page one, but printed on the next page a column declaring that such a proposal revealed the "impure conscience of its authors." That column, probably prepared by the Ministry of Foreign Affairs or at even higher levels, had obviously been written earlier in the day, and the editors had simply erred and failed to delete it when receiving the Turkey-Cuba message at the last minute. The second message, by this evidence, represents a step back from the stiffer positions earlier that day.

Tatu concludes that the premier, who favored greater moderation, was outvoted on Saturday and did not approve of the Turkey proposal. By this hypothesis, the shifts on Saturday resulted from other factions in the Kremlin who were bargaining, and the hardliners did not retreat until Sunday, when Khrushchev regained control and accepted the American proposal that he had suggested on Friday.

If the Cuban missiles were not an imminent military threat, then another set of questions becomes even more important: Why didn't Kennedy accept the missiles? Why did Kennedy react so strongly, bar private negotiatons, and strike out on the course that entailed a dangerous public confrontation between the two great powers?[68]

At one point, Sorensen tells us, the Ex Comm "seriously considered" either doing nothing about the missiles or simply taking diplomatic action. As some Pentagon advisers pointed out, "we had long lived within the range of Soviet missiles, we expected Khrushchev to live with our missiles nearby, and by taking this addition calmly we could prevent him from inflating its importance." Presumably this counsel was unsuccessful, because Kennedy believed that in world affairs "appearances contribute to reality." The *political* balance had been overturned. Khrushchev's act of putting missiles in Cuba, if not reversed, would have been an international political victory for the Soviet Union and therefore a defeat for the United States—because the Soviets had successfully challenged the United States.[69]

Even granting temporarily that this explains satisfactorily why the missiles could not be allowed, we may still ask, Why did Kennedy bar private negotiations and stage a public confrontation? To this question, the answer is allegedly that the administration could not have launched the same strategy—of quarantine and threat—and have had the same success if the Soviet Union had believed that the United States knew about the missiles and if the Soviets first announced the presence of missiles. (The administration believed that the Soviets might well announce the missiles if it moved first to private negotiations.) This is a weak, even suspect, argument. Roger Hilsman, for one, notes that he and his assistants in the Bureau of Intelligence even concluded that Khrushchev by October 16 (the day that Kennedy learned of the news) probably assumed that the United States knew about the presence of missiles[70]—which makes the initiative theme even more suspect. At worst, for the United States, a private American warning, even if followed by a Soviet announcement of missiles in Cuba, would have meant only a temporary loss of initiative and a brief blow to American prestige. In turn, a private warning would also have provided time for the Soviets more calmly to consider their response to American demands. Presumably, such a strategy would have had a great advantage: the Soviets, having time to consider a response, would have been less likely to act precipitously, and therefore nuclear holocaust would have been less likely. The Soviet leadership, by not being forced to back down publicly, might have had less of a vested interest in maintaining a dangerous position. Given the splits within the Soviet leadership and the likely efforts by some to seize upon this crisis as an opportunity for gaining an advantage within the Kremlin, the American tactics risked compelling those Soviet leaders who had devised or endorsed the plan of putting missiles in Cuba to choose between public humiliation and military confrontation. Put simply, private negotiations—if tried first by Kennedy—would have reduced the danger.

The international costs would have been minor and short-run—assuming that the United States would still have sought withdrawal of the missiles. Of course one cannot discount that Kennedy may have wanted publicly to humiliate Khrushchev, much as the president felt threatened with humiliation. This cannot be proved, but it is true—despite some later statements to the contrary—that requiring Khrushchev to back down publicly did constitute humiliation.[71]

There is another strong influence on Kennedy that cannot be dismissed—politics at home. "Politics," Theodore Sorensen, the president's friend and speech writer, reminds us, "pervades the White House without seeming to prevail. It is not a role for which the President sets apart certain hours. It is rarely the sole subject of a formal presidential meeting. It is instead an ever-present influence—counterbalancing the unrealistic, checking the unreasonable, sometimes preventing the desirable, but always testing what is acceptable."[72] Politics did not mean simply the forthcoming elections and the prospects of maintaining or losing a majority in Congress, whose approval was seen as vital to the New Frontier at home and abroad. But this was certainly an important part of politics. Roger Hilsman admitted that if the missiles did not constitute a military peril, the United States "might not [have been] in mortal danger but the administration most certainly was."[73] Later, in denying that the election or partisan politics was a serious consideration, he wrote, "I meant that the Administration would be faced with a revolt from the military, from the hardliners in other departments, both State and CIA, from not only Republicans on Capitol Hill but from Democrats, too. . . ."[74] Hilsman, while adding this often-neglected dimension of bureaucratic politics, is too quick to deny the importance of electoral politics. His own reference to opposition on the Hill underlines the administration's fear that the wrong kind of Congress might be elected, thereby dooming Kennedy's programs. In acknowledging bureaucratic politics, Hilsman was also focusing upon the very kind of discontent, beginning with the Bay of Pigs, which led to leaks and helped create the electoral pressure whose influence he denied. Such anti-Castro crusaders as Senators Hugh Scott and Kenneth Keating, among others, cited as their sources administration personnel (military and intelligence) who were unhappy with the administration's Cuban policy.[75]

These senators were the men who helped fan the raging political fire. Even without their help, Cuba was the number one political issue in 1962. It was the Achilles heel of the administration. According to one official, it was about 70 percent of the Republican campaign. In state after state, *New York Times* reporters, surveying politics before the missile crisis, concluded that Cuba was the "major issue." The GOP was successfully attacking Kennedy for his policy of "tragic irresolution." The major news magazines roasted Kennedy for allowing the Soviets to violate the Monroe Doctrine and to set up a military base in this hemisphere. The president was accused of being weak and spineless; in short, he would not defend America's interest.[76]

In fact, it was these intense political pressures, increased by the calls for another invasion from men like Senators Homer Capehart, Strom Thurmond, Barry Goldwater, and Kenneth Keating, that contributed to Kennedy's public statements to the Soviet leadership. Two days after Capehart's call in late August for invasion, Kennedy said that it "would be a mistake to invade Cuba . . . [for it] could lead to very serious consequences. . . ." On September 4, while denying that there were Soviet troops, bases, or "offensive ground-to-ground missiles" in Cuba, he warned, "Were it to be otherwise, the gravest issues would arise." On September 13, he renewed this warning, announcing that the United States "will do whatever must be done to protect its own security and that of its allies . . . [if Cuba becomes] an offensive military base of significant capacity for the Soviet Union." These statements, his former associates generally acknowledge, were directed primarily at the domestic scene. Kennedy, under pressure from Capehart and others, sought to draw a line, allay fears about the Soviet buildup, and remove Cuba as a political issue.[77]

With the ever-present danger of leaks, particularly from those hostile to the administration's Cuba policy, the president could not risk trying for long to conceal or deny the presence of missiles in Cuba. Indeed, by Wednesday evening, October 17, about thirty-six hours after the president first learned of the missiles, British intelligence was beginning to piece together the facts, and by Saturday at least two newspapers had the story.[78] Forced to act partly by his own statements, Kennedy could no longer afford politically to do nothing. Nor could he risk private negotiations, for either disgruntled members of the government or the Soviets might leak the information, probably create a panic in America, and undoubtedly cost Kennedy the election.[79] This point is made dramatically by Sorensen, who tells us of a note that a Republican member of the Ex Comm, C. Douglas Dillon, passed to him during deliberations: "Have you considered the very real possibility that if we allow Cuba to complete installation and operational readiness of missile bases, the next House of Representatives is likely to have a Republican majority? That would completely paralyze our ability to react sensibly and coherently to further Soviet advances."[80] Kennedy could not announce the presence of the missiles without also announcing a policy that would demolish Republican charges of "tragic irresolution." The actual importance of the missiles—in military or international political terms—was not long a subject for analysis in the Ex Comm. Robert McNamara, who had pointed out that a "missile is a missile" and stressed that a missile fired from Russia was as deadly as one fired from Cuba, soon learned his lesson. His "initial attempt to frame the issue in strategic terms struck Kennedy as particularly inappropriate, given the President's problem," concludes Graham Allison.[81]

For those who examine the crisis there are a few other themes (suggested earlier) that merit sustained consideration: Kennedy believed that Khrushchev was testing his, as well as America's, courage. Arthur Schlesinger has written: "What worried . . . [Kennedy] was that Khrushchev might interpret his reluctance to wage war as a symptom of America's loss of nerve. . . . 'If Khrushchev wants to rub my nose in the dirt . . . it's all over.' "[82] Kennedy, more than any president since Theodore Roosevelt, had a way of personalizing challenges, of perceiving threats to manhood and to courage. Kennedy's rhetoric bristled with the words of bravery, the denial of weakness, the assertions of forcefulness and purpose.

His personal fear was easily linked to the challenge to national credibility. In foreign affairs, at least in theory, the president makes the decision to go or not to go to the "nukes," to use the then-familiar vulgarism. The whole system of deterrence depended upon the enemy's conviction that the United States (the president) would go to war if necessary. The paradox, as the missile crisis suggests, is that a nation may go to war in order to maintain the very credibility which is being protected in order to avoid war. The felt need to prove America's (Kennedy's) mettle could mean nuclear disaster. Even the strain to remain credible might lead to dangerous miscalculations, flawed perceptions, and, ultimately, war.

There was a related fear: unless the United States got the missiles out of Cuba, the nation's will would be found wanting, its prestige injured, its word worthless, its commitments to allies suspect. Actually, aside from some Latin American governments and Adenauer's Germany, most nations were not initially impressed by the missiles in Cuba or by Kennedy's bold response. (Prior to the crisis, according to Sorensen, "Most West Europeans cared nothing about Cuba and . . . had long accustomed themselves to living next door to Soviet missiles. Would they support our risking a world war, or an attack on NATO member Turkey, or a move on West Berlin, because we now had a few dozen hostile missiles nearby?")[83] The Canadian government was so reluctant to get involved that it would not let United States planes use its airfields. Macmillan's government was also cool, in part because Europeans had grown so accustomed to living under the nuclear gun. While the British publicly backed Kennedy, they also feared miscalculation and holocaust and wanted the United States in the middle of the crisis to accept U Thant's proposal for a relaxation of the blockade.[84] De Gaulle, who received the news of the American decision with haughty dignity, later cited Kennedy's Cuba policy as an example of the danger of the NATO alliance: it intruded upon the independence of sovereign states, and could drag them into nuclear holocaust—even without their approval and against their will.[85] The missile crisis seemed to prove what some Europeans had warned earlier could be the price of an alliance with the United States: annihilation without representation. Rather than strengthening America's alliances, the handling of the crisis may have weakened them. It certainly failed to strengthen NATO.

What the crisis did accomplish is that it contributed to a detente in Soviet-American relations, helped undermine Khrushchev's position at home, strengthened the Soviet faction that wanted a much larger military budget, and ultimately helped accelerate the arms race. Khrushchev's defeat in the missile crisis and his apparent reluctance to accelerate greatly the Soviet ICBM program contributed to the decline in his political fortunes, and probably to his ultimate removal from office. The Soviet setback in Cuba stressed to the Soviets the dangers of America's great strategic superiority, for the crisis indicated that America's coercive diplomacy could succeed in many situations unless the Soviets approached nuclear parity. Khrushchev's successors moved energetically to close the missile gap, and by 1968–69, the Soviets and the United States were near parity. Thus, ironically, the crisis contributed to a dual, seemingly contradictory, legacy—the cooling of passions in Soviet-American relations and an escalation of the arms race.[86]

In 1962 the crisis also raised world respect for John Kennedy. He was viewed as bold, wise, and courageous. The world loves a victor, and he carried his triumph with modesty and grace. His administration was widely heralded for its skill in crisis management, and few worried that the decision making was carried out in virtual isolation from the public and the Congress. Having triumphed, he refrained publicly from calling his victory by its name—for his actions had already so defined it. He did not gloat, nor did he question publicly his own means or standards. For example, why was he prepared (on Saturday) to go to war rather than publicly trade the useless missiles in Turkey for the missiles in Cuba? Why was an attack on Cuba justifiable in order to remove missiles that did not add greatly to the America's peril? Was this plan the stuff of greatness?

Eight months after he had humiliated Khrushchev, Kennedy offered the sage lesson that he had partly violated: "Above all, while defending our vital interests, nuclear powers must avert those confrontations which bring an adversary to a choice of either humiliating retreat or nuclear war."[87] What, we may ask, would have happened if Khrushchev had not backed down on that Sunday over a decade ago? If the missile crisis was Kennedy's greatest triumph, as many scholars and memoirists contend, how many more similar victories can America afford to seek?

NOTES

This essay grew out of a long-standing interest in the missile crisis, and has benefited from the criticisms of my views by my students at Bennington College, 1963–64 and at Stanford University, 1966–67, 1968–70. John Langer, who wrote his honors thesis on the subject, effectively challenged some of my earlier views, for which I am grateful. My own interpretation has changed over time, and the shifts can be viewed in: Bernstein, "The Background of the Crisis," and (with Roger Hagan), "Comments on Dewart," as well as Hagan, "Triumph or Tragedy? The Crisis Reviewed," *Council for Correspondence Newsletter,* No. 21 (Oct., 1962); Hagan and Bernstein, "The Military Value of Missiles in Cuba," *ibid.,* No. 22 (Nov., 1962), which appeared in revised form under the same title in *Bulletin of the Atomic Scientists* 19 (Feb., 1963); and Bernstein, "Their Finest Hour?" *Correspondent,* No. 32 (Aug., 1964). An earlier draft of the present essay was criticized by Waldo Heinrichs, Allen J. Matusow, Edward Friedman, and Martin Sherwin, and I am grateful to them for their generous counsel.

1. Khrushchev speech of December 12, 1962, reprinted in *Current Digest of the Soviet Press* 14 (Jan. 16, 1963), pp. 4–5.

2. Rusk, quoted in Roger Hilsman, *To Move a Nation* (Garden City, N.Y.: Doubleday, 1964), p. 226.

3. Kennedy, quoted in Theodore Sorensen, *Kennedy* (New York: Harper & Row, 1965), p. 705.

4. In addition to the volumes by Hilsman and Sorensen, the chief memoirs are: Robert F. Kennedy, *Thirteen Days* (New York: W. W. Norton, 1969); Arthur M. Schlesinger, *A Thousand Days* (Boston: Houghton Mifflin, 1965); Pierre Salinger, *With Kennedy* (Garden City, 1966); Dean Acheson, "Dean Acheson's Version of Robert Kennedy's Version of the Cuban Missile Affair," *Esquire* 71 (Feb., 1969); and Nikita Khrushchev, *Khrushchev Remembers* (Boston, 1971), a volume of dubious source. Among the more important interpretations are: Robert Crane, "The Cuban Crisis: A Strategic Analysis of American and Soviet Policy," *Orbis* 6 (Winter, 1963); Leslie Dewart, "Russia's Cuban Policy and the Prospects for Peace," *Council for Correspondence Newsletter,* No. 21 (Oct., 1962), and "The Cuban Crisis Revisited," *Studies on the Left* 5 (Spring, 1965); Alexander George, "The Cuban Missile Crisis, 1962," in George *et al., The Limits of Coercive Diplomacy* (Boston, 1971); Arnold Horelick, *The Cuban Missile Crisis* (Rand 3779-PR, 1963), which is summarized in "The Cuban Missile Crisis: An Analysis of Soviet Calculations and Behavior," *World Politics* 16 (April, 1964); Roger Hagan, "Triumph or Tragedy," *Dissent* 10 (Winter, 1963); Graham Allison, *Conceptual Models and the Cuban Missile Crisis,* Rand P-3919 (Santa Monica, Calif.: Rand Corporation) which is partly summarized under the same title in *American Political Science Review* 63 (Sept., 1969) and expanded substantially in *Essence of Decision* (Boston, 1971); I. F. Stone, "The Brink," *New York Review of Books* 6 (April 14, 1966); Ronald Steel, "Endgame," *New York*

Review of Books 12 (March 13, 1969); Hilsman and Steel, "An Exchange of Views," *New York Review of Books* 12 (May 8, 1969); Henry Pachter, *Collision Course* (New York, 1963); Adam Ulam, *Expansion and Coexistence* (New York, 1968). Jerome H. Kahan and Anne K. Long, "The Cuban Missile Crisis: A Study of Its Strategic Context," *Political Science Quarterly* 87 (Dec., 1972); Charles Bohlen, *Witness to History, 1929–1969* (New York: W. W. Norton, 1973); and W. W. Rostow, *The Diffusion of Power, 1957–1972* (New York: Macmillan, 1972), appeared too late to be fully integrated into this analysis, though it deals with most of the issues they raise.

5. Elie Abel, *The Missile Crisis* (Philadelphia: J. B. Lippincott, 1966), p. 31 n. For some doubts about when the administration actually first learned of the presence of the missiles, see Dewart, "The Cuban Crisis Revisited," pp. 24–32. The IRBM sites, according to later statements, were first photographed on October 17.

6. For the members of the Ex Comm, see Abel, *The Missile Crisis,* pp. 44ff; and Kennedy, *Thirteen Days,* pp. 30–31.

7. Quoted from Kennedy, *Thirteen Days,* pp. 33 and 31; see also Sorensen, *Kennedy,* pp. 682–83; and U. Alexis Johnson oral history, p. 43, Kennedy Library. On the military significance of the missiles, see also Acheson, "Robert Kennedy's Version," pp. 76–77.

8. Kennedy, *Thirteen Days,* pp. 33–39; Abel, *The Missile Crisis,* pp. 47–65; and Allison, *Essence of Decision,* pp. 124–25; see also Llewelyn Thompson oral history, p. 11, Kennedy Library.

9. Kennedy, *Thirteen Days,* pp. 43–50; Abel, *The Missile Crisis,* pp. 67–105; and Allison, *Essence of Decision,* pp. 174–200.

10. Kennedy, *Thirteen Days,* pp. 53–55.

11. Speech of October 22, reprinted in *Public Papers of the Presidents: John F. Kennedy, 1962* (Washington, 1963), pp. 806–9.

12. The relevant Soviet statement reads: ". . . there is no need for the Soviet Union to shift its weapons for the repulsion of aggression, for a retaliatory blow, to any other country, for instance Cuba." (*New York Times,* Sept. 12, 1962) Kennedy, in turn, interpreted this as a Soviet assurance "that the Soviet Union had no need or desire to station strategic missiles on the territory of any other nation." Given this carelessness, and the frequent habit of administration memoirists to cite and claim to quote conversations with the Soviets in which they allegedly promised not to place "offensive" weapons in Cuba, and were presumed to understand and accept the American meaning of "offensive," it is possible that the Soviets never even lied privately on this matter. See, for examples of the confusion, the somewhat different reports, Kennedy, *Thirteen Days,* pp. 25 and 109; and cf. Hilsman, *To Move a Nation,* pp. 165–66; and Sorensen, *Kennedy,* pp. 690–91.

13. Speech of October 22.

14. Ronald Hilton, among others, concluded that unanimous support was won partly because an endorsement was regarded as a sine qua non for American financial aid. ("A Note on Latin America," *Council For Correspondence Newsletter,* No. 21 [Oct., 1962], pp. 42–44.)

15. Abel, *The Missile Crisis,* pp. 132–33.

16. *Ibid.,* p. 134; Schlesinger, *A Thousand Days,* p. 820; Kennedy, *Thirteen Days,* p. 66.

17. Quoted from Abel, *The Missile Crisis,* p. 133. Reprinted by permission of the publishers.

18. *Tass,* Oct. 23, reprinted in *New York Times,* Oct. 24.

18a. Moscow to Secretary of State, Oct. 23, with embassy translation of Khrushchev's letter to Kennedy, file 611.3722/10-2362, Department of State Records (copy in my possession).

18b. Kennedy, *Thirteen Days,* pp. 67–71, and quotations from pp. 67, 69, 70.

19. Hilsman, *To Move a Nation,* p. 214.

20. Khrushchev letter to Russell, October 24, reprinted in *New York Times,* Oct. 25.

20a. Moscow to Secretary of State, Oct. 25 (received Oct. 24), with embassy translation of Khrushchev's letter to Kennedy, file 611.3722/10-2562 (copy in my possession). Kennedy, *Thirteen Days,* p. 80, wrongly places this letter on Oct. 23. Kennedy replied very moderately, saying, "I regret very much that you still do not appear to understand what it is that has moved us to this matter," and then claiming that the Soviets had violated their private and public promises and his warning that they would not send offensive weapons to Cuba. (Kennedy to Khrushchev, Oct. 25, file 611.3722/10-2562 (copy in my possession).

21. Khrushchev reply to U Thant, October 25, reprinted in *New York Times,* Oct. 26.

22. Schlesinger, *A Thousand Days,* p. 820. Copyright © 1965 by Arthur M. Schlesinger, Jr. All quotes from this volume reprinted by permission of Houghton Mifflin Company and Andre Deutsch Ltd.

23. Kennedy, quoted in Hilsman, *To Move a Nation,* ˙p. 215.

24. Kennedy, *Thirteen Days,* pp. 76–77.

25. Abel, *The Missile Crisis,* pp. 157–75.

26. Hilsman, *To Move a Nation,* pp. 216–19, and quotations on p. 218.

27. Quoted in *ibid.,* p. 219. Copyright © 1964, 1967 by Roger Hilsman. All quotes from this volume reprinted by permission of Doubleday & Company, Inc., and Candida Donadio Literary Agency, Inc.

28. Khrushchev message, October 26, Department of State Records (copy in my possession).

29. Acheson, "Robert Kennedy's Version," pp. 44 and 77; Robert Lovett oral history, p. 6, Kennedy Library.

30. Kennedy, *Thirteen Days,* pp. 93–95.

31. Hilsman, *To Move a Nation,* p. 220.

32. Kennedy, *Thirteen Days,* pp. 97–99.

33. *Ibid.,* p. 95.

34. Hilsman, *To Move a Nation,* pp. 223–24. Sorensen maintains that the phrase "Trollope ploy" was not used at the meeting (*Kennedy,* p. 679).

35. Kennedy, quoted in Hilsman, *To Move a Nation,* p. 224.

36. Scali, quoted in *ibid.,* p. 222.

37. Kennedy, quoted in Schlesinger, *A Thousand Days,* pp. 829–30. George, "The Cuban Missile Crisis," pp. 126–31, doubts that the administration would have attacked Cuba without first trying other tactics if Khrushchev had not met the deadline.

38. Kennedy, *Thirteen Days,* pp. 108–9, and see also pp. 124–27 for assertions of caution; *Khrushchev Remembers,* pp. 497–98.

39. Khrushchev message, October 28, reprinted in *New York Times,* Oct. 29, 1962.

40. Kennedy, in interview of December 31, in *Public Papers of the Presidents . . . 1962,* p. 898.

41. Sorensen, *Kennedy,* p. 678.

42. McNamara, quoted in Hilsman, *To Move a Nation,* p. 195, and Hilsman, *ibid.* For a challenge by Nitze, see *ibid.*

43. Hagan and Bernstein, "Military Value of Missiles," pp. 8–10, 12.

44. Cf. Albert and Roberta Wohlstetter, *Controlling the Risks in Cuba* (Adelphi Papers), No. 17 (London, 1965), who conclude that the vulnerability of the Soviet missiles means that they could be used only for a first strike. Their reasoning is dubious, for they have actually established far less: only that the missiles, in the whole, were not useful for a retaliatory strike. It does not follow, necessarily, that a first strike was the only other possibility.

45. There were forty-two MRBMs, twenty-four missile launching positions for them, and twelve launching positions being prepared for IRBMs, meaning presumably that twenty-four IRBMs were scheduled for Cuba. None of the IRBMs had arrived before the missile crisis. During the crisis, the administration did not know how many offensive missiles were in Cuba, but the upper limit of the nuclear threat could be calculated on the basis of the number of missile sites. Subcommittee on Department of Defense Appropriations, *Department of Defense Appropriations,* House of Representatives, 88 Cong., 1 Sess., pt. 1, p. 7; cf., Wohlstetter and Wohlstetter, *Controlling the Risks,* pp. 11–12, for a careless reading of the testimony. There were also forty-two IL-28 bombers, but the administration had known about them since at least October 9. None was operational, even by the end of the crisis. (*Department of Defense Appropriations,* pt. 1, pp. 16–17).

46. For estimates of the number of Soviet ICBMs, see Institute of Strategic Studies, *The Communist Bloc and the Western Alliances: The Military Balance, 1962–63,* p. 3.

47. Data on American nuclear weapons from the Senate Committee on Armed Services, which received them from the Pentagon. (Nancy Bearg to George Bullock, May 25, 1971). In addition to the 177 ICBMs in the operational inventory, there were twelve more at Vandenberg Air Force Base available for use. The Titan and Atlas D missiles were grouped in clusters, thereby meaning that a number of missiles could constitute one target.

48. Many strategists assumed, because of the probability of some inaccuracy, that the kill ratio of Soviet missiles to American targets was 3:1 or 4:1, and that the ratio for American hardened targets was higher,

about 6:1 or 8:1. In this analysis, however, I am relying upon the far more pessimistic official Pentagon figures: 1:6 for six Atlas D's in a cluster of six; 1:3 for Atlas D's in clusters of three; 1:1 for Atlas E's, 4:3 for Titan I's, which were in clusters of three; and 4:1 for Atlas F's. Cf. Wohlstetter and Wohlstetter, *Controlling the Risks,* for doubts which even most of their Rand colleagues cavalierly rejected in practice. See, for example, Horelick, *The Cuban Missile Crisis,* pp. 28–29.

49. Gilpatric, quoted in *New York Times,* Nov. 12, 1962.

50. Data from House Subcommittee on Military Appropriations, *Department of Defense Appropriations,* 88 Cong., 1 Sess., pt. 2, pp. 416, 436, 479; House Committee on Armed Services, *Hearings on the Military Posture,* 88 Cong., 1 Sess., pp. 244, 308, 316. The IRBMs, according to later estimates, were not scheduled to be operational until December 15, but during the crisis, intelligence estimates placed the date at mid November (if the missiles had been available.) Even if the Soviets had installed the additional six MRBMs and the twenty-four IRBMs, which had not arrived, and if two complete salvos could have been fired (which is quite unlikely), only another thirty Atlas F missiles might have been eliminated—if one assumes a (unlikely) perfect kill ratio. That would have left the United States dependent upon 144 Polaris missiles, eight Atlas F missiles, about twenty Minutemen, and about a dozen other ICBMs (and at least thirty-two SAC bases)—which in numbers, but not megatons, would have roughly equaled the Soviet first strike. Admittedly, there would have been a point at which the United States might have been left dependent exclusively upon its Polaris missiles for a second strike, but that would have required the continued introduction of Soviet missiles in Cuba. How many more? Presumably the Soviets would not have wished to rely upon firing two salvos, for only one was likely before an American retaliatory attack, or upon the (unlikely) perfect kill ratios, especially not in the case of hardened American targets. Obviously, at a distant point, the United States might have been placed in a secondary position, but that was not an imminent danger. Cf. Horelick, *The Cuban Missile Crisis,* pp. 27–28, for the "quick fix" theory and some of its limitations.

51. Khrushchev messages of October 23, 25, 26.

52. Hagan and Bernstein, "Military Value of Missiles," pp. 10–13. This theory, however, does not adequately explain why the Soviets—if they were astute about strategic theory—felt they needed thirty-six, forty-two, or seventy-two "soft" missiles in Cuba, since a dozen or two should have seemed sufficient to establish credibility. Perhaps the Soviets deployed the larger number of missiles in order to make an American attack even *less* likely on the grounds that this larger number would make it more difficult for the United States to destroy *all* these missiles and launchers. Perhaps also, at the level of determining the number of missiles and launchers, bureaucratic politics operated, and those implementing the basic decision to place missiles in Cuba found it desirable and possible to add more.

53. Kennedy himself accepted this view in part, though he stressed the challenge to the United States, which was essential to a Soviet success.

(Schlesinger, *A Thousand Days*, p. 811; cf. Sorensen, *Kennedy*, pp. 676–78.)

54. Carl Linden, *Khrushchev and the Soviet Leadership* (Baltimore, 1966), pp. 147–57; cf., Roman Kolkowicz, *Conflicts in Soviet Party-Military Relations* (Rand, 1963), pp. 9–32; and Roman Kolkowicz, *The Soviet Military and the Communist Party* (Princeton, 1967), pp. 160–71. See also Rostow, *Diffusion of Power*, pp. 252–53, who also takes literally Krushchev's later claim that the missiles in Cuba would have equalized the balance of power.

55. For a view of bureaucratic practices, see Graham Allison, *Essence of Decision*, pp. 108–13.

56. *Defense Department Appropriations for 1964*, pt. 1, pp. 8, 25.

57. Statement of September 13, in *Public Papers of the Presidents . . . 1962*, p. 674. Notice also that Kennedy indicated that one criterion was whether a buildup "were to endanger or interfere with our security." For other doubts about America's clear drawing of the line, see Dewart, "The Cuban Crisis Revisited," pp. 24–37; and Allison, *Essence of Decision*, pp. 235–37, who also notes that Bundy publicly declared on October 14 that the administration was willing to accept at least one of these "offensive" systems, the IL-28 bombers.

58. White House press release of September 4, 1962, in Kennedy Library.

59. *Department of Defense Appropriations for 1964*, pt. I, pp. 21–22.

60. Kennedy, *Thirteen Days*, p. 26.

61. Anatoly Gromyko, "U.S. Manipulations Leading to Cuban Missile Crisis Exposed," *Voprosy Istorii*, No. 7 (July 7, 1971) (American translation), p. 13; the article is summarized in *New York Times*, July 29, 1971. The article in modified form is in V. V. Zhurkin and M. Primakov, eds., *Mezhdunarodnyye Konflikty* (Moscow, 1972).

62. Ulam, *Expansion and Coexistence*, pp. 670–78. Steel, "Endgame," p. 20, also finds this theory "intriguing" but perhaps too imaginative.

63. Mark Frankland, *Khrushchev* (London, 1966), p. 193, first called to my attention by John Langer.

64. Khrushchev statement of December 12; cf. George, "The Cuban Missile Crisis," pp. 118–21.

65. Quoted in Kolkowicz, *Conflicts in Soviet Party-Military Relations*, p. 14.

66. Khrushchev message of October 26.

67. Michel Tatu, *Power in the Kremlin: From Khrushchev to Kosygin* (New York: Viking Press, 1969), p. 270. Copyright © 1968 by William Collins Sons. Reprinted by permission of The Viking Press. The next two paragraphs draw upon *ibid.*, pp. 265–70; cf. George, "The Cuban Missile Crisis," pp. 122–24.

68. Dispersal of missiles to satellites (whether American or Soviet) increases the danger of miscalculation or technical error. Therefore it is desirable, in order to protect world peace, to prevent such dispersal or to achieve withdrawal of the missiles if the cost of such action appears inconsequential. That was not the case with the missiles in Cuba. All analysts of the crisis seem to agree, when they address the matter, that

the danger of war during the crisis was much greater than the likelihood of a war resulting from an accident if the missiles had stayed in Cuba.

69. Sorensen, *Kennedy,* pp. 682–83. Bohlen urged private negotiations first. *Witness to History,* pp. 491–92.

70. Hilsman, *To Move a Nation,* p. 167. Sorensen, *Kennedy,* p. 691, provides some evidence that Kennedy may have doubted that the Soviets concluded that he knew about the missiles.

71. Tatu, *Power in the Kremlin,* pp. 273–82. Also see Walter Lippmann, *Washington Post,* Oct. 25, 1962, for the suggestion of the Turkey-Cuba deal.

72. Theodore Sorensen, *Decision-Making in the White House* (New York: Columbia University Press, 1963), p. 44.

73. Hilsman, *To Move a Nation,* p. 197.

74. Hilsman, "An Exchange of Views," p. 37. Reprinted with permission from *The New York Review of Books.* Copyright © 1969 Nyrev, Inc.

75. Bernstein, "Background of the Crisis," pp. 7–16.

76. *Ibid.,* pp. 10–16.

77. Hilsman, *To Move a Nation,* pp. 196–97; Sorensen, *Kennedy,* pp. 670–71.

78. Abel, *The Missile Crisis,* pp. 66, 98–99.

79. For earlier statements of the influence of politics, see: Bernstein, "Background of the Crisis," p. 16; Bernstein and Hagan, "Comments on Dewart," p. 26; Bernstein, "Their Finest Hour?" pp. 119–20; Stone, "The Brink," pp. 13–15; Steel, "Endgame," pp. 15–17; cf. Pachter, *Collision Course,* p. 13.

80. Sorensen, *Kennedy,* p. 688. See also George, "The Cuban Missile Crisis," p. 39n.

81. Allison, *Conceptual Models and the Cuban Missile Crisis,* p. 52.

82. Schlesinger, *A Thousand Days,* p. 391. Kennedy had uttered these words before the missile crisis.

83. Sorensen, *Kennedy,* p. 681.

84. *Washington Post,* Oct. 26, 1962.

85. *The Times* (London), Jan. 15, 1963; *Washington Post,* Feb. 22, 1966; Bernstein, "Their Finest Hour?" pp. 120–21; and Stone, "The Brink,'" pp. 15–16.

86. Arnold Horelick and Myron Rush, *Strategic Power and Soviet Foreign Policy* (Chicago: University of Chicago Press, 1966), pp. 154–56; Thomas M. Wolfe, *Soviet Power and Europe, 1945–1970* (Baltimore: Johns Hopkins University Press, 1970), pp. 182–84, 431–37; Rostow, *Diffusion of Power,* pp. 259–60; Kahan and Long, "Cuban Missile Crisis," pp. 586–90.

87. Kennedy speech (American University), June 10, 1963, in *Public Papers of the Presidents . . . 1963* (Washington, 1963), p. 462. For the opposite interpretation from mine, see: Kennedy, *Thirteen Days,* p. 126; Sorensen, *Kennedy,* p. 717; Schlesinger, *A Thousand Days,* p. 841; Hilsman, *To Move a Nation,* p. 157; and Salinger, *With Kennedy,* pp. 346–47.

Richard J. Barnet

7
The Cold War and the Arms Race

EDITORS' NOTE. Among its other aftereffects, the Cuban missile crisis proved to be an important landmark in the intense armaments competition between the United States and the Soviet Union. Its significance in this regard, however, should not mask the fact that it was but a single event in a long and complex history. Indeed, one of the major characteristics of the Cold War years as a whole, from the concern over large land forces and atomic weapons in 1945 to the Moscow summit of 1972, has been the ever-mounting arms race of the major antagonists.

Arms races are nothing new in history, and generally arise whenever international political tensions are great. So it is here. The arms competition between the United States and the Soviet Union began in earnest with the outbreak of Cold War, and has continued to the present day.

But in other respects, the current arms race is historically unique: first, the buildup of armaments has long since passed the point at which the weapons systems of the superpowers might reasonably be used to achieve politico-military goals. When we entered the "age of overkill," we left—so far as nuclear warfare is concerned—the world of Clausewitz, in which war could be described as the "continuation of politics by other means." However irrational the arms races of the past, today's turns reason upside down in that it centers almost entirely on the construction of weapons systems so potentially destructive that they can never be employed to further the interests of the state. Second, as Richard J. Barnet notes in the following chapter, "the arms race . . . is now independent of the Cold War and has a life of its own." Several unique factors account for this fact. In the Cold War, the real competition has been limited to two actors, each with vast military establishments focusing on the purported capabilities of the other. This situation has encouraged each to base its own quest for superiority on a projection of the most that the enemy is assumed capable of spending, designing, and deploying. When the other contestant fails to translate all its presumed military potential into new weapons systems, it finds that it has fallen behind, since its opponent is now involved in weapons programs designed to offset the hypothetical (or imaginary) capability of its opponent. As a result, the second antagonist feels compelled to go ahead with the kinds of programs that the first assumed it would launch. A self-fulfilling prophecy has come into being, and it is then nurtured by the mutual suspicions of the antagonists, their lack of accurate information about each other's intentions, and the technological gap in the arms arena, which may make some weapons obsolete even before they are deployed.

In this chapter, Mr. Barnet analyzes the beginnings of the United States–Soviet arms race, and examines the ingredients, particularly on the American side, that set it in motion. His interpretation has clearly revisionist implications. He notes, for example, that the heavy American emphasis on being able to "negotiate from strength"—a phrase most often associated with Secretary of State Dean Acheson, but adhered to by his successors—gave considerable impetus to the competition in armaments, and that insistence on such a posture came originally less from the Defense Department than from the State Department. The Eisenhower years are seen to be a period of warlike rhetoric but limited spending for defense, whereas President Kennedy was responsible for a greatly increased defense budget. Finally, Barnet views the Cuban missile crisis of 1962—in a somewhat unorthodox interpretation of Soviet intentions in Cuba—as a milestone in the arms race, for its aftermath encouraged greatly increased Soviet spending for defense and an accelerating arms competition. Today, with the deployment of multiwarhead missiles capable of striking different targets, we have taken a quantum leap in the arms race by passing numerous coils in the upward spiral of armaments.

Since Barnet's chapter was completed, the first round of the Strategic Arms Limitation Talks (SALT) has borne fruit in the completion of two United States–Soviet arms control agreements. One agreement, in treaty form, bans all but two comparatively small antiballistic missile systems for each country, thus rendering each largely defenseless against nuclear attack from the other. On

the positive side of the ledger, the treaty should help: reduce in-
centives on both sides to launch a new round in the quest for better offensive weapons; reinforce mutual deterrence through the
recognition that neither side can defend itself effectively; and call
a halt to the effort to "improve" the technology of missile defense
systems—at staggering costs to United States and Soviet taxpayers.
Yet a potential negative feature of the treaty is the permission it
gives the United States to build an ABM system, in addition to
the one under construction in North Dakota, near Washington,
D.C. Even though few are currently pressing for the construction
of such a site, its permissibility within the terms of the treaty could
become a sufficient excuse in the future for vastly increased arms
expenditures to make such an ABM system a reality.

The second part of the SALT accords—the interim agreement
limiting offensive weapons—is both more complex and more con-
troversial. It is not a treaty, but an executive agreement ratified—
in the case of the United States—by a joint resolution of both
houses of Congress. The agreement places quantitative restrictions
on the buildup of certain intercontinental ballistic missiles, mis-
sile-launching submarines, and submarine-launched ballistic
missiles.

Yet, it may actually encourage a stepped-up arms race on two
counts: (1) It does not touch on a number of important strategic
weapons questions, such as long-range strategic bombers, aircraft
carriers, and forward-based systems, nor does it prohibit the development of new offensive weapons. Even before Congress acted
on the interim agreement, the secretary of defense strongly urged
support for increased arms expenditures and an accelerated
buildup of every strategic weapon not covered by the interim
agreement. (2) No restrictions are placed on qualitative improvements of existing weapons systems. In particular, this means that
both countries are given a free hand to continue to develop and
deploy multiple warheads (MIRVs)—the United States is several
years ahead of the Soviets in this technology—and are, in fact,
given a positive incentive to do so under the terms of the agreement.

Both sides appear to regard such qualitative improvements as
creating bargaining chips for the next round of SALT discussions.
Certainly, such improvements can have no other purpose, since
each country now has more than ten times the number of warheads

needed to deter or destroy the other. What each ignores is that this process perpetuates the arms race, makes early agreement in SALT II more difficult, and assures that if a second agreement does come, it will do so only by placing much higher limits on offensive strategic weapons than would be necessary if mutual restraint were exercised now.

Finally, successful discussions in the second round of SALT may also have been impaired by a congressional amendment attached to the interim agreement. A number of senators expressed alarm over the fact that the agreement permitted the Soviets numerical superiority in certain weapons systems and an overall advantage in megatonnage of their total missile payload. (These critics generally ignored the enormous American advantage in MIRVs as well as the fact that the advantage permitted the Soviets in numbers of weapons is far less than they were capable of achieving under their 1971–72 construction rate.) The result was the passage of the Jackson Amendment, which stipulates that in any future treaty governing offensive missile systems, numerical equality should be maintained in the weapons controlled. One can speculate that this formula may complicate mightily the already complex factors that render strategic arms limitations so difficult to negotiate.

On balance, SALT I may have some impact in stabilizing nuclear deterrence between the superpowers, but it can hardly be said to have stabilized the arms race (unless somewhat greater predictability is a mark of stabilization). The costs of the arms race will be shifted a bit, but there is little indication that these will be markedly reduced, and, indeed, they may increase in certain areas. As long as the concerned governments continue to regard the expansion of weapons programs as creating bargaining chips, rather than as wasteful and needless expenditures, arms limitation agreements will never keep pace with weapons spending and development. Perhaps the beginning of wisdom is the recognition that the situation is not analogous to a poker game, terminology to the contrary notwithstanding. Controlling nuclear armaments is not a zero-sum game, in which one party wins whatever the other loses. Here the stakes are such that there can be no winner if there is to be survival.

I would like to review the question of the arms race in the Soviet-American rivalry and, in the process, to look at the sweep of a generation of history. It is really impossible to discuss this issue, I think, without keeping two factors in mind. The first is the nature of the Cold War rivalry itself. Second, I think it is necessary to have some understanding of the workings of internal national security bureaucracies in both the United States and the Soviet Union. While it is true that the arms policies of both the Soviet Union and the United States reflect their basic foreign policy positions, including their views of their own roles in the world and their views of the rival nation, such policies also reflect a whole series of internal developments and internal dynamics within the bureaucratic structures of the two states involved.

Let me indicate first what I think the Cold War is about. It is the story of two great powers, each with a set of expectations as to how the other should behave which neither was willing to fulfill. I think that the roles the United States and the Soviet Union assumed for themselves and expected of each other have to be understood in the context of the immediate postwar period.

The United States emerged from World War II the most powerful nation in the history of the world. By any historical definition, the United States was supreme. This was the result not only of the possession of the monopoly of the atomic bomb, short-lived as that monopoly was, but also of the extension of American military power during the war. At the end of the conflict, the United States occupied military bases—which it retained—on every inhabited continent. Many of these bases were in fact legally turned over to the United States in the form of Strategic Trust Territories. Many had been part of the Japanese forward military empire in the Pacific. The war, which had brought all other participants—victors and vanquished alike—to economic ruin, had restored the American economy and left the United States in a position to play the managerial role in the reconstruction of the world economy. This point cannot be emphasized enough: the United States was the only nation to benefit directly and handsomely from the war, and the war worked an extraordinary transformation on American society.

RICHARD J. BARNET is Co-Director of the Institute for Policy Studies and a former member of the United States Arms Control and Disarmament Agency. His most recent book is *The Roots of War*.

Although I remember thinking, as a child, that we were all sacrificing during the war because we had ration cards, the fact was that meat consumption went up dramatically, and that by a number of other indicia that the Bureau of the Budget prepared at the end of the war, the standard of living took a big rise in the United States during the war years. And of course the war solved for the United States its major critical economic problem—the nearly 18 percent unemployment that still plagued the economy in 1937 and 1938. The United States was in a position at the end of the war, with its economy restored, to substitute the dollar for the pound as the global currency. The United States was the number one banker and creditor and consumer of resources.

The picture of the Soviet Union in 1945 could not provide a greater contrast. With more than fifteen million of her people dead, her relatively primitive industrial facilities largely in ruins, and her territory wasted by four years of scorched-earth war, the Soviet Union had purchased survival at a terrible price and was still vulnerable. True, she was unquestionably the number two power in the world: this was so because of the impressive Soviet victories over Hitler and, more particularly, because victory had spelled the end of the British and French empires that had dominated European politics, along with, of course, the German, Japanese, and Italian.

The United States came into the postwar era with a well-developed imperial creed. The United States, President Truman declared in 1945, should take the lead in running the world the way the world ought to be run. From that point on, the twentieth century, to use Henry Luce's famous phrase in his widely circulated 1941 pamphlet, was to be the American Century. This theme was repeated over and over again, not just from the lips of conservatives or businessmen but from liberals like Henry Wallace. Walter Lippmann warned in 1943 that America now stood at the center of world civilization, that she must now assume the role of guarantor of the whole Atlantic community or face the prospect that Europe would fall to an expanding Soviet Union. In 1943 also, the secretary of the navy concluded that the United States must police the seven seas in the postwar period, and that it should exercise its power—in a phrase that was common during this period—as a trustee for civilization.

How was the Soviet Union to fit into the American Century?

American attitudes toward the Soviet Union had evolved since the days of the 1917 revolution. When the policy of military intervention under Wilson failed, the policy of nonrecognition that was tried by subsequent administrations finally ended with the resumption of relations in 1933. But suspicion and hostility toward the self-proclaimed revolutionary state continued in the United States, and were deeply imbedded in our society. Even during the war, attitudes among the general population toward the Soviet Union fluctuated widely, although there was a considerable amount of general goodwill toward the Soviet ally, much of which was fostered and promoted by official propaganda.

But there were within American society pockets of deep and continuing hostility to the Soviet Union which continued to have an important political impact. Their impact was, in fact, disproportionate to their numbers in the population. If one reads the Catholic press, for example, during World War II, one sees a line toward the Soviet Union that is different from the official line of the United States government and, indeed, from that generally accepted by the press. The Catholic press made strong ideological attacks on the Soviet Union as the godless state. So too the Eastern European ethnic minorities—Poles, Czechs, and others—brought with them to the United States some of the deep-seated antagonisms, fears, and suspicions of great Russia that they had known in Europe.

The national security managers in charge of American policy during World War II—men like James Forrestal, Will Clayton, John McCloy, Robert Lovett, Averell Harriman—were in general suspicious of the Soviet Union throughout the war for many reasons. The Kremlin had its own diplomatic style, and under the very best of circumstances, their diplomats' personal relations were far from easygoing. The very existence of a powerful Socialist state, legitimated by its struggles with Hitler, professing an alternative model for achieving the consumer affluence and social justice which the American system also set as a goal—this too posed a threat to the concept of an American Century. Yet the men who managed American foreign policy at the end of the war prided themselves above all in being realists. They knew that they would have to deal with the Soviet Union as the number two power. So the real question for them was how much power it would be necessary to share with the Soviet Union.

The Truman administration was certainly committed to the

recognition of the Kremlin as the legitimate ruler of the prewar Soviet empire. But it was extremely reluctant to acquiesce in any further territorial expansion as a result of the Soviet victory. The State Department believed that it would be possible to adopt what amounted to a double standard in the development of postwar spheres of influence—that is, that the United States would not accord to the Soviet Union in Eastern Europe the same kind of exclusive sway that it had demanded for itself in Latin America since the promulgation of the Monroe Doctrine. The managers of the Truman administration saw nothing particularly anomalous about insisting on the very rights for the number one nation that they would deny to the number two nation. "I think it's not asking too much," Secretary of War Stimson remarked to an associate in May, 1945, as the war was ending, "to have our little region over here which has never bothered anybody." He was referring to the United States sphere in Latin America.

Stalin emerged from World War II resolved to preserve the Soviet state in what he believed to be an increasingly hostile environment. He was suspicious by nature. He had been betrayed, as he saw it, by the only man he ever trusted—Hitler. And he was convinced that a fundamentally anti-Soviet, capitalist state would continue to put pressure on him. Stalin's position was anomalous because, despite the great weakness of the Soviet Union vis-à-vis the United States, its international prestige had never been higher. His innate caution and his traditional view of revolutionary movements kept him from exploiting the considerable political advantage which he might well have been able to exploit in Western Europe. In Eastern Europe, he moved with hesitation, despite his overwhelming military power over the area. In Poland, for example, he ruthlessly purged politicians of an independent bent, including many Communists. But as Louis Halle, who was in the State Department at the time, has since written, he was generally reluctant to make Poland a satellite. A Communist Poland, brought into being over the clear objections of the West, was something of a provocation, whereas he thought a non-Communist Poland with a "friendly foreign policy" preferable because it could serve as a buffer. A country with an acquiescent foreign policy would, like Finland, nonetheless be independent in its domestic organization and not part of a Soviet bloc as such.

This pattern was visible elsewhere in Eastern Europe. In Romania, Vyshinsky descended into the midst of a chaotic situation in 1945, and demanded the premiership for a man who was actually a conservative but who was willing to work with the Communists. As late as November, 1946, the Romanian Communist newspaper was wishing the king a long life, good health, and a reign rich in democratic achievements. Then, as the Cold War developed and as pressure from the West built up, Stalin clamped down his hold on Eastern Europe. But even then, it was not until August, 1947, that Hungary became a People's Republic. In the intervening years, there had been reasonably free elections, in which the Communists had lost.

This, then, was the political background against which the first moves in the arms competition must be observed. Where the Red Army came into a country, the Soviet Union moved to tighten its hold and finally to consolidate the area into a Soviet bloc. But—and this is an important distinction—beyond the reach of the Red Army, Stalin followed his prewar policy of discouraging Communist revolutionary movements that could not be tightly controlled from Moscow or that could embarrass the Soviet Union in its diplomatic relations with other states. Thus I think it is no accident, as the Soviets themselves like to say, that two of the three Communist governments which were established by local revolutionaries without the aid of the Soviet Army—China and Albania—became enemies of the Soviet state, and the third—Yugoslavia—once also an enemy, is now still a wary neighbor.

Stalin did begin to make some moves elsewhere on the periphery of his empire. It was here that the arms competition began. In Iran and in Turkey, he made some political moves to try to get Azerbaijan as a province, and he made some demands on the Turks for return of provinces which had been Russian between 1878 and World War I. But in the face of a strong American reaction—which was immediate and forceful—he backed down. These moves, which were highly tentative in the sense that Stalin, I think, at no time indicated he would go to war over either one of these issues, were taken in Washington as the occasion for projecting the American fleet into the eastern Mediterranean. In 1946, the United States first sent a battleship on a trumped-up visit to Istanbul to return the body of the Turkish ambassador, who had died a couple of years earlier in Washington. The ship stayed there, and was soon joined by a permanent flotilla. According to

Forrestal, Truman was already talking at the time about World War III. This was in August, 1946. Truman said to his cabinet that we might just as well find out now as in five or ten years whether the Russians are bent on world conquest. So inconceivable was it to members of the Truman administration, that Stalin could make the moves that he made in Turkey and Iran without having that be the prelude to a Hitler-like plan for European or world domination, that they saw this as the beginning of a worldwide struggle.

What role did the military situation play in this gathering struggle? The first factor was the United States monopoly of nuclear weapons. I rather subscribe here to a part of Gar Alperovitz's thesis, but not all of it. There seems no doubt that the bomb was dropped on Nagasaki and Hiroshima for reasons having nothing to do with the Soviet Union, but it was also clearly used then as what Secretary of War Henry Stimson called our master card in dealing with Stalin.

Although the Soviets tried to minimize the significance of nuclear weapons in that early period, they were aware that possession of these weapons was an enormous military advantage to the United States. The Soviets reacted by developing a policy of deterrence of their own which, I think, has to be seen in three stages. The first stage was the maintenance of a conventional military force capable of occupying Western Europe in the event of a United States nuclear attack on the Soviet Union. One need only read the Soviet military journals of the late 1940s and early 1950s to see clearly their doctrine of deterrence. They recognized that they were powerless to prevent the United States from dropping a nuclear bomb on the Soviet Union, but felt that once that happened, the Soviet Union would at least be in a position to march to the English Channel. The second stage of deterrence, from the Soviet standpoint, was the development of a short-range nuclear missile capacity. In 1949, the Soviet Union exploded its first nuclear weapon. This was about the time when the best-informed scientists thought they would do so, but it was considerably in advance of what the government bureaucrats thought, because in this situation, as in so many others, those who were in charge of American military policy had consistently ignored unfavorable news or projections. Even when the Soviet Union exploded its bomb in 1949, it still did not have any capability of delivering it to the United States. Nor was it to have such a capability for many years to come. It did begin to develop, first, an aircraft and, then, a missile capability which would in effect make Europe a nuclear hostage. Whereas Europe had been vulnerable in the early postwar period to a Soviet invasion by the Red Army, it was now under the nuclear gun.

It was not until the early 1950s, with the simultaneous development of a long-range bomber force and the hydrogen bomb (which again the Soviets developed far in advance of what many in the United States anticipated), that the Soviets were in a position to pose a nuclear threat to the United States.

American policy makers in the 1946–47 period concluded that they should maintain a defense budget of somewhere around fifteen billion dollars, which was fifteen times the last prewar budget. They would rely on a few nuclear weapons, which would be stationed in forward bases in Britain capable of easily hitting the Soviet Union. They would maintain a small occupation force in Europe, and they would keep most of the bases that were acquired during the war.

It is interesting that during this period the military services themselves had rather modest visions of the role of American military power, and certainly of what the size of the defense budget was going to be. It was, rather, the State Department and the managers of the American postwar Cold War strategy who began to exert pressure, starting in 1946, for a sharply increased defense budget. This rested on a theory of the Soviet Union which is best exemplified in the famous memoranda which George Kennan sent from Moscow in 1946 and which Clark Clifford later put into an extremely influential memorandum for President Truman in September, 1946. This memorandum said that the language of military power is the only language which disciples of power politics understand. The reference was to the Soviet Union. The United States must use that language in order to make the Soviet leaders realize that "our government is determined to uphold the interests of its citizens and the rights of small nations." Compromise and concessions are considered by the Soviet Union to be "evidence of weakness," and they are encouraged by our retreats to make new and greater demands. According to this analysis, Stalin was considered to be a paranoid ruler who believed that the nations of the West were out to encircle him with bases. Thus the only way to deal with him was to fulfill his paranoid fantasies.

That view of course became the very basis of military policy throughout this period. Anything that looked like a concession would have to be rejected because it would merely encourage the buildup on the Soviet side. The assumption was that if, in fact, the Soviets were confronted with enough superiority and preponderance of military power, they would "mellow"—which is Kennan's word—and eventually they would become easier to deal with. I interpret that to mean that they would be willing to play the role of number two power which the United States had in mind for them in the American Century.

The first attempt to maintain the military superiority of the United States was manifested in the nuclear disarmament proposals of the Baruch Plan, which, I think, nobody in the United States government seriously thought that the Soviets would accept. At least, United States officials understood that if they did accept them, by some remote possibility, it would bring about a profound internal change in the Soviet Union. The very essence of the plan was an international management that would have subjected Soviet industry and, in large measure, the Soviet economy not only to inspection but literally to supervision and control by an international institution in which the United States had every right to believe that it would play the dominant role. That was the reason why the Soviets turned it down.

I think that the Soviet Union had no expectations that the United States would agree to disarmament, and that the whole discussion of disarmament in the first ten years of the postwar period was a pure propaganda exercise on both sides. The situation began to change as the second decade of the Cold War began, because of the development by the Soviet Union of nuclear weapons— including the hydrogen bomb—and because the United States had begun to recognize, at the very moment when the rhetoric of rollback had become the official policy of the United States government under Dulles, that that policy was doomed to failure. Indeed, the Eisenhower administration gave up the pretense that it would be possible to free Eastern Europe from the Soviet bloc or even to reduce Soviet influence there materially by bringing diplomatic and military pressure to bear.

So there appeared to be a kind of standoff—what Churchill called the "balance of terror" in the mid 1950s—and the Soviet Union for the first time began to show some interest in arms control. In 1955, it made some proposals which took up many of the offers that the United States had put on the table in the earlier period. Once that happened, the United States immediately placed a reservation on its previous positions and began to rethink its whole disarmament strategy. At that time we had a negotiator, Harold Stassen, who was genuinely interested in bringing about a limited disarmament agreement. He had advanced far in discussions with the Soviet Union on some limited agreements with respect to Europe, with respect to inspection, and, indeed, had gone so far as to initial a document with the Soviet Union. When John Foster Dulles learned of this development, he immediately flew to London; within a few weeks, Stassen was no longer the disarmament negotiator.

The Soviet Union, under Khrushchev's leadership, also began to rethink at that time the doctrine of nuclear war, recognizing that such war would be catastrophic for both sides. Khrushchev advanced the thesis that a nuclear standoff was possible at lower levels, and in the next few years he proposed a substantial variety of disarmament and arms control programs which were generally not considered seriously by the United States.

The American policy at this point in the early 1950s was to urge the buildup of conventional forces in Europe and the rearming of Germany through NATO. The Eisenhower philosophy was essentially that of a minimum deterrence posture, which is strategists' jargon for the view that there ought to be some kind of arbitrary limitation on the defense budget. Eisenhower believed that strict limitations would have to be imposed on the actual use of military power by the United States. It is interesting to note that during the Eisenhower period, the only military operations actually undertaken were the evacuation of some islands in the Pacific and the invasion of Lebanon, where the troops were in and out within three months. This was so partly because Eisenhower was interested in keeping the budget down, partly because, I think, he had a real sense of the limitations of military power and a real horror of nuclear war which goes back even to his first reactions to the dropping of the bomb on Hiroshima and Nagasaki.

But it was also because of changes that had taken place in the internal bureaucracy of the United States. The Eisenhower period was the period of the great ascendancy of the CIA, the era of covert activities and paramilitary operations. Allen Dulles, the brother of the secretary of state, was the director of the CIA, and a key adviser in the Eisenhower administration. These years saw a succession of paramilitary operations in Iran, in Guatemala, in Indonesia, and in many other places, where the emphasis was on the discreet and minimal use of military power. It was in effect an attempt to limit the risk and to limit the costs.

Under this policy, the fate of the army began to suffer, because the budgets went to the CIA and to the Air Force, which was building up its big deterrent posture. The whole notion behind Dulles's massive retaliation doctrine was risk limitation and cost control. I think John Foster Dulles needs to be understood as Khrushchev's counterpart—they were both great believers in bluff. In fact, there was a considerable symmetry in the 1950s in the military policies of Dulles, Eisenhower, and Khrushchev, involving a great escalation of rhetoric on both sides. The challenge of massive retaliation existed on our side, while Khrushchev warned that the rockets would fly and bragged that he could hit a fly in outer space. But it was also a period in which a lid was kept on the military both in the United States and in the Soviet Union. And the top political leaders were interested in doing that. Despite Dulles's strong feelings about the Soviet Union—an intense, religious fear and hatred of the Soviet Union and of Communism as an ideology—he also had a realistic sense of what the Soviets were really prepared, or likely, to do. He believed that bluff backed by overwhelming nuclear power would be enough to keep them from attempting to challenge the American position in the world.

The 1960 election now became critical. Kennedy campaigned for office on the promise to get the country moving again. As his campaign speeches reveal, his major point was that the Eisenhower administration had let the country down on the issue of defense, as evidenced in the alleged missile gap. The prestige of the United States—something Kennedy constantly referred to in his campaign speeches—had suffered because Eisenhower had not followed the advice of the generals. This was also the time when some of the leading generals—Maxwell Taylor, James Gavin—who later would become key advisers to Kennedy, wrote books denouncing the Eisenhower administration.

Kennedy made much of the missile gap—and this was a pure election fraud. The figures on the relative missile strength of the United States and the Soviet Union in 1960 showed that the

United States had something like three hundred, while the consensus of the intelligence community in 1960 was that the Soviets had no more than sixteen. It was later decided by some of the intelligence people that the most likely figure was four.

Yet, the Air Force had concluded, on the basis of actual photographic evidence that they had from the U-2, that if the Soviet Union were the United States, and if the Soviet Union organized its production as the United States did (even though there was very clear hard evidence that it did not), it should have something like two hundred or three hundred missiles; then they assumed the possibility of a margin of error and doubled or tripled their figures, "just to be on the safe side." It was the Air Force projections leaked to Kennedy by some Democratic senators who were on the Armed Services Committee that became the basis of the "missile gap" campaign.

When Kennedy came to office, it was prefectly clear that the missile gap existed in reverse. To claim that one existed was, indeed, a rather self-defeating policy from the standpoint of deterrence. We were spending billions of dollars trying to convince the Russians that we had military superiority, while we were telling the American people that the Soviets were ahead. Therefore, the Kennedy administration immediately attempted to correct this discrepancy, and United States officials began to make speeches about the great superiority of the United States in military power.

It was at about this time that Khrushchev put forward some of his most plausible disarmament proposals, calling for limited agreements for a freeze on missiles. Yet the Department of Defense was unwilling to consider these proposals, because they said that the superiority of the United States in military power was an enormous asset which could not be given away. Then came the Berlin crisis of 1961, in which there was a real threat, at least, so it was felt in Washington, that we might be moving toward a nuclear war with the Soviet Union. As a result of this pressure, the United States moved fast to increase its superiority substantially. In the first year of the Kennedy administration, the military budget was increased by about four billion dollars, which meant substantial increases in nuclear weapons and of course in the big new development of the Kennedy administration—counterinsurgency, which led to our increasing involvement in what was soon to become the major war in Indochina.

The Soviet Union in the early 1960s was faced, it seems to me, with a critical choice. It could either greatly increase its military power or attempt to save the money, which was desperately needed for the buildup of industry and for consumer goods in the Soviet Union, by continuing the Khrushchev policy of the bluff or the grandstand play. It is in this context that I see the Cuban missile crisis.

It seems to me that what Khrushchev tried to do in the Cuban missile crisis was to protect Cuba in order to protect the ideological position of the Soviet Union. But, I think, a more important consideration was that he tried, by means of a dramatic step, to close the real missile gap which had now been exposed. If the missiles had been allowed to remain in Cuba, he would have greatly increased the Soviet missile force capable of striking the United States without having had to build an extensive force of intercontinental missiles.

The United States has viewed the resolution of the Cuban missile crisis as an enormous American success and one that vindicates the policy of maintaining nuclear superiority. I think it is possible to read the outcome in quite a different way. In fact, in the resolution of the Cuban missile crisis, the United States ended with a victory but no fruits of victory. That is, the United States gave a pledge not to invade Cuba, and it agreed privately to remove the missiles from Turkey, which it had in fact already decided to remove—indeed, the orders had been given to remove them. As McNamara himself said during the early days of that encounter, the missiles in Cuba did not, in a military sense, change the balance. The Soviet Union had an effective deterrent and enough force by that time to destroy the United States. The importance of the missiles in Cuba was in their psychological and political value, and the significance of their removal was psychological and political. The United States was able to show to the world that it could maintain the double standard. It was possible for the United States to continue to ring the Soviet Union with bases, but the United States could compel the Soviet Union to remove its bases and military weapons from the Western Hemisphere.

The aftermath of the crisis has been different, I think, from what the United States could have hoped for. It led directly to the downfall of Khrushchev, for, despite what he may have said in his memoirs or what the official excuses were, he was clearly humiliated not only in the eyes of the world but, I suspect, also in the eyes of his own military. Since then, the power of the military in the Soviet Union, by all the evidence that we have, has greatly increased. The best evidence is of course the very dramatic rise in the military budget which Secretary Laird often mentioned. In the Cuban missile crisis, the United States tried to cash in its chips on the basis of its nuclear superiority, but it resulted in the ending of that superiority.

This led, I think, to the recognition on both sides of the standoff in the nuclear arms race and of the dangers in the use of nuclear weapons to influence policies of the other side. There is now a far more realistic view on both sides. But the fact is that we have now set up in the United States and in the Soviet Union mechanisms for the continuation of the arms race which are now independent of the politics of the Cold War. The sense of detente has greatly increased—that is, the United States today is prepared to accord to the Soviet Union something like the duopoly, the two-power supremacy of the world, with the United States as senior partner, that Stalin was looking for at the end of the war. But we are now in a period in which the arms race is going to escalate gigantically with the arrival of the MIRV system and the ABM. These systems involve not only quantitative changes in the likely increase from four thousand to eleven thousand nuclear warheads capable of hitting the Soviet Union but also qualitative changes that will alter the whole technique of nuclear warfare. The arms race, which started as an instrument of the Cold War, is now independent of the Cold War and has a life of its own.

Lynn H. Miller

8

The United States, the United Nations, and the Cold War

EDITORS' NOTE. One of the chief characteristics of the Cold War has been its pervasiveness in nearly every aspect of the world arena during the past quarter-century. Not only have East-West political tensions intruded into areas once regarded as nonpolitical (such as cultural exchange programs and international competitions), they have also infected the domestic politics of countries far from the centers of Soviet or American power. The result has been to globalize even local issues and to render insoluble those matters requiring cooperation—or at least not active opposition—on something like a global basis.

Nowhere have the debilitating consequences of this infectious political process been more apparent than in the activities of the United Nations. Founded in 1945 as the hoped-for instrument of greater international cooperation, the UN soon found itself nearly torn apart by the East-West conflict. Its founders had designed it to work effectively on issues where great power cooperation could be assured; without that cooperation—the necessity for which was made particularly explicit in the provisions to maintain and restore international peace—it was assumed that the organization could not act authoritatively, if it could function at all. In light of these facts, it is no wonder that the United Nations has not functioned exactly as the Charter framers hoped it would. It is perhaps little short of astounding that it has not only survived tht Cold War but has evolved in some important respects to meet the challenges of a hostile environment.

In the chapter that follows, Professor Lynn H. Miller offers a brief assessment of the impact of the Cold War on the United Nations, with special emphasis on the ways in which United States policy makers have sought to further the Cold War goals of the United States through use of the international organization. There is nothing innately villainous in this attempt of a state to pursue its own foreign policy aims in the UN; indeed, every member state does precisely that, for the UN is, at base, simply an instrument of multilateral diplomacy. But the very nature of the United Nations invites hypocrisy and deception in this pursuit, for the organization is intended also to provide the foundation for a more viable international community, in which the anarchic reliance on self-help no longer prevails. Therefore it is tempting for states to behave selfishly at the UN and to describe that behavior as selfless—as designed to further the goals of the Charter and strengthen the United Nations.

Professor Miller argues that United States leaders have had few peers in this kind of rationalizing of their policy goals at the UN. They have succeeded in convincing large segments of the American public that it is the United States—sometimes almost alone—that has sought to inject life into the nobler aspects of the Charter in the face of the destructive opposition of the Soviet Union and her allies. Such a presentation of the United States posture is unfortunate not only because it is untrue; it heightens Cold War tensions and leads to unrealistic expectations as to what the UN should accomplish, and encourages acceptance "at face value [of] the supposition of American officials that they alone are able to interpret correctly the extent to which United States interests can be served through the United Nations."

In short, the Cold War, by its nature, has served to emphasize competitive rather than cooperative interests among the nations of the world. Yet the true self-interest of nations may often lie in cooperative action, and it was precisely this insight upon which the United Nations was erected. Had cooperative behavior been cultivated more fully, the United Nations would no doubt be a stronger institution today than it is.

Yet, paradoxically, the United Nations has often proved to be of importance not in spite of but because of the Cold War, which molded it. It has more than once demonstrated its ability to prevent Cold War conflicts from spreading and has, in fact, been an important instrument in stabilizing the bipolar world. Now that the most virulent aspects of the East-West conflict are receding, the real question for the future is whether the great powers will abandon the United Nations as no longer as relevant to their immediate problems as it used to be and once again ignore its potentiality for creating a less anarchic world.

Many interpretations of American foreign policy describe America's approach to the world as oscillating widely between vigorous involvement in the international arena and introspective withdrawal from world affairs. It is a theme that emphasizes the tendency toward the extremes of quietism and activism in American foreign policy as a recurring historical phenomenon. The pendulum swings, in the words of one commentator, "from phases of withdrawal (or, when complete withdrawal is impossible, priority to domestic concerns) to phases of dynamic, almost messianic romping on the world stage."[1] This interpretation implicitly or explicitly views the American approach to foreign policy as somewhat unsophisticated, idealistic, and guided by a strong conviction of the goodness of the American way of life. Thus quietistic periods reflect the notion that we must not dirty our hands in the tawdry game of power politics but, turning inward, should make ourselves an exemplary model for the rest of the world; zealous activism follows when we become convinced that we have a noble mission to perform on the world stage; then, disappointed by the fruits of our involvement, a rather petulant withdrawal follows once again.

It is the purpose of this essay to discuss a variation of this theme of oscillation in the United States' participation in the United Nations. At one level of analysis, it is true that the United States was rather consistently activist in its approach to the UN from its creation until the advent of the Nixon administration. Our refusal to participate in the work of the League of Nations was generally viewed as an error by the time of World War II, and undoubtedly generated the reverse response—that of dynamic leadership and active participation—when the United Nations came into being. But this observation tells us little or nothing about the nuances of United States policy in the UN, its impact on the organization, and, more specifically, the relationship of American participation there to the Cold War. Even within the brief historical framework of America's participation in the United Nations, there are discernible patterns of American oscillation between the attempt to dominate the scene and to retire from it. These patterns are not so much chronological, however, as they are issue-oriented.

LYNN H. MILLER is Associate Professor of Political Science and Associate Dean of the Graduate School, Temple University. A specialist in international law and organization, he is the author of *Organizing Mankind*.

It is not that the United States has shifted over time from strong support for all UN programs to disenchantment with, and opposition to, them; rather, the United States has been zealously active in ostensible support of some kinds of UN activities, and has refused to give more than token support to others. An analysis of these patterns should tell us much about American leaders' conceptions of the national interest, the role of the UN in U.S. foreign policy, and the effect of both on the evolution of the United Nations.

To understand the way in which the American oscillation between quietism and activism has made itself felt in the world organization, it may be useful to consider briefly the fundamental dualism that is at the heart of the conception and evolutionary potential of the United Nations. When the UN was created, it was conceived to be both an instrument for the cooperation of sovereign states and, at the same time, a vehicle which, at least potentially, might aid in the transformation of the nation-state system. This fundamental dualism, in other words, is between the conservative attempt to make viable the traditional structure of international policies and the radical vision of a transformed international system built upon world community.[2] In the words of one commentator, "the very ambition of the Charter turned it into a two-faced instrument. One face looks nobly toward the beginnings of a super-State well beyond the League of Nations; the other looks grimly backwards to the anarchic self-help of the old world, well before the foundation of the League of Nations."[3]

Obviously, the quietism/activism in American foreign policy and the conservatism/radicalism inherent in the UN charter are not comparable concepts. Quietism is not necessarily equatable with conservatism; nor is activism with radicalism. But in an important sense, the two dualisms are interrelated: in the UN context, inaction, little action, or stalemated action reduces the organization to the lowest common denominator, "the anarchic self-help of the old world," or the "conservative" face; dynamic action that produces authoritative policy, on the other hand, does not necessarily contribute toward the "beginnings of a super-State," but it at least seems to enhance supranational processes for the short run, thereby revealing the "radical" face. Since the United States is not the sole actor in the United Nations, there has of course never been any simple correlation between the intent of United

States policy and the eventual outcome for the United Nations. But as the dominant actor within the organization, the United States clearly has had a primary role in determining the course of the UN's evolutionary development. What has that been?

The United States was the chief architect of the United Nations, just as the League of Nations had been principally the inspiration of an American president, Woodrow Wilson. But in the creation of the post–World War II organization, the United States had an even stronger hand. One of the prime concerns of both the Roosevelt administration and the Allied leaders was that the United States should not turn its back on the new international organization, as it had on the League of Nations. Hence, United States leadership in the creation of the Charter was deferred to at every step. The chief preparatory conference was held at Dumbarton Oaks, in Washington, D.C.; the Charter itself saw the light of day in another American city, San Francisco; and there was little opposition to the proposal to place the headquarters of the new organization in the United States.

At a more intangible level, the role of the United States in bringing the new organization into being was at least as important. The major European powers had been through it all before with the League of Nations, and, as a result, both their leaders and their peoples were understandably less optimistic than the Americans about the prospects for an organization to take the place of the League. They supported the idea, but surely did not regard it as a likely panacea. In contrast, the United Nations was sold— some would say oversold—to the American public with enthusiasm, and in general that public responded enthusiastically. The Charter was constructed largely on the twin attempts to provide collective security and social welfare, both of which are concepts that were, if not American inventions, perfectly compatible with the American political tradition.[4]

Once the United Nations came to life, it was not long before American disappointment set in. The first illusion shattered was that great power harmony could be maintained in the postwar world to provide the basis for collective security. Before the organization was a year old, the five permanent members were well on their way toward stalemate over the attempt to implement the crucial provisions of Chapter VII of the Charter, those dealing with the creation of a permanent international armed force to be placed at the disposal of the Security Council's Military Staff Committee for its use in meeting breaches of the peace.[5] No agreement on the composition of the force could be reached. As Claude has observed, "American suspicions were aroused by the Soviet Union's evident urge to 'sneak into' United Nations military ventures while the Soviet Union was alarmed by the apparent Western intent to monopolize those ventures, 'squeezing out' the Soviets."[6] Had Chapter VII been implemented as intended by the Charter, the fledgling organization would have developed police powers far superior to any that have ever existed at the international level. The "radical" face of the Charter would have shown itself in this area (although one might legitimately ask whether such a development would have been an unmixed blessing for the world's smaller states, the likely objects of international police action). As the above quotation suggests, however, this stalemate was perhaps the first clear example in the United Nations of the fact that American activism in the work of the organization often meant an attempt to steal the show. Conversely, Soviet behavior here and later often manifested the Kremlin's desire not to be crowded off the stage. Both attitudes may have been understandable, self-protective ones, given the relative influence of each of the giants and of their growing and deep-seated distrust of each other. What was less than objective, however, was the way in which Americans and other Western leaders placed all the blame for inaction on the Soviet Union, seeing it as indicative of a desire to destroy the UN.[7] It was, more plausibly, indicative of a Soviet desire to maintain it as a forum for the promotion of their interests in more or less the way the West wished to use the organization for its own purposes. Regardless of the fact that the stalemate may have been foreordained, given the depth of the political cleavage, there seems little reason to suggest that one side was entirely wrong and the other entirely right simply because the former wished to maintain a place in the military planning that seemed to have been guaranteed it by the Charter.

Meanwhile, on other fronts of UN activity, the United States took the lead in the early years in the apparent attempt to strengthen the authoritative structure of the organization, including efforts to bring atomic weapons under effective international control and to promote the acceptance of universal standards for human rights.

At the first meeting of the UN's Atomic Energy Commission in June, 1946, the United States representative, Bernard Baruch, proposed that an International Atomic Development Authority be created and entrusted with all phases of the development and use of atomic energy. This authority would have had genuinely supranational powers, for it would have been given exclusive control over every step in the production of atomic energy, including the power to restrict states to licensed activity and to inspect national atomic establishments without hindrance. Its activities were not to be subject to the veto. In conception, it went much farther in the direction of limited world government than any of the provisions of the Charter.[8] Crucial to the proposal, however, was the requirement that the authority's control system should become fully operable *before* the United States—with its monopoly of atomic weapons—would undertake its own atomic disarmament. The Baruch Plan was indeed a radical proposal to create meaningful political authority at the international level, but it demanded the legalized acceptance of the American atomic monopoly in the transition period.

The Soviets soon countered with proposals demanding United States atomic disarmament as a first step, to be followed by the establishment of an international authority with much weaker regulatory powers. The reason for the reversal of priorities in the Soviet plan was clear: the Russians did not wish to accept on faith the American pledge to destroy their arsenal only at a stage when other states would have lacked the sanctions to force them to do so. And their rejection of an authority with truly governmental powers reflected their own conservative bias in international affairs. As leaders of the minority in international society, their own interests seemed to demand as much freedom of action for the individual nation-state as possible.[9] The positions of the two superpowers were irreconcilable, and the moment for controlling atomic technology was lost. Once again the American attempt to thrust international society into a brave new world foundered on the Soviets' natural reluctance to enter what to them must have appeared to an overwhelmingly American world.

In the area of human rights, the activism of the United States in the early years was thwarted not by external but by internal voices of dissent. The activist stance was expressed by President Truman at the closing session of the San Francisco conference when he called for the United Nations to develop an international bill of rights that "will be as much a part of international life as our Bill of Rights is part of our Constitution."[10] The leading foreign policy spokesman for the Republican party, John Foster Dulles, took a similar position. By 1949, the first of the specialized conventions on human rights, that dealing with genocide, was adopted by the General Assembly and opened to ratification by states. President Truman forwarded it to the Senate for its advice and consent, urging speedy ratification. In the words of Deputy Under Secretary of State Dean Rusk, the United States should take the lead in ratifying the convention because of the "inescapable fact that other nations of the world expect the United States to assert moral leadership in international affairs."[11]

That assertion of moral leadership was, however, not to be. In the Senate, opposition to ratification of the convention soon took the form of a pseudo-constitutional debate. Conservative states' rights advocates, obviously fearful of the precedent that might be involved in social legislation through the treaty-making power, argued that such conventions were an illicit intrusion into the domestic jurisdiction of the United States and a usurpation by the executive of the legislative powers of Congress. After a long period of debate, the controversy came to a head when Senator John Bricker of Ohio proposed a constitutional amendment that would have limited the president's treaty-making powers. With that, the Eisenhower administration, thoroughly alarmed at the potential mischief of such an amendment, agreed not to submit any more human rights treaties to the Senate in return for the defeat of the Bricker proposal. The genocide convention was left unratified, and the United States largely dropped out of international human rights efforts.[12] On this front, the quietism of the United States became a deathlike silence. Even today, the United States ranks near the bottom of the list of states in terms of the number of human rights conventions ratified—and this in spite of the fact that most of the conventions in question simply uphold at a world level individual rights already protected in the American Constitution.

The year 1950 brought the Korean conflict and with it a resurgence of American activism in the UN—this time by reviving the dormant collective security provisions of the Charter. The Soviet representative had been boycotting the Security Council for several months to express opposition to the UN's failure to seat a Chinese Communist delegation in the permanent seat reserved for "China." The United States therefore went to the council and introduced resolutions calling for a cease-fire and withdrawal of troops in Korea and, several days later, for support of United States military action against the North Korean army. In a move of dubious constitutionality, the resolutions were passed on the grounds that the Soviet absence did not constitute a veto. For the first time, it was argued by American spokesmen, the United Nations was to be marshaled to take collective security action of a sort that had been anticipated by the framers of the Charter.

This argument rather neatly ignored the fact that the founding fathers had assumed collective security would be possible only in the event of agreement among all the permanent members as to its purpose and direction. The Soviet absence in effect permitted the United States to transform the international organization into a huge anti-Communist alliance, at least for the moment. The involvement of other UN members in the military operation itself never went beyond the token level; it was essentially an American war sanctified by the flag of the United Nations. As such, it soon became clear that the Korean precedent would not encourage the authoritative growth of a UN police power. The operation was much too transparently partisan in nature for that and, as such, was not likely to be repeated.

American leaders, however, were quick to see the benefits for themselves and, apparently, the world when United States policy could achieve its goals through effective UN action (although they generally rationalized their action as simply upholding the Charter). Therefore, when the Soviet representative returned to the Security Council and began to block further resolutions on Korea, the Truman administration went to the General Assembly and secured passage of a proposal—known as "Uniting for Peace"—permitting the assembly to take action with regard to international peace and security once the Security Council was deadlocked by the veto. In the assembly, where the veto did not exist, a simple majority could pass a resolution. The measure was adopted over the protests of the Soviet bloc, whose representatives objected that it was an unconstitutional distortion of the Charter, which had specifically entrusted conflict management to the council. Underlying the opposed positions were the obvious facts that the United States could command a nearly automatic majority on virtually any issue it brought before the assembly, whereas the Soviet Union was almost certain to be in the minority. American appetites clearly had been whetted by the quirkish transformation of the Security Council into an anti-Communist alliance; now they sought to do the same for the General Assembly.

All this seemed to suggest that American leaders sanguinely—or perhaps piously—assumed a natural identity of interests between the United States and the United Nations as a whole, at least in the area of conflict management. What was good for the United States was good for the United Nations. As the Korean conflict dragged on, however, second thoughts began to arise in various quarters. First of all, the American civilian and military command had increasing difficulty in behaving in accordance with their purported claim to be the mere agents of the international organization, rather than an independent belligerent power. Once the American decision was made to cross the 38th parallel and pursue the North Korean forces back into their territory, the entire justification of the UN operation as a defense of the territorial status quo against aggression began to lose whatever force it had originally had.[13] With that, it became abundantly clear that no organ of the United Nations could make effective policy for what was a national army in virtually all but name. (For that matter, given the conflicts that arose between President Truman and General MacArthur, it was not even clear that the American chief executive could make effective policy for his own army.)

Second as a result, many UN members that had supported the original American initiative were forced to reexamine their positions in light of the growing extremism of United States military action. These states quickly perceived that it was dangerous—for themselves and for the future of the United Nations—to accept at face value the American identity-of-interests argument. This reaction was no doubt largely responsible for the fact that none of them went ahead with contributions of troops to the organization as they had been urged to do under the Uniting for Peace resolution. To have done so might have given an American-dominated assembly all the excuse it needed to take belligerent action anywhere in the world it wished.

Third, as UN members became increasingly critical of the United States conduct of the war, the identity-of-interests arguments also began to lose force within the United States. Generally this took the form of expressions of disgust on the part of the most nationalistic and anti-Communist elements in the society at the way in which the United Nations was hamstringing the American effort in Korea. An almost random example of this attitude can be seen in the following quotation from Senator Thomas J. Dodd:

> It was in deference to our United Nations allies that we refrained from bombing the Yalu River bridges, across which the Chinese Communists were supplying their 1-million-man army in Korea. Because they feared that the war might be enlarged, we refrained from attacking staging areas or airfields in Communist China and even gave up the right to pursue Chinese aircraft to their privileged sanctuary across the frontier. And when the tide of war turned against the Chinese Communists and they went reeling back in defeat, it was primarily in deference to our allies that we consented to an immediate cease fire instead of pressing our military advantage. . . .
>
> The result was that a war that could and should have ended in a decisive triumph for the free world, wound up, instead, in an armistice agreement that enabled the Communist negotiators to rush from the tent in Panmunjom shouting: "We have won. We have won."[14]

The kind of attitude expressed here is clearly blind to the possibility that there may be a preferable goal ror the international community, including the United States, to that of a "decisive triumph for the free world." For Americans sharing Dodd's attitude—and they were at least as numerous in the early 1950s as they are today—it became tempting to look for scapegoats to blame for the fact that the United Nations was not always perfectly subservient to the policy goals of the West.

By 1952, this search for villains took the form of a vicious attack on the integrity of the UN secretariat. In the summer of that year, a special federal grand jury was impaneled in New York to investigate potential violations of United States laws by Americans employed at the UN. When several employees refused to answer questions about their affiliations with the Communist party, important segments of the American public were aroused to demand not only that the employees in question be fired but that the United States institute stricter security checks over American citizens employed by the UN.[15] After a prolonged and heated controversy, the Secretary-General submitted to United States pressure and fired the American staff members suspected of political unorthodoxy. The action, however, was declared illegal by the UN's Administrative Tribunal, which ruled that the dismissed employees were entitled to full payment of their salaries to the date of the tribunal's judgment.

More significant for the long run was the resulting American requirement that all United States applicants for employment at the UN must be processed by the American security system. In spite of the fact that there have been no further controversies of the sort that came close to wrecking the independence of the organization in 1952–53, it is still true, as Stoessinger has pointed out, "that the U.S. government wields significant potential power over UN personnel policy, which may border on an infringement of the Secretary-General's role as the UN's chief administrative officer."[16] The myopia of the American position is obvious when one considers that it has scarcely encouraged effective opposition to the Soviet government's maintenance of stringent controls over their nationals employed at the UN—a policy that American leaders have generally decried without apparent regard for the beams in their own eyes. In this affair, as in United States treatment of the UN throughout the Korean war, the message of the American government seemed to be, "Either you play the game by our rules, or we won't play the game at all."

As was to be expected, Korean-type action has never been repeated by the United Nations. But in 1956, there broke out a new international conflict that prompted UN action squarely based upon the attempt to ameliorate, rather than to exacerbate, the political tensions of the Cold War. The Anglo-French invasion of Egypt in the Suez, accompanied by an Israeli attack on Gaza and Sinai, was generally viewed in the rest of the world as the kind of aggression that the UN was specifically designed to prevent. Soviet leaders immediately so branded it, and threatened an atomic attack on the offenders if it were not halted immediately. United States officials, shocked by the attack, quickly concluded that their allies were in the wrong, and that not to say so publicly would increase the danger of a Soviet reprisal. The United States therefore introduced a resolution in the Security Council calling upon all member states to "refrain from the use of force or threat of force."[17] When that resolution was vetoed by both Britain and France, the Uniting for Peace resolution was invoked with the support of both the United States and the Soviet Union, to permit the General Assembly to consider the matter. In that forum, a compromise United States–Soviet draft resolution was finally adopted, calling for a cease-fire and the withdrawal of all troops behind armistice lines.

At this point, the Canadian representative introduced a draft resolution calling upon the Secretary-General to submit a plan within forty-eight hours for the creation, "with the consent of the nations concerned," of an international force "to secure and supervise the cessation of hostilities." The United States supported the plan strongly, and the Soviets did so somewhat more reluctantly (they continued to insist that more coercive action should have been taken against the attackers). As a result, the United Nations Emergency Force (UNEF) came into being; it permitted an orderly withdrawal of foreign troops in accordance with the General Assembly resolution, and remained in the area to police the armistice line for nearly eleven years.

This was the first full-fledged example of United Nations peace-keeping, and it showed a remarkable ability for innovation and adaptation within the basic framework of the Charter, permitting the UN to adjust to a different world from that anticipated in 1945. UNEF was made possible by the fact that, for the first time since the outbreak of the Cold War, both the superpowers discovered that UN intervention in a trouble spot was a preferable alternative to the intervention of a rival's power bloc, which would have invited a countervailing intervention from the other side. UN intervention, in other words, gave some assurance that the situation could be stabilized without a radical shift in the East-West power balance. Based as it was upon this understanding, UNEF was an innovation in many respects. It was not collective security or enforcement action, but rather was designed to prevent the spread of the Cold War into new power vacuums. As a result, the major Cold War antagonists were carefully excluded from direct participation in the force. It was authorized by the General Assembly, not the Security Council, and the Secretary-General was made responsible for its administration.[18]

The establishment of UNEF was made possible because of the comparative restraint of the superpowers and their mutual deference, in the final analysis, to important Charter principles. For the United States, the contrast was particularly obvious in comparison with Korea; in the Suez case, it was clear from the start that the organization could not be transformed into an anti-Communist alliance, and no attempt was made in that direction. Yet in the process of encouraging a neutral UN role in Suez, the UN was given vital duties to perform in helping to stabilize the balance of terror and improve the quality of world order.

When independence came to the Congo in 1960, a new crisis erupted of a sort that seemed to parallel the Suez conflict, demanding a similar kind of peacekeeping role for the United Nations. There again, the threat of Western intervention in a new nation brought the prospect of a countervailing move from the Soviets and a dangerous Cold War confrontation. At the initiative of the Secretary-General, a UN peacekeeping force was authorized—this time by the Security Council—to enter the Congo and to act as an interpositionary force between rival domestic factions. Before long, however, the resemblance to the Suez case began to fade. The United Nations operation soon found itself in a vastly more complicated situation, where rapidly changing political fortunes within the Congolese state made it nearly impossible to maintain the original neutrality of the peacekeeping operation. What had begun as a unified central government quickly split into rival factions, one distinctly pro-Western and the other pro-Soviet. With that, each of the superpowers stepped up its support of the group it favored, thereby leaving the UN force caught in the middle.

At this point, a decision was taken by a secretariat official—who happened to be an American, Andrew W. Cordier—that had far-reaching consequences. In the effort to prevent the outbreak of civil war between the Kasavubu and the Lumumba factions, Cordier ordered that all Congolese airports be closed, the radio station shut down, and all troops immobilized. Whether intentional or not, the end result of the action was to benefit the pro-Western Kasavubu government, since the Lumumba faction was by this time ousted from the government and thus denied access to the principal avenues by which it might have returned to power.[19] The Russians, infuriated, charged that the neutrality of the operation had been betrayed, and called upon the Security Council to direct the United Nations to cease interference in the internal affairs of the Congo. The resolution was defeated, superpower consensus had broken down, and the General Assembly was called into session to consider the situation.

In that forum, United States policy generally received the support it was looking for. After a heated debate, the representatives of the Kasavubu government were seated as the legitimate spokesmen for the Congo, and the peacekeeping operation was continued. With those basic decisions made, a long and costly effort still lay ahead before much order was restored to the Congo—separatist rebellions in Kasai and Katanga provinces were among the complications faced—and it was not until 1964 that the Congo operation was completed. Meanwhile, the Soviets and their allies, convinced that the secretariat had behaved in pro-Western fashion, launced their troika proposal for a three-headed secretary-generalship and refused to pay any of the costs of the Congo operation.

From the Soviet point of view, what had started as an impartial peacekeeping force on the Suez model was soon distorted into anti-Communist coercive action that more nearly resembled Korea. But in this case, the success of Western policy must have seemed even more insidious because of the different expectations with which the operation began. Here the transformation of the UN into an anti-Communist alliance, because it was far more subtle, was able to mask itself as no transformation at all. For the Russians, the only alternative seemed to be to oppose this evolution toward peacekeeping as contrary to the Charter, and to demand that all future actions in this field remain firmly under the control of the Security Council, where the veto could prevent activities opposed to Soviet interests.

Officially at least, the United States has always maintained that the Congo operation was a genuinely neutral peacekeeping measure whose effect was to prevent the spread of the Cold War to central Africa. As was the case in Korea, the American administration was able to argue not that it had captured the operation to further American interests but that it had acted with moderation in resisting strong domestic pressures raised by disenchantment with the fact that the United Nations effort did not go farther in support of supposed anti-Communist elements.[20] American spokesmen have tended to cloak their satisfaction with the outcome of the Congo operation in arguments that speak in more lofty terms of the usefulness of peacekeeping, its constitutionality under the Charter, and the legal obligation of member-states to support it. As one commentator has said of the assembly's decision to seat the Kasavubu representatives, "the United States, of course, insisted that it was supporting a disinterested UN operation that sought to restore peace and order in the Congo. One wonders, however, what American policy might have been had the Credentials Committee and the General Assembly seated Lumumba instead of Kasavubu."[21]

On balance, the East-West controversy over the Congo operation has led to a deadlock about United Nations peacekeeping comparable to the earlier deadlock over implementation of Chapter VII. It is true that peacekeeping operations have been mounted since then—in Cyprus, in the aftermath of the Indo-Pakistani war of 1965, and again the Middle East in 1973—but these have been authorized by the Security Council and paid for on a voluntary basis. The underlying stalemate has nonetheless been manifested in the so-called financial crisis, which grew directly out of the Congo operation and its aftermath.

Article 19 of the UN charter provides that a member-state shall lose its vote in the General Assembly "if the amount of its [financial] arrears equals or exceeds the amount of the contributions due from it for the preceding two full years." Because of the Soviet Union's refusal to pay for peacekeeping operations which it considered to be illegal, its debt to the UN had met the conditions under which Article 19 was to be applied by the opening of the 19th General Assembly in 1964. (France was in the same position, because of her similar refusal to pay for peacekeeping.) The United States took the position that Article 19 should apply "automatically" to recalcitrant states, and urged the Assembly to deny the vote to the affected states. Whatever the merits of the United States position from a legalistic point of view, it was clear that the United States hoped, in pressing the issue, to secure acceptance of the doctrine that peacekeeping was legitimate and that member-states were obligated to support it. What was unspoken was of course the view that peacekeeping did benefit the West.

With the issue drawn in these terms, the Soviets naturally refused to budge, and, in effect, dared the General Assembly to face the consequences for the organization should two permanent members of the Security Council be deprived of their vote in the assembly. The United States worked zealously to marshal a majority in support of its position, but was unsuccessful in doing so. The

days of an automatic American majority in the assembly were
over, thanks largely to the recent influx of new states into the organization. After an assembly session in which no votes at all were
taken in order to avoid the application of Article 19—and the
business of the assembly ground nearly to a halt—the United
States reluctantly admitted defeat. With the opening of the 20th
General Assembly, Ambassador Arthur Goldberg announced that
"the United States regretfully accepted the simple and inescapable
fact of life that a majority of the 114 member states was unready
to apply Article 19."[22] He specifically stated that in the future the
United States would also reserve to itself the right to decide
whether or not to support specific peacekeeping measures.

The American about-face was a realistic retreat from an untenable position, but, more important, it marked a new recognition
by the United States that its dominant position within the organization was losing strength: it would not be possible indefinitely—
thanks to the changing composition of the membership—to
mobilize the organization to enter the fray in pursuit of the kinds
of goals desired by the West. The radical insistence that members
were Charter-bound to support even peacekeeping action of which
they disapproved was replaced by the far more conservative acceptance of the fact that major states could still decide pretty much
on an ad hoc basis which activities to support and which to
oppose.

Since the American capitulation on Article 19, two United
States administrations have shown a greater disinclination than
ever before to work to expand the authority of the United Nations.
Under the Johnson administration, this often meant that lip service
continued to be paid to some of the progressive goals most
ardently desired by a General Assembly majority, but that no commitment of American power was made to help implement those
goals. A classic example was the strong United States support, in
1966, for a resolution declaring South-West Africa legitimately
under the jurisdiction of the United Nations until such time as
it could be given independence. Yet the United States balked at
Security Council efforts to implement that goal in any effective
way—which would have meant a show of great power force to
wrest the territory away from South Africa—with the result that
the quasi-legislative potential of the General Assembly was reduced to a charade in this case. In another somewhat cynical

move, the Johnson administration attempted, in 1966, to dump the entire Vietnam war issue in the lap of the Security Council, professing only a righteous desire to see peace and security restored to Indochina. When that move was rejected as a transparent desire to get the United States off a most uncomfortable hook—essentially by accepting the American rationale for the war and multilateralizing the American effort—administration spokesmen were able to describe the result as another example of the failure of the United Nations.

Under the Nixon administration, the place of the UN in United States policy has been downgraded even further. The only obvious example of United States "leadership" at the UN in this period came in the rearguard effort to prevent the expulsion of the Nationalist Chinese representatives at the time mainland China was seated. However explainable the United States action in terms of historical alliance relationships, had that effort succeeded, it almost certainly would have created enormous roadblocks to the effective functioning of the United Nations. Otherwise, United States representatives increasingly vote against anticolonial majorities in the General Assembly, rather than abstaining, as they often did in the past. The first use of the American veto in the council was on a measure condemning aspects of British policy toward Rhodesia—a draft resolution that the British were already committed to veto; hence, the American action was unnecessary. Late in 1971, the United States Congress deliberately violated UN sanctions against the illegal regime in Rhodesia by passing legislation to permit the United States to import Rhodesian chromium. That action, which later became law, brought a General Assembly resolution condemning the American move.[23] These are but a few examples of recent actions indicating that the Nixon administration has largely written off the United Nations as an institution worth cultivating by the United States.

At one level, it is possible to explain this American shift to a negative quietism on virtually all fronts at the United Nations as the logical response of a state that is no longer able to dominate the organization as it once did. In this respect, it can be argued that the defensive conservatism characteristic of Soviet policy in the organization through most of its history is now being emulated by the United States, and for similar kinds of reasons.[24] But that kind of argument accepts at face value the supposition of American officials that they alone are able to interpret correctly the extent to which United States interests can be served through the United Nations. In fact, these official interpretations have been consistently suspect since the organization's founding, for they have been built largely on mixtures of nationalism and hubris.

As this brief survey has attempted to show, the United States has adopted the most activist stance in the United Nations, urging the organization into a radical authoritative posture precisely in those areas of conflict management where such action was seen to benefit the American position in the Cold War. This was as true of peacekeeping as of the anti-Communist enforcement action in Korea, for stabilization of the status quo is a primary aim of a status quo power. For all of Washington's attempt to portray its leadership in these fields as a simple commitment to the principles of the Charter, the fact remains that, on balance, UN action to keep or restore the peace has produced positive benefits for the United States and often setbacks for the Soviet Union.

In other areas of UN activity, United States leadership has been much less forceful, if not nonexistent. Refusal to ratify important human rights conventions is an obvious case in point. In the economic sphere, the United States initiated moves in the late 1940s that led to establishment of a UN Technical Assistance Program, but the Eisenhower administration then refused to support the creation of a Special United Nations Fund for Economic Development. With the gradual expansion of UN assistance programs over the past two decades, the United States has remained a rather reluctant donor, preferring to channel vastly more of its aid monies directly through bilateral programs outside the control of the United Nations. Assistance targets established for two UN Development Decades have not been met by the United States. Yet the United States has not been reluctant to bring all the pressure it could to bear to prevent United Nations development assistance from going to governments not approved in Washington.[25]

The negativism of the American roles in these areas can seem reasonable only to those who assume that direct, unilateral action by the United States—presumably with immediate payoffs—is always preferable to indirect, multilateral action where the payoffs may not be visible for years or, more simply, where the results are not recognized as foreign policy gains. Such an attitude fails to consider the possibility that the effective implementation of human rights standards, the commitment to close the gap between the rich and the poor internationally, or the efforts to protect the world environment—all may promote long-range interests of the United States far more effectively than exclusive, unilateral action by this country possibly can. It is an attitude that often dimly perceives the desirability of strengthening the community aspects of international life but fails to acknowledge that to build such a community requires conscious effort, imagination, a willingness to compromise, and a deference in some cases to the values of others. In this regard, Senator Fulbright has written gloomily: "The global community which the Charter assumed exists today neither in fact nor in prospect. If the social fabric essential to institutions does not exist, even the most brilliant statecraft cannot create it."[26] One might reply that brilliant statecraft can at least play a constructive, rather than destructive, role in helping to strengthen the social fabric essential to the establishment of authoritative international institutions. To assume that the task is hopeless is to condemn the United Nations in advance to shipwreck on the shoals of national sovereignty and self-help. It is the latter attitude that has too often characterized American policy.

Because of the long-dominant position of the United States within the United Nations (and it still remains the most influential single member), American officials have long been able to delude themselves into thinking that their most radical mobilizations of the organization constituted proof of their commitment to a strong United Nations. They have generally ignored the implications of the fact that they wanted a strong organization only to the extent that it could be made so on American terms. In some respects, it is true, the United Nations has been strengthened by United States support, but it has also suffered from the violent extremes of United States participation. American governments have periodically pushed the organization into untenable positions, escape from which only made more apparent the UN's obvious weaknesses. At the same time, American governments have done little to overcome those weaknesses, because they have refrained from participating fully in the kinds of UN programs designed to strengthen the world's social fabric and, hence, the viability of the United Nations.

It would be naïve to imply that the United States has been the only villain in the undermining of the United Nations. Among other great powers, certainly the Soviet Union has been even more conservatively sovereignty-oriented, because of its more defensive position, in its approach to the organization. France, under the nineteenth-century–style leadership of de Gaulle, showed even more disdain for any effort to strengthen the United Nations. It is, in fact, safe to say that no state, when it feels an important interest threatened by the will of the organization, will acquiesce meekly in the community decision. To admit all this is simply to acknowledge the continued force of notions of self-help and national sovereignty in international affairs. The point should be, rather, that if this creaking, decentralized international system is no longer adequate to provide minimal standards of world order, then it is the duty of statesmenship to develop a more imaginative vision of the potential areas for harmonizing individual national interests with those of the larger community of nations.

NOTES

1. Stanley Hoffmann, *Gulliver's Troubles* (New York: McGraw-Hill Book Co., 1968), p. 191. See also Dexter Perkins, *The American Approach to Foreign Policy*, rev. ed. (New York: Atheneum, 1968), Chap. 7. A comparable view is expounded with regard to the American attitude toward war in Robert W. Tucker, *The Just War* (Baltimore: Johns Hopkins University Press, 1960).

2. For an elaboration of this point elsewhere, see my *Organizing Mankind* (Boston: Holbrook Press, 1972), Chap. 1.

3. Julius Stone, *Legal Controls of International Conflict* (New York: Rinehart, 1954), p. 280.

4. And a case can be made for saying that collective security was overwhelmingly an American invention, at least if one wishes to credit Woodrow Wilson with its authorship. At base, collective security is an attempt to transcend the balance of power politics that Americans have always found so distasteful.

The strong emphasis in the Charter on improving social conditions throughout the world has been said to reflect "a kind of international New Dealism, an adaptation of the welfare state philosophy to the realm of world affairs," Inis L. Claude, Jr., *Swords into Plowshares*, 3d ed., rev. (New York: Random House, 1964), p. 72. Copyright © 1956, 1959, 1964 by Inis L. Claude, Jr.

5. For the hoped-for role of the Military Staff Committee and the international armed force, see Articles 43 and 47 of the Charter.

6. Inis L. Claude, Jr., *The Changing United Nations* (New York: Random House, 1967), p. 31. Copyright © 1967 by Random House.

7. For example, in a speech in the House of Commons on February

5, 1962, Prime Minister Harold Macmillan asserted that "the Military Staff Committee and the air force contingents have never been set up, again because of the Russian objection." Technically speaking, the prime minister was incorrect in his first statement; the MSC simply has not functioned meaningfully for nearly twenty-five years.

8. See *The United Nations and Disarmament* (New York: United Nations Office of Public Information, n.d.), Chap. 1.

9. A useful analogy may be made here to the states' rights emphasis of political groups in the United States federal system that feel themselves to be in the minority with regard to important social issues. No unitary, or fully integrated, political system would have tolerated Jim Crow politics in the American South for nearly a century after ratification of the 14th Amendment. Similarly, no genuinely integrated international system would accept the argument that states cannot be coerced into accepting certain kinds of controls for the good of the community.

10. See *Documents of the United Nations Conference on International Organization, San Francisco, 1945* (London: United Nations Information Organizations, 1945), vol. 1, p. 683.

11. U.S. Congress, Senate Committee on Foreign Relations, *The Genocide Convention.* Hearings before a Subcommittee, 81st Congress, 2d Session, on Executive Order 1950, p. 19.

12. For a fuller account of this controversy in the United States, see Vernon Van Dyke, *Human Rights, the United States, and World Community* (New York: Oxford University Press, 1970), Chap. 7.

13. For an account of the factors that went into this decision, and its consequences, see Walter LaFeber's chapter in this volume.

14. Thomas J. Dodd, "Is the United Nations Worth Saving?" in Raymond A. Moore, Jr., ed., *The United Nations Reconsidered* (Columbia: University of South Carolina Press, 1963), pp. 101–2.

15. For an account of the American attack on the secretariat, see John G. Stoessinger, *The United Nations and the Superpowers,* 2d ed. (New York: Random House, 1970), Chap. 3.

16. *Ibid.,* pp. 47–48. Copyright © 1970 by Random House.

17. U.N. Doc. S/3712 (October 29, 1956).

18. For a fuller discussion of the implications of peacekeeping, see Miller, *op. cit.,* Ch. 4.

19. For fuller discussions of this episode, see King Gordon, *The United Nations in the Congo* (New York: Carnegie Endowment for International Peace, 1962); and Stoessinger, *op. cit.,* Chap. 5.

20. For example, right-wing leaders in this country insisted that the United States should not have opposed, but supported, Tshombe's pro-Western secessionist movement in Katanga.

21. Stoessinger, *op. cit.,* p. 88. Copyright © 1970 by Random House.

22. Quoted in Stoessinger, *op. cit.,* p. 113. For an account of the World Court's involvement in the financial crisis, see also Stanley Hoffmann, "A World Divided and a World Court Confused," in Lawrence Scheinman and David Wilkinson, eds., *International Law and Political Crisis* (Boston: Little, Brown, 1968), pp. 251–73.

23. General Assembly Res. 2765 (26), 16 Nov. 1971.

24. See note 9, above, and my discussion of the Soviet reaction to the Baruch Plan.

25. The most blatant case of this kind came in the early 1960s when the United States tried to halt a UNDP project for Cuba. For a discussion of the case, see Stoessinger, *op. cit.,* Chap. 9.

26. J. William Fulbright, "For a Concert of Free Nations," *Foreign Affairs* 40 (Oct., 1961), 8–9.

Richard A. Falk

9

Counterrevolution in the Modern World:
Soviet-American Consensus and Continuities
between Counterinsurgency Abroad and at Home

EDITORS' NOTE. It is unlikely that most Americans are persuaded
that theirs is an imperialistic country. It is true that at the end
of the nineteenth century's era of imperialism, the United States
annexed the Philippines, Puerto Rico, and some scattered island
territories, while concomitantly asserting a right of control over
the political life of Cuba that was tantamount to annexation. But
this flirtation with classical imperialism could be dismissed as comparatively short-lived: the Philippines, it could be argued, eventually achieved independence with the encouragement of the
United States government; Puerto Rico received a good deal of
autonomy as it moved to "commonwealth" status; the Platt
Amendment, by which America exercised a large measure of control over Cuba, was repudiated in the 1930s; and the earlier significant acquisitions of Hawaii and Alaska moved to statehood and
assimilation into the republic. Thus, with only minor exceptions,
by the 1950s the United States might be said to have divested
itself of empire and had even urged its great European allies to
do the same.

In contrast, the Soviet creation of "satellites" in Europe after
World War II appeared to most Americans as a particularly brutal
example of empire building in the traditional sense. With pleasant
notions of United States traditions, it seemed outrageously implausible to Americans in the early years of the Cold War that
Soviet leaders, of all people, blithely used the epithet "imperialist"
in virtually every denunciation of the policies of the United
States.* According to the official American doctrine, they were
the imperialists, while we opposed imperialism.

* The concept of imperialism of course has a special significance in the
theory of Marxism-Leninism, since it describes what is thought to be the
final, decadent phase of capitalism. See Lenin's "Imperialism: The Highest
Stage of Capitalism."

That this official view has always been much too simplistic has become increasingly apparent to a public that has had to confront—through air strikes, pacification programs, and body counts—the destructive impact of American hegemony over distant peoples that we do not rule in the formal sense but allegedly protect. Mined harbors, napalm, and the bombing of dikes have grated many a conscience and yielded searching moral questions. The existence of an American imperialism without annexation has been accepted by many, and debate focuses on whether this has been deliberate (as revisionists are inclined to argue) or mindless (as liberal critics generally believe). Certainly the issue is of vast importance to American society—it can tell us much about ourselves and the interests that actually control American foreign policy.

Where the United States has exercised hegemony, its impact has been pervasive and overwhelming by any standard of measurement, even when it can be rationalized as beneficent. And where the effect of American hegemony is as catastrophic for the social and economic life of a people as it has been in Vietnam, it is difficult to escape the conclusion that American governments have been guilty, at the least, of nearly unparalleled hubris in the exercise of American power, whatever the real motivations behind their policy.

In the following chapter, Professor Richard A. Falk argues, first, that the repressive elements of recent United States foreign policy are not novel but have broken to the surface in the past; second, that these features are the outgrowth of certain traditional repressive tendencies in American domestic politics—most notably evidenced by a history of racism and the practice of genocidal policies toward American Indians; third, that this regressive streak has long vied with the progressive tradition of American liberalism for dominance in both domestic and foreign politics; and fourth, that "by making the imperial mission explicit [as it appears to him to be today] a domestic conflict is provoked, because the external policies activate the liberal democratic elements in the American tradition and contradict values regarded as dominant and desirable by a large portion of American society."

While describing the nature of American foreign policies in the Cold War years, Professor Falk also reaches significant conclusions concerning those of the Soviet Union. Indeed, he argues that several decades of rivalry have demonstrated how much the two great protagonists have in common. By the 1970s, after plentiful examples of Soviet behavior in Eastern Europe and American behavior in Southeast Asia and Latin America, "there is a recognition that the main revolutionary center of power is no more revolutionary than the main center of counterrevolutionary power. . . ." Both powers have shown themselves determined to preserve their respective empires, and have struggled with each other over tangential areas not firmly tied to either.

The regressive foreign policies Falk discusses both reflect and reinforce regressive domestic policies. In this connection, it is both ironic and troubling that the basic instrument for the promotion of regressive United States foreign policies today—the counterinsurgency mission that has been the essential component of the American involvement in Indochina—is itself the direct outgrowth of the doctrine of Communist containment developed at the outset of the Cold War. In its early years, containment tended to be supported by progressive elements in American society because of its apparently limited, pragmatic goals, and to be opposed by regressive elements as insufficiently committed to victory over Communism. Vietnam has completed the process of the containment doctrine's transmogrification, with the result that, in Professor Falk's words, "we seem to be at a turning point in the effort of the country to take account of what has been happening to it."

A painful decade of warfare in Southeast Asia has climaxed America's policy of response to revolution. Starting from a set of antirevolutionary sentiments, this country's foreign policy has crystallized around a counterrevolutionary posture and stimulated the development of a full-blown counterinsurgency mission reinforced by a coherent doctrine and set of military capabilities. I will discuss this political evolution and argue that the ongoing dialogue about revolution between the Soviet Union and the United States provides both governments with an ideological facade that serves to obscure their common concern with the maintenance of their respective spheres of imperial control. The current phase of international politics is characterized principally by the imperial techniques of these two dominant states. Their international rivalry is becoming less significant in revolutionary situations around the world than are their mutual acknowledgment and mutual toleration of zones of influence.

These two main imperial forces are not symmetrical. The United States is stronger economically and militarily than is the Soviet Union. The definition of American imperial interests has been somewhat more global than has the Soviet conception of its interest, although the disparity has been diminished by the contraction of the United States role and the expansion of the Soviet role. The danger of superpower warfare is greatest where both sides are committed to the maintenance of unstable or ambiguous boundaries. It is significant in this connection that the main confrontations involving Soviet and American interests since the end of World War II have taken place at the ambiguous edges of empire. These confrontations have concentrated particularly around the future and destiny of the four divided countries, where the boundaries are ipso facto unstable, being drawn in defiance of popular aspirations for national unity that exist in each of these countries. These divisions are associated with wider strategic patterns of competition in world society. It is no accident that China, Germany, Vietnam, and Korea have been the scenes of the most vigorous confrontations between the Soviet Union and the United States, either directly or indirectly. It is my contention that the

RICHARD A. FALK is Albert G. Milbank Professor of International Law at Princeton University. Among the most recent of his many books are *Legal Order in a Violent World, The Status of Law in International Society,* and *This Endangered Planet.*

only sustained issue between these two imperial actors has been to define clearly the edge of their respective domains of influence and control. Where problems emerge in their relations with one another, in their most dramatic form, they are connected with the attempt of either to change a boundary or to maintain an unstable boundary in the face of overwhelming popular opposition. The divided countries represent a set of geopolitical compromises between the two superpowers that are quite unacceptable to important factions in the affected countries.

In order to understand how this development has taken place, it is necessary, first of all, to take account of the continuity between domestic politics and foreign policy. It is exceedingly difficult to maintain a revolutionary policy abroad and a repressive or counterrevolutionary policy toward one's own population. Both the Soviet Union and the United States, to varying degrees and for quite different reasons, have been responding to domestic political pressures by adopting repressive internal policies. These policies have influenced and structured the role they have played with regard to many political developments.

The Soviet Union has sustained the Stalinist direction of domestic repression, and has, in my judgment, significantly undermined its capacity and willingness to encourage or even tolerate the success of the sorts of progressive forces that were initially identified with in its own revolution.

The United States, in contrast, has maintained a relatively permissive domestic society, but has always been afflicted domestically with contradictions that have impaired the credibility of its creed. The most blatant of these contradictions of course lies in the treatment of racial minorities and, at the base of American history, the brutal and self-interested elimination of the American Indians from the land. In other words, the genocidal and racist roots of American history have always been intertwined with the liberal democratic revolutionary heritage. There is, then, a confusion or split attitude at the heart of America's political identity that has existed throughout the history of the country, and has expressed itself periodically in foreign relations in a manner not drastically dissimilar from the crisis provoked by the Indochina war. A consistent pattern of uncertainty keeps recurring as to whether the United States in its external policies will identify with the progressive or the regressive side of its domestic political character. The quest for influence in its foreign relations has complicated its task of resolving its ethos and of projecting into foreign policy the dominant values of national culture.

The war with Mexico in 1848 dramatically illustrates this schism in American thought and, more generally, foreshadows the quasi-imperialistic relationship between the United States and Latin America. This imperialistic attitude was even more blatantly adopted in the Spanish-American War at the end of the nineteenth century and in the policies that the United States carried out in the Philippines, which bear a disturbing resemblance to the policies that the United States has been pursuing in Indochina. Although the rhetoric was different, a similar recourse to counterinsurgency strategies was pursued in the Philippines in the name of pacification: a decimation of the countryside, a failure to take prisoners, a kind of body count assessment of counterinsurgency efforts, and, as with the Mexican-American war in the middle of the century, a significant hostile reaction domestically in the United States.

In other words, by making the imperial mission explicit, a domestic conflict is provoked, because the external policies activate the liberal democratic elements in the American tradition and contradict values regarded as dominant and desirable by a large, if minority, portion of American society. Moreover, the exposure of blatant imperialism is at odds with the myth that America has believed about itself—a myth of beneficence that has been shattered many times and yet survives as a potentially progressive liberalizing force both domestically and internationally. Serious domestic questioning of the reality of this myth has probably never been more vigorous than at present. The conception of America as a progressive, liberalizing force in the life of its own people and in relation to the rest of the world has been drawn into serious contention. The public outcry against the conviction of Lieutenant Calley indicated the extent to which the myth is under attack. The confused reactions to the Calley conviction and the passions released by it suggest a popular sense that America's official policies—as demonstrated so dramatically in the Indochina war—have resulted in a deep descent into evil for which the public as a whole refuses to accept responsibility. More specifically, to punish Calley for murdering innocent civilians is to punish everyone who has fought in the war, because the essence of the counterinsurgency mission in Vietnam is indiscriminate slaughter. To treat Calley as a criminal was to stir deep resentment in ordinary citizens, who were already agitated by a losing war effort, a thankless and dangerous assignment that had never made much sense militarily or politically. For the politicians who conceived of such a war to punish Calley who had been sent over to fight in it is, in this context, an outrage, a scapegoating of the man at the bottom, and is understandably interpreted as an exercise in official hypocrisy.

We seem to be at a turning point in the effort of the country to take account of what has been happening to it. The question really becomes whether a moral consensus can be built to repudiate the regressive and counterrevolutionary roles, domestically and internationally, that governing elites in this country have played. It asks whether the event of such a moral consensus will produce a political consensus that can translate this negative experience into a redefinition of American objectives both internally and abroad.

I would suggest that the primary historical background of this present crisis is the international civil war that has been continuing more or less since the Russian Revolution of 1917. It was not accidental that even under a liberal president, Woodrow Wilson, the United States after World War I planned and participated in the Allied intervention in the Soviet Union to reverse the outcome of the Russian Revolution and, when the revolution was won, refused to accord diplomatic recognition to the Soviet government until 1933. The effort to isolate the Soviet Union clearly anticipated the comparable effort recently to isolate the People's Republic of China. The United States, from the beginning, as the dominant non-Communist state in the world, regarded the success of the Russian Revolution as a primary challenge to its own role and interests in the world, and tended, because of this challenge, to identify its foreign policy goals with the contradiction of everything that the Russian Revolution stood for. The initial effort was to reverse the outcome and to restore a conservative government; the second-order strategy has been, with a specially induced pause during World War II, to contain the revolutionary movement within its existing domain of influence; we now may be moving into a third-order strategy of mutual accommodation in which there is a recognition that the main center of revolutionary power is no more revolutionary than is the main center of counterrevolutionary power, and that the locus of revolutionary energy has shifted to the poor countries of the Third World. Such a shift creates the basis for tacit cooperation between the United States and the Soviet Union in a new sequence of interventions and containments directed at damping revolutionary flames or at least building firebreaks. As the United States increasingly defined its global interests in counterrevolutionary terms, it has been led to neglect those elements in its own tradition that were progressive and, in rhetoric, even revolutionary. This neglect was noticed, and formed the undercurrent of the allegation of ideals betrayed that has been a theme of the American antiwar movement.

I would also argue that, independent of the Russian Revolution, there was a de facto kind of imperial, counterrevolutionary role being played by the United States that was manifested in its objective position as powerful and rich in relation to subordinate parts of international society, such as Latin America. In short, contributing to the development of the policy lines that culminated in the Cold War were: first, the domestic ingredients of repression directed toward subordinate groups in American society; second, the external policies of dominance that were developed for America's economic, diplomatic, and military advantage in the Western Hemisphere in particular but also in the Pacific; and, third, the specific challenge to a conservative governmental orientation that was presented by the Russian Revolution, which was viewed by early Soviet leaders as a movement that could not be confined to any one country, but as one representing the best interests of people everywhere. Consequently, world Communism was seen as a movement that in the right circumstances would spread to other countries.

In accordance with the kind of analysis that I am undertaking here, World War II, during which there was a temporary alliance between the United States and the Soviet Union, involved an effort by rational power wielders of distinct ideology to deal jointly with a pathological challenge to their position in international society. The challenges posed by Germany and Japan combined with certain regional pressures to threaten fundamental Western geopolitical and economic interests. These challenges produced the wartime alliance between the Soviet Union and the United States. Once the pathological phenomenon of Nazism was eliminated, however, the international civil war resumed almost immediately.

It is evident from what we now know about the history of attitudes and actions on the part of both the United States and the Soviet Union that there were strong pressures on both sides to resume the civil war. Once it became plain that World War II would lead to an Allied victory, a substantial portion of the elites on both sides looked to the postwar period as a time of resumed central struggle between the Soviet Union and the United States.

Initially, the arena of struggle was principally the developed world, particularly Europe, which was obviously the most important contested area in the postwar period. In general, each side succeeded in achieving a sympathetic orientation from those portions of Europe that it occupied militarily, though this link was more manifest in relation to the Soviet Union than to the United States. The USSR imposed political regimes as a direct outgrowth of its military domination, which it has used to maintain control over Eastern Europe. The United States succeeded largely through economic assistance, but also by supporting within the principal Western countries those anti-Communist political groupings who ultimately were able to beat off the formidable radical challenges of the immediate postwar period.

The situation in Europe was essentially stabilized by the time that Stalin died (except for the geopolitical stalemate in Berlin), when the center of political struggle in the world shifted from Europe to Africa and Latin America, but particularly to Asia. In the interim, the most important phenomenon that occurred was of course the outcome of the Chinese revolution, which produced a second principal country with a Marxist-Leninist ideology and orientation. This led to a confirmation of the general interpretation of world history as one in which the powers of the West were locked in a mortal struggle with the powers of Communism and were confronted by a further threat of revolutionary expansionism. Therefore this event contributed significantly to the sense that the overall purpose of Western foreign policy was the containment of Communism, and that this objective should take precedence over every other consideration of values or preference as to the kind of political outcome and political orientation that should prevail in any part of the world.

The Chinese revolution was followed by the Korean War, and this event, especially as interpreted by American leaders, confirmed the general thesis that the United States and its allies were challenged by an expansionist and unified enemy, and that they must coalesce all forces in order to neutralize the Communist menace. In this period, the assumption prevailed that the Communist world was monolithic, that Communist states acted cooperatively in trying to expand their spheres of control. The United States reacted by defining its essential interests as including the maintenance of a ring of anti-Communist countries on the periphery of the Communist world in Asia.

It seems to me that this constellation of forces set the stage for the developments since the late 1950s that have culminated in the long American involvement in the Indochina war. A central question remains: What converted the defensive character of containment as a geopolitical doctrine into a basis for aggressive warfare in Vietnam during the 1960s? When the arena of struggle was shifted to Asia and the rest of the underdeveloped world, a counterrevolutionary policy began to express itself as a counterinsurgency mission. This, it seems, is the decisive shift in recent international history that is responsible for provoking the present crisis in American political consciousness. One catalyst for it was an overreaction to the statements and actions of the leaders on the other side. When Khrushchev said in 1961, "We will bury you," in the context of Soviet support for wars of national liberation, it was taken literally in Washington. Some of the most important occurrences were those that took place in the early years of John F. Kennedy's presidency.

One feature of the milieu in the late 1950s was a tendency by the Democratic party leadership in the United States to criticize Republican foreign policy because of its excessive reliance on nuclear weapons and its failure to meet emergent challenges to American primacy in international society. In the pre-1960 electoral period in the United States, the Democrats emphasized a force gap in the military capabilities of the United States that would make it ineffectual in relation to challenges that, while representing a threat to the maintenance of America's world position, did not warrant massive nuclear retaliation.

This sense of underlying anxiety was activated, first, by the recognition that Mao Tse-tung had won his extraordinary victory in China through the successful employment of the tactics and doctrine of people's war; and, second, by a much-publicized and

-studied speech by Nikita Khrushchev on January 6, 1961, in which he said, among other things, that the working class, which already leads an enormous part of the world, cannot allow the doomed forces of capitalism to drag hundreds of millions of people into the grave with them, and that a world war in present-day conditions would be a nuclear war and the most destructive in the history of warfare. Khrushchev's speech emphasized that it was exceedingly important for the Soviet Union to lead the struggle for liberation and for the expansion of socialist influence in the world, but that the means for this must avoid raising risks of general war to high threshholds. Hence, by the time of the 1960 American elections, the other side emphasized "wars of national liberation" as virtually the sole means of carrying forward the socialist revolution in the nuclear era.

Khrushchev continued in this speech to say there would be wars of liberation as long as imperialism and colonialism existed. Meanwhile, as a reality, revolutionary wars were not only possible but inevitable, since he was convinced that the colonialists would not voluntarily grant the people independence. Therefore the only method for these people to win their freedom and independence was through struggle, including armed struggle. Khrushchev concluded that Communists fully and unreservedly supported such just wars and marched in the vanguard of the peoples fighting wars of national liberation.

In my judgment, this speech was as much directed toward sustaining some kind of ideological cohesion within the Communist world as it was designed to communicate a credible threat to participate actively in revolutionary struggles—incipient and ongoing—throughout the world. But it was taken literally and seriously by the security planners in the Kennedy administration. Kennedy's response was given clearly in a speech in 1962 to the graduating class at West Point, where he noted the importance of guerrilla warfare as a new type of warfare in its origin. He described this as war by guerrillas, subversives, insurgents, and assassins, war by ambush instead of by combat, by infiltration instead of by aggression, where victory is sought by eroding and exhausting the enemy instead of engaging him. To counter this warfare required, according to the president, a whole new kind of strategy, a wholly different kind of force, and therefore new programs of military procurement and training. As the result of this kind of analysis, there emerged in the Kennedy years the idea of a counterinsurgency doctrine. The Greeen Berets were formed, and a febrile attempt was made to develop a capacity to frustrate wars of national liberation and to deter Communist intervention in such wars by making credible counterthreats. The models for American counterinsurgency were a mixture of economic and military responses to revolutionary challenges drawn especially from European experience as embodied in the Greek civil war and the Marshall Plan. In geopolitical terms, the objective was to close off wars of national liberation as an avenue for Communist expansion as securely, it was conjectured by policy planners in the early 1960s, as the defense of South Korea had closed off the avenue of direct military expansion. The central problem with this conception was that it involved deterring an external actor as a principal means of justifying response to an internal situation of struggle. Many of the contradictions and deceits in American foreign policy toward Vietnam arose from this underlying pressure to treat the external threat as the fundamental one in a context in which the dynamics of struggle were dominated by internal factors. And, indeed, the early military efforts in Vietnam in the 1960s were so ineffectual because they were made as if the enemy were the external actor (North Vietnam) rather than the internal actor (the National Liberation Front).

The idea with regard to wars of national liberation was to build up the capacities of governments to deal with internal challenges directed at their control of a national society. It was in this spirit that Vietnam was looked upon as a way of communicating to the Soviet Union the determination of the United States to resist any attempt to expand Communist influence. It was seen as an opportunity that would allow the United States to use its military capabilities effectively to meet the most urgent challenges being presented in international society at the time.

Therefore, in the early stages of the discussions about Indochina, Vietnam was generally regarded as a test case for wars of national liberation. It was even blatantly asserted that Vietnam constituted a laboratory to test the doctrines and weaponry of counterinsurgency. For instance, in 1963, one of the chief architects of this doctrine in the Kennedy period, General Maxwell Taylor, said:

Here we have a going laboratory (Vietnam) where we see sub-versive insurgency, the Ho Chi Minh doctrine being applied in all its forms. This had been a challenge not just for the armed forces, but for several agencies of government, as many of them are involved in some way or other in South Vietnam. On the military side, however, we have recognized the importance of the area as a laboratory. We have had teams out there looking at the equipment requirements of this kind of guerrilla warfare. We have rotated senior officers through there, spending several weeks just to talk to people and get the feel of the operation. So even though not regularly assigned to Vietnam, they are carrying their experience back to their own organizations.

This was, one must remember, ten years ago, in 1963, when this war was looked upon as a relatively minor investment by the United States which would yield a big geopolitical dividend.

In this context, it is also worth taking account of the fact that the war in Vietnam was seen too as a way of signaling to Peking the insufficiency of its conceptions of how to project its influence internationally. Lin Piao's speech in 1965 had an impact on Washington policy makers only slightly less than that of Khrushchev. Lin Piao talked about the peoples of the underdeveloped world aggregating their forces and gradually surrounding and defeating the forces represented by, and allied with, the developed portions of the world. Lin Piao said that in a sense the contemporary world revolution presented a picture of the encirclement of the urban centers of industrial power by the impoverished rural areas. In the final analysis, the whole cause of world revolution hinged on the revolutionary struggles of the Asian, African, and Latin American peoples, who make up the overwhelming majority of the world's population.

The lesson of this speech, as it was read by United States policy makers, was that the counterinsurgency arena was the primary one in which to carry out the response to the revolutionary challenge. The basic analysis of what counterinsurgency entailed was again based on an intellectual reading of what the other side was saying, and then trying to reverse it and use it to Western advantage. In this case, this was a perverse misreading. Lin Piao's basic message to the Vietnamese, for instance, was to base their plans on self-reliance and not to count on Chinese help to offset American intervention; and the more general interpretation of revolutionary struggle on the world scene could have been read, as it was surely intended, to emphasize the extent to which the Soviet Union as an industrial urban power was part of the problem rather than part of the solution.

Mao Tse-tung's famous notion—that the guerrillas are fish, and the people are the water in which they swim, and that if the temperature of the water is right, the fish will thrive and multiply— was also influential in the structure of our response to insurgency. Originally the American response was expressed in the benign rhetoric of pacification, the idea being that the guerrillas could be separated from the people, the fish from the sea, by relatively nonviolent modes of intervention, such as programs of pacification, providing fortified villages in which people could live in safety, and by generally trying to improve the capability of the government to govern.

But in Indochina it became clear that benign forms of counterinsurgency could not succeed, given the circumstances of the struggle. Therefore the counterinsurgency effort was increasingly converted into a purely military response to a broad-based insurgent challenge, and eventually became a genocidal war effort carried on against the population; the population—the sea—is the enemy that must be dried up so as to destroy the fish. It is in this context that we learn that in northern Laos virtually all villages have been destroyed by American airpower. It is in this context too that American officials learned that the only way to deal with the base of power that insurgents have in the countryside is to destroy their homeland to such an extent that they must abandon their villages and move to the city and become refugees. The result of such policies was to generate an extraordinary refugee population in Indochina amounting to a cumulative total of nearly seven million; nearly a third of the civilian population in South Vietnam has been displaced at some point in the struggle. A similar proportion of the population in Cambodia and Laos was also turned into refugees. And we have seen that counterinsurgent attitudes eventually lead the people of the countries on whose behalf the war is supposedly being conducted to be regarded and treated as the principal enemy. Progress in the war was measured by reference to a body-count set of indicators in which every dead Vietnamese is treated as a Vietcong, where "the dink complex" defines all Vietnamese as inferior; all Vietnamese become gooks who, when killed, are enemy combat soldiers. All these things are part, it seems to me, of the overall effort to use a high-technology military capability to frustrate movements of revolutionary nationalism, movements deeply rooted in the aspirations of the population for independence, national unity, and peace.

Therefore this counterrevolutionary posture and orientation has gone from a mere ideological position of resistance to a conventional military strategy, which has evolved into a counterinsurgency mission, culminating in genocidal attitudes, tactics, and effects.

During this same period of international relations, largely for reasons of maintaining domestic control, the Soviet Union has increasingly been led to a betrayal of its own revolutionary origins and, most manifestly in its interventions in Hungary in 1956 and in Czechoslovakia in 1968, to play what amounts to a counterinsurgency role in relation to those areas of the world, including its own society, which it regards as its sphere of influence. As a result, in both the Soviet Union and the United States, there has been a drift toward counterrevolutionary policies leading to counterinsurgent tactics, with its concomitant, a domestic counterinsurgent doctrine, disposition, and capability to deal with antigovernment tendencies in their own population.

This has been much more obvious in the Soviet Union, which has been more explicitly authoritarian-totalitarian, but there are signs that a counterrevolutionary attitude is being imported into the United States, and that a domestic counterinsurgency temperament is beginning to emerge in the centers of government and to influence budgets, law enforcement, and official ideology. One sees this attitude, for instance, in the greatly expanded reliance by the government on surveillance of its population and in the encroachment of the FBI and other security agencies on legitimate domestic political activities. One sees this tendency in the obsessive focus of military journals upon domestic urban guerrilla warfare. One sees it, for instance, in the recent reports that the Pentagon has been releasing on how to deal with urban guerrillas in a city that is described to a contracting company as Montevideo, Uruguay, but which has all the characteristics of Detroit, Michigan. The real identity of the city is disguised because of the jurisdictional inability of the Defense Department to investigate how to deal with an uprising in Detroit. One also sees it, it seems to me, in the initiation of such political trials as the conspiracy cases against those who were active in the Pentagon Papers disclosures and in the charges against Father Philip Berrigan and others. All forms of antiwar activities that have taken a prolonged position of opposition find themselves drawn into litigation. The Berrigan trial has been aptly called a domestic Gulf of Tonkin incident, because it tried to build public support for coercive tactics against the enemy—in this case, domestic dissenters—by deceptive accusations, including, in this instance, reliance on a paid informer and provocateur as the main witness for the prosecution. In the Camden 28 case, the government went so far as to have its informer also provide the skills and equipment needed for the draft board raid after the defendants had abandoned the project as impractical. Such official policies are designed to intimidate the antiwar movement and to pacify the public—to Americanize the war. Therefore the situation at the present time is one of domestic cleavage, a dissenting minority appalled by what has been done in Indochina and an official effort to crush this awareness by importing counter-insurgent attitudes and policies that were initially developed to deal with external challenges.

In this situation, President Nixon has tried to give the American public the illusion that there are only two external choices. The first is to withdraw from the world and adopt the kind of isolationist posture which is simply not a realistic possibility, given the size of the United States in relation to the world, given the way the world economy functions, and given the way the world communication systems operate. He has distinguished such neo-isolationism, which he rejects, from what he modestly calls the Nixon Doctrine, which he favors. The Nixon Doctrine sets forth a series of steps to sustain the American counterrevolutionary presence in the world without entailing what appear to be the domestic political costs of the earlier efforts to implement that posture—namely, without entailing the loss of American lives and without requiring very high budgetary appropriations. It has been complemented by a new era of great power moderation as a result of Nixon's trips in 1972 to Peking and Moscow.

The point of the Nixon Doctrine is that the United States has to get out of Vietnam and out of Indochina in a way that shows we are nonetheless serious about all our other comparable commitments to between forty and fifty foreign governments, which clearly is Orwellian doublethink rhetoric for not getting out at all.

Many of these governments, like the Saigon regime, are isolated from their own populations and dependent on external military support to maintain power in relation to the balance of forces within their own societies. In other words, the pattern of commitments that the United States has made includes a dependence on the American external military capability to give the counterinsurgent, counterrevolutionary side a reasonable prospect of success. This seems to involve, in the Nixon Doctrine, the substitution of American naval and air power for American ground forces going, for example, to Cambodia and Laos, the first two countries that have experienced the implementation of the Nixon Doctrine. It entails destruction, at least as extensive as that which has taken place in South Vietnam, the large-scale creation of refugees, and an equal effort to destroy the people—the sea—within which the insurgents—the guerrillas—might live.

In my view, neither the kind of continuity provided by the Nixon Doctrine nor the isolationism that he presents as its alternative is a tenable response to the bankruptcy, political and moral, that our long period of counterrevolutionary reaction to the Russian Revolution has produced in the United States. I think that what is essential, and what I alluded to at the outset, is that a dominant consensus emerge which recognizes that what happened in Indochina and what has been happening generally in the Third World has entailed the United States' undertaking the wrong mission as well as the wrong tactics. By and large, until recently all the mainstream dissent on the war has underscored the failure of the war on cost-effective grounds—that it has cost too much; that it was the wrong place to fight a large-scale counterinsurgency war; that the Saigon regime was not good enough to support; that the effects on American domestic society were bad; that it took away money that we needed for the cities; that the level of commitment involved a distortion of international and domestic priorities; that we should have been worrying about the Middle East and Europe as more important to American interests than Southeast Asia. All the debate, in other words, has focused on the pragmatic grounds of whether the means were adequate and whether the undertaking was desirable in view of its burdens and costs. No questioning has yet been done by people in mainstream American politics, including those who have lately described themselves as opponents of the policy, such as Arthur Schlesinger, Roger Hilsman, McGeorge Bundy, and others, of the mission itself. These planners have not questioned the intrinsic impropriety of relying upon external military capabilities to reverse the political relation of forces in Vietnam; nor have they been willing to acknowledge that victory by our "enemy" would have been generally more desirable than victory by the incumbent regime. They have not dealt with the fact that we are allied with regressive and repressive forces in many parts of the Third World whose success we should not promote, because upholding the integrity of American domestic society depends on seeking to enhance the welfare of people externally. A viable world order system depends on such progressive outcomes in domestic societies everywhere.

Therefore, in my judgment, in order to generate any kind of positive response to the Indochina experience, it will be necessary to build a moral and political consensus around the repudiation of the counterinsurgency mission and the counterrevolutionary perspective. This will be possible only if a progressive vision of the future of American domestic society is ascendant and linked with this consensus. A serious and credible domestic policy of liberation from repression will have to develop to provide the intellectual and political foundations for a progressive vision of foreign policy. A progressive foreign policy for the United States would not entail relinquishing all prospects of response to the Soviet challenge. In my judgment, it would, indeed, put the United States in dramatic opposition to the real orientation and role of the Soviet Union in the world system arising from Soviet recourse to counterinsurgency and a counterrevolutionary perspective at home and abroad.

This reorientation of American foreign policy perspective can occur only after present policies are exposed and perceived as criminal. The role of the war crimes issue is to draw a sharp boundary within the domain of government action between that which is intrinsically acceptable and that which is intrinsically unacceptable. Only if that boundary is drawn by the dominant political forces in this country will it be possible to have a clear break with the past that produced Indochina and related policies throughout the Third World. The adoption of a progressive vision domestically and internationally would lead the United States in the direction of identifying positively with such liberation causes as those in southern Africa, although not militarily, because the external uses of force represents a form of diplomatic hubris that almost invariably produces destructive results. The new perspectives have to identify diplomatically, economically, and psychologically with the success of repressed peoples engaged in liberation struggles.

The adoption of such a progressive vision would lead also to a much greater effort to achieve drastic disarmament, and to construct international institutions that were concerned with problems of war and peace, problems of economic development, and problems of ecological balance.

Such a world order movement could build on the growing sense of ecological danger that is emerging domestically and internationally. It would recognize that to prevent ecological catastrophe, an organization of world affairs is required that shifts the emphasis of political concern from an exclusive focus on the relations of men with other men to the relation between people and nature, and that some kind of central guidance system must be developed to embody this new order in institutional form. Once a foreign policy is formed that has a strong ecological, and necessarily globalist, element in it, it will naturally lead away from the parochial approach to political concerns and responses that has so often influenced American foreign policy to adopt destructive modes of behavior. We are quickly learning about the continuity of domestic and foreign policy, and that we, any more than the Soviet Union, cannot long insulate our domestic society from the means and ends we deploy abroad. So, by repudiating Vietnam, we would be repudiating an international stance of counterrevolution; and by repudiating this stance, we would notice the seeds of counterrevolution in the governing process in the United States, and realize that counterrevolutionary postures breed counterinsurgent doctrines and methods as surely at home as abroad. Such postures are inevitably bloody, indiscriminate, and destructive of values worth cherishing. In this fundamental respect, the indiscriminate rain of bullets at Attica Prison is joined indissolubly with the disclosures of indiscriminate killing at My Lai. The bicentennial celebration in 1976 is an apt occasion on which to reconsider the options for America in the years ahead. The best of these options is to rehabilitate the wisdom and vision of the early republic, and to give it a new global application that is responsive to the interdependence and fragility of our planetary society.

Index